Hot Type, Cold Beer and Bad News

ALSO BY MICHAEL D. ROBERTS

Thirteen Seconds: Confrontation at Kent State
(with Joe Eszterhas)

Hot Type, Cold Beer and Bad News

A CLEVELAND REPORTER'S JOURNEY THROUGH THE 1960S

Michael D. Roberts

GRAY & COMPANY, PUBLISHERS
Cleveland

Gray & Company, Publishers
www.grayco.com

ISBN: 978-1-59851-102-4

Printed in the United States of America
1

For Patricia, with love

Contents

Hot Type,
Cold Beer and
Bad News

Prologue

It is 12:45 a.m. on January 31, 1968, at Nha Trang in the Republic of South Vietnam. A hand shakes my shoulder and I awake with a start. The voice in the darkness is an urgent whisper, an order really, and it insists I roll from the cot to the tile floor of the military press camp. The tile is cold and my senses are caught in that abyss between sleep and consciousness. I wait for the comforting realization that this is just a nightmare. Instead, my mind retraces the last couple of days until reality comes into focus.

"Stay on the floor and be quiet," the voice says. It belongs to an Army captain with a pistol in hand. "A Viet Cong platoon just walked by the house."

I am less than 100 hours out of Cleveland and haven't even begun to adjust to the climate and culture, let alone the war that is about to confront me with all its force and fury.

Eddie Adams, a photographer from the Associated Press, is with me on the floor. He is a veteran of this work of covering wars. In two days he will take a picture of an execution that will horrify the world and forever symbolize the Vietnam War. But now we are lying there waiting in the dark.

"This shit will either kill you or give you nightmares forever," he says.

In the distance an enormous firefight breaks out. To the uninitiated, the first sounds of combat are startling. They are loud and fierce and terrifying.

"It's not like the movies, is it?" Adams whispers. Outside we can see the arcing fall of tracers glowing red and green in the night.

We lie on that cold floor for what seems like hours, and then with the onset of dawn the firing tapers off and the shooting is punctuated by long silences.

Finally, with quiet prevailing, we make our way to the battle-ground in the heart of this seacoast city, not far from the beach. The area is strewn with bodies, some in uniform, but most in the black pajamas worn by the Viet Cong. Later, officials will provide a death count of 377. The bodies are in ugly repose, limbs akimbo, eyes wide open, wounds black with blood, the beginning of that stench associated only with death.

Workers hurriedly go about collecting the corpses, swinging the dead bodies into piles in the back of Army trucks. Vietnam-ese Boy Scouts help with the body parts. Those tending to the dead wear baby-blue cloth gloves and clean their hands and arms with an alcohol wash from large glass jugs. They hurry with their work before the tropical sun reaches its zenith.

I wander among the bodies and destruction in contempla-tion. Not Adams, who has seen this before many times and doesn't bother to think about it. He records the scene with his camera, searching for the one photo that will tell the story of this morning. The snap of his shutter is an intrusion upon the silence of the dead.

A Special Forces sergeant motions to me. He points to a body riddled with shot.

"This one was an officer," he says. "You can tell by his belt buckle with the star. Look how his brains burst out of his skull."

I don't want to look. The soldier reaches down and takes the belt from the body and hands it to me. "Keep it as a souvenir. You could get some money for this in Saigon."

I survey the scene again and determine that the attack was aimed at the center of town where the government and military advisers are housed. It appears a curiously blatant assault. It will take another day to understand that this was the first act of the nationwide battle that will come to be known as the Tet Offensive.

As I stand amid the carnage taking notes, a hand tugs on my sleeve. It belongs to an elderly Vietnamese woman whose face is contorted in such sorrow that even today it remains fresh in my memory. She motions for me to follow her. The language barrier prevents me from fully understanding her lament.

We walk away from the center of the city and down a narrow street. At the end stands a small house that has been damaged by an explosion. The woman takes me to an outhouse in the back. She is crying, her face a mask of grief.

When she opens the outhouse door, I finally understand. There on a latrine sits a dead man, literally cleaved in half by an errant rocket from a helicopter. It is probably her husband. The woman's mournful wail pierces the air. I stand there, embarrassed that I cannot offer the simplest condolence, knowing that I will never forget this moment. This is my first day at war, and the woman's awful agony will forever symbolize the violence that made the 1960s such a pivotal time in history.

*   *   *

It was a decade dedicated to destruction, death and dissension. It was a decade when a newspaper reporter could find a story that reflected the times just down the street or around the world. For a journalist, technology had yet to alter the way one worked. You just needed a pen, a notebook, a typewriter, carbon paper, a pay phone and a pocketful of change. The national television networks were making their first great impact on public opinion, and 24-hour fake news networks weren't around to cloud objectivity. Social media consisted of a landline telephone. And the print media still followed the same model it had followed since the Civil War.

That era would end with the 1960s. In an arcane way, the events of that decade made it the best of times for a reporter, times filled with hot type, cold beer and bad news.

This is the story of the period just before technology changed the way news was covered—the final years before the widespread use of fax machines and mobile phones, before the Internet united the world. It was a time of incredible upheaval, a decade that changed Cleveland and America forever. It was also my time, and this is the story of how I became a journalist and what I witnessed in that turbulent age. I covered civil rights violence, the Tet Offensive in Vietnam, the agony of the Middle East and the shootings at Kent State. It is also the story of how those mean times tormented the soul of a newspaper.

This is the way it was.

CHAPTER 1

Making the Team

It is Tuesday, November 12, 1963, a few minutes after 5 p.m. I sit in the city room of the *Plain Dealer* at East 18th and Superior Avenue in Cleveland, watching as the reporters return from their beats with gleanings that will be digested and shaped into the news for tomorrow's paper.

The reporters are a polyglot, ordinary in dress, loud, somewhat profane, many with cigarettes dangling from their lips as they peruse their notes, figuring their leads and the pitch to the city editor, who will decide the value of their day's endeavors. They are of various ages, most in their 30s or 40s with an occasional senior citizen in the mix. They wear their inch-and-a-half-wide ties askew, collars open. There are a few women in the cluster around the city desk. Women's liberation has yet to take hold in the city room. There are no African Americans.

My afternoon had been spent dealing with the trivialities of employment, filling out forms with my Social Security number and next of kin. My weekly pay, I learned, would be $110 a week, more than twice as much as I had made in my previous job at the *Ashtabula Star-Beacon*. I listened as a managing editor spoke to the advantages of being a *Plain Dealer* employee. He outlined the responsibilities as well as the need to be a good citizen and a charitable soul, especially when it came to helping the paper meet its annual community campaign goal. For a moment I thought I was talking to a guidance counselor or a Methodist minister, for the man wore a tweed sport coat with leather elbow patches and spoke with the soft lilt of the truly concerned. Given the hard-boiled newspaper setting, the familial tone was disconcerting.

Conversely, about this same time a lapsed divinity student, Lute H. Harmon, was at East 9th and Lakeside applying for a job at the *Cleveland Press*. When Louie Seltzer, that paper's legendary editor, asked Harmon what he had ever written, the applicant offered a folder holding 30 of his best sermons. "I don't have time to read that shit," Seltzer said with a pained expression. "Go find yourself a desk." (Ten years later I would join with Harmon in the creation of *Cleveland Magazine*.)

Despite my somewhat listless interview, I felt deeply appreciative to be at the *Plain Dealer*. In those days you needed a lot of experience to land a real newspaper gig. Had it not been for one story from my year in Ashtabula, I would hardly have gotten an interview let alone a job. A stroke of luck had brought me here.

I had wanted to be a newspaper reporter since the age of five. That was the year I contracted polio on August 4, 1944. I was in a room at old City Hospital, Metro General now, with a boy in an iron lung beside me. For a month, I listened to the machine breathe for him. After I returned home, my mother, Rose, would regularly wrap my legs in hot packs made from strips of wool that gave off an odor I can still smell. My days were spent listening to radio news broadcasts about World War II. I knew all the famous commentators: Raymond Gram Swing, Lowell Thomas, Gabriel Heatter.

The *Cleveland Press* was delivered around 3:30 p.m., six days a week. That was the high point of my day. Though I could not yet read, just looking at the paper provided a special excitement. There were maps that let me follow the war. Lying there with the hot packs, day in and day out, between the radio and the newspaper I began to make out words. Television was five years away.

Neighbors brought magazines. Few things were more exciting than paging through a photo-packed issue of *Life*. The *Saturday Evening Post*, *Look* and other long-gone publications left an indelible impression. As I endured yet another smelly hot-pack treatment, I wondered what it would be like to work for a magazine or a newspaper. My father, Jim, was a steelworker. His descriptions of the fiery furnaces and dangerous conditions in the mill also inspired me to seek a different vocation.

I remember the day that President Franklin Roosevelt died. Arthur Godfrey broadcast the funeral, his mournful voice heard over muffled drumming in the background. For a while, I wanted to be a radio broadcaster. Roosevelt had been paralyzed by polio and I feared I would be, too. You didn't need to move as a broadcaster, I reasoned. Thankfully, I recovered from the disease without complications.

The day the war ended a huge bonfire was built in the middle of Blythin Road, our street in Garfield Heights. Neighbors came forth clanging pots and pans and sharing their rationed liquor. As the flames of the fire reached skyward, I thought it a signal of relief to the heavens. The long war had been hard on everyone.

As the news of war ebbed, my interests turned closer to home. The daily appearance of the *Press* began to feed my fascination for Cleveland. Eventually I would learn a lot about the city, but not before traveling down a long road.

CHAPTER 2

A Beer and a Byline

Ashtabula is Ohio's largest county area-wise, but it is terribly short on population and jobs. In the summer of 1962 it was in economic malaise. A booming titanium plant had closed; missiles were replacing bombers in the nation's arsenal and the metal was no longer in demand. The city of Ashtabula's once teeming waterfront was quiet. I got a job on the *Ashtabula Star-Beacon* on August 5, 1962, the day Marilyn Monroe died. In those days the *Beacon* was a six-day afternoon paper with a circulation of nearly 20,000.

Given my $50-a-week paycheck, I existed on hot dogs and chicken wings and lived for a time in a dingy room at the YMCA. My social life was stagnant. And the small-town environment severely restricted the scope of news that was fit to print. The day I arrived, I promised myself I'd leave as soon as possible.

To get to a larger newspaper, though, I would need to impress editors with clips of major stories. Such stories were hard to come by in a place like Ashtabula. But I managed to stumble into one.

After a few months on the job I was assigned to the city hall beat, where I found a great source in the police chief, Gordon

Arvidson. A bluff, good-natured man, Arvidson was thoroughly amused by my naïveté involving municipal matters.

On Sundays the chief often invited me to his home, where I dug into thick, grilled steaks that tasted way better than hot dogs. We drank beer, his wife scolding us from the kitchen not to drink too much. "Honey, we're still on our first one," the chief would say over his shoulder. This was true, but what he did not say is that he was pouring shots of Jack Daniels into the beer bottles, and we were halfway to the moon.

One day, making my rounds through city hall on a slow news day, I stopped in to see Arvidson and lingered a bit. While checking the police reports I noticed several shoeboxes on a shelf above his desk. I pointed to them and asked what they contained.

"That is the judge's work," Arvidson said. I knew the chief had a running feud with the municipal court judge over some long-standing dispute. "Those are hundreds of parking tickets accumulated by a lawyer here in town, a friend of the damned judge, and he's let him get away without paying them."

There is a rush that comes with the discovery of a good story. And at that moment I was almost breathless with pure elation over the prospect of a front-page headline. I felt like I'd won the lottery.

There was one problem, though. During my short time in Ashtabula I had learned about the sometimes hidden restraints of a small-town newspaper. Relationships in a small town tend to be clannish and congenial. Virtually every person of any importance knows everyone else. Vast networks of families are interlocked through marriage. I had come across stories that were quashed for these reasons, so despite my initial euphoria, I tempered my hopes for the shoeboxes of tickets.

When I finally tallied the tickets there were $25,000 worth

of unpaid violations. After some prodding of editor Ross Smith, he agreed that the story should appear, but without names. Not only was that disappointing, it was a mistake. And since we were not going to name names, we could not provide background on the violators—another mistake. It was a feeble journalistic effort, but it was better than nothing.

What we did not know was that a few days before the article ran, the same local lawyer who was a friend of the Ashtabula municipal court judge had been appointed an assistant U.S. attorney in Cleveland. He had amassed 133 parking tickets. We also did not know that on the basis of the *Star-Beacon*'s revelations the lawyer would be subsequently and suddenly fired by U.S. Attorney General Robert F. Kennedy.

It was Kennedy's action that interested the *Plain Dealer*, and when the paper called I knew that my story was also my ticket out of Ashtabula. But before I left, the dispossessed lawyer confronted me at the paper one day and accused me of every vile act one could conceive. It was the First Amendment in reverse.

CHAPTER 3

Plain Dealing

As the reporters returned from their beats on that November day when my *Plain Dealer* career began, I witnessed a startling transformation. Within minutes the city room morphed from a semi-deserted space into a veritable madhouse. Scurrying copyboys clutched sheaves of paper or sour coffee in sullen cups, answering to cries of "Boy!" A copyboy's main occupation was preparing "books": three pieces of copy paper with two pieces of carbon paper sandwiched in between. A reporter would roll the entire five-page wad into his typewriter and bang away. The actual typewritten pages, or "hard copy," were edited and sent to the printer, while the two carbon copies were filed for reference.

Telephones rang ceaselessly, voices rising to be heard over the cacophony while cigarette smoke collected in a cloud beneath the unblinking fluorescence overhead. On summer nights, I would later discover, the lingering smell of burnt lead from the linotype machines on the floor above permeated the city room. It would be a decade before cold type and computers rendered the machines museum pieces. As the clock moved relentlessly toward the first deadline at 7:20 p.m., the staccato click-clack of dozens of manual typewriters reached a crescendo.

At the center of this sound and fury was the city desk, actually three side-by-side desks occupied by the city editor in the center and two flanking assistants. The city desk was the newspaper's veritable sanctuary, a sacred place shrouded in cigarette smoke and (unlike most other sacred places) awash in profanity and the harangue of reporters begging for column inches. The uninitiated approached the desk with a mixture of reverence and fear.

The desks were occupied by men who had been in World War II. One of them had covered the Cleveland Clinic fire of 1929 in which 123 people died, another Eliot Ness when he was Cleveland's safety director during the infamous Head Hunter of Kingsbury Run murders, and, of course, the Sheppard murder case which would haunt the city forever. Those manning the desk had both seen and written history.

A neophyte reporter advanced toward this triumvirate gingerly and with trepidation. World War II had produced men steeled not only for combat, but for life itself. For the most part they were tough, no-nonsense and of few words. You did not converse with them. You listened carefully and then went about your work. Political correctness was a half century away.

From here assignments were dispatched and copy collected and edited, scrutinized carefully for even the smallest error. The *Plain Dealer* required a middle initial for any name mentioned in news stories and compass points identifying each unnumbered city street.

It was a compelling scene, and over the next decade I would always find this moment in a newspaper's day exciting. This was the convergence that examined the soul of a city and laid bare its failures and its triumphs, its secrets and its lies. Those in this gathering studied the very essence of news ingredients, many of which would never be made public. They traded their discoveries among themselves like dealers in an exotic bazaar. While they could not prove all they knew, their cynical views of the city and its public officials were as finely honed as a tempered chef's knife.

That day I envied them, wanting so much to join their ranks and be part of their fraternity. Their easy manner belied the difficulty of the work, and their sharp retorts masked the fragile egos that both propelled and restrained them.

It was clear, however, that this was not an altogether fraternal place. Over in a corner near the mailboxes was Don Robertson, the newspaper's quintessential writer and bad boy, loudly berating Roy W. Adams, the military/religion writer and a captain in the U.S. Army Reserves. Adams had made some comment about President John F. Kennedy that struck a liberal nerve in the redoubtable Robertson.

Robertson was quick and mean and took no prisoners. He cut into Adams with slice-and-dice invective that rendered the man a stammering victim. Frustrated and angry, Adams finally turned the tables on Robertson with these words: "I'm going to tell your mother on you." Whereupon he spun on his heel and walked back to a desk where sat Josephine Robertson, the newspaper's medical writer and Don's gentle mother. Adams promptly informed her that the son she had brought up had no manners or moral fiber.

Don Robertson bellowed a cascade of obscenities that froze the city room and brought the tableau to the attention of the entire staff. They witnessed the further verbal dismemberment of Adams, a trauma from which he would never recover throughout the rest of his long *Plain Dealer* career. I made a mental note never to engage Robertson's wrath.

Neophyte *Plain Dealer* reporters suffered a painful sense of insecurity, one perhaps unique to this field of employment. You were profoundly aware that you would not be trusted until you proved yourself worthy. A sense of competitiveness crackled in the air. There was the competitiveness of deadlines; the competitiveness of the dreaded *Cleveland Press*, which dominated the morning newspaper for decades; and the competitiveness of your colleagues, especially the feisty younger ones like yourself who were intent on making the team.

Years later, Tom Wolfe would write a perceptive essay about "New Journalism," a movement meant to enhance newspaper and magazine writing through the use of literary devices that were the staple of novels and short stories. Wolfe and others on the *New York Herald Tribune* and the *New York Times* had pioneered this style of journalism in the early 1960s. Soon the movement spread across the country among younger writers eager to express themselves with more freedom.

Wolfe wrote about the cadre of journalists who practiced this new form of writing and labeled them "aces"—those vying for the merest flicker of fame in a silent competition with the rest of the aces. The competition was not so much the *Press* down the street, but instead the guy at the desk next to yours.

At the *Plain Dealer*, young, aggressive journalists with neon-bright egos resented any suggestion of tamping down their ardor for glory. In the back of many of our minds we were the clarions of truth, justice and the American way, defenders of the oppressed, discoverers of deceit and purveyors of purity. The copy editors, generally older and consigned to a life of comma crunching, looked upon the younger reporters as an English 101 remedial class. Conversely, the aces viewed the copy desk as the Taliban, a priestly lot bent on destroying precious works of journalism that were this side of the Dead Sea Scrolls.

At one point *Newsweek* picked up on this intense atmosphere and sent a writer to Cleveland to do a magazine piece on the emergence of the *Plain Dealer*. In an article entitled "Tigerish," executive editor Philip Porter was quoted as saying the newspaper was staffed by a group of young tigers. Their work, he said, was eating into the circulation lead of the *Cleveland Press*.

The *Newsweek* piece forecast what would become an ace race. The idea here was to gain as many page-one bylines above the fold as possible so you could lord it over the city room and summon copyboys for coffee as if they were indentured servants. The copyboys studied this behavior with some curiosity, as well as envy, for many were understudies for the next generation of hubris.

I didn't know it yet, but from the very beginning I had put myself in the *Plain Dealer*'s ace race. In the morning on that first day at the paper, I quietly dropped a story and a set of photographs into the city desk's in-basket. In the ensuing confusion I lost track of the copy and figured one of the editors had discarded it.

I felt odd being there. My first choice of employment would have been the *Press*. I had a long acquaintance with that paper, having delivered it for several years, and having read it daily as I recovered from polio. I loved the *Press* with its clean type style and bold headlines. No paper covered murder better. Highlighting crime and corruption, it gave the city the aura of film noir.

The *Press* also wrote at length about racketeering crime figures, making a local man named Shondor Birns a public enemy worthy of any big city. Birns was portrayed as the boss of Cleveland's numbers game, an enforcer of such ferocity that he would blow up cars and houses on a whim. The *Press* used telephoto lenses to capture Birns' hard face as he smoked a cigar on the sidewalks of Short Vincent, an avenue that the newspaper portrayed as so vile and dark that I could not imagine walking its length in safety.

I became an employee of the *Press* in 1950 when I acquired a route of 50 customers on Blythin and Horton Roads in Garfield Heights. My boss was deliveryman Joe Vaclavic, a husky cigar smoker who would heft bales of newspapers with ease and snap the wire bindings with cutters to reveal that day's headlines. Oftentimes the byline on the top story was that of a reporter named Bus Bergen. Bergen was a legend. He was the subject of two episodes of *The Big Story*, a nationally televised show that dramatized real stories by real newspapermen, sponsored by Pall Mall cigarettes. The honor of being featured on the show was almost as good as winning a Pulitzer. He was my hero. God, would it be great to be like Bergen.

After graduating from Baldwin-Wallace College, I interviewed for a job at the *Press* and was told by a very good editor that I did not have the experience to join its staff. Get some, come back, and we will talk again, he said. I remember walking out of the newspaper's offices on a lovely summer day feeling dark, gloomy and lost.

Irony can be a funny thing. In about a year, I would feel very differently about the *Press*.

My city editor in Ashtabula, Howard Mobley, had approached me with a grim face when he learned I was leaving for the *Plain Dealer*. A gentle and knowledgeable man, Mobley had once taken the same journey to the *Plain Dealer*, regretted it, quit the paper, and returned to the somnambulism of Ashtabula. He told me he left after a few months on the police beat. He could not tolerate the chief police reporter, Robert Tidyman, and warned me to beware. I anticipated Tidyman's arrival in my life like I would a draft notice from the government, summoning me to its newly created quagmire in a place called Vietnam.

My first day at the *Plain Dealer* ended with an incredible surprise. The story that I had slipped into the in-basket was about a policeman named Joe Dober, who directed traffic on Euclid Avenue in front of the May Company department store. Dober performed his job with such zest that crowds would gather to watch him flourish his jacket in front of a bus in the manner of a bullfighter performing a veronica, then bow as the vehicle drove on. He was fun and I had captured him on film.

The next morning the story ran at the top of page one with three pictures! I could not help but congratulate myself. It was a hell of a first day. And in another way, it was merely hell in general, for I had brought unwanted attention to myself and incurred the wrath of the *Plain Dealer* photographers, who had an agreement with the Newspaper Guild that no reporters were permitted to take pictures. For all my eagerness to succeed, I was sometimes viewed as a grandstander by my contemporaries. Just another aspiring ace, I would think.

CHAPTER 4

The Cop House

Years later mature men, and some women, would talk about the police beat with the fondness of matriculation, a rite of passage through the thickets of journalism. A ritual in the golden days of newspapers, they would say at Nighttown over wine or at a Press Club of Cleveland Journalism Hall of Fame dinner where the past was painted with romance.

As for me, I wanted to get the hell off the police beat before I ever got there. There were few bylines to be had out of that shabby carbuncle of an office in Central Station on Payne Avenue, where everything smelled of urine, disinfectant and stale tobacco. You were afraid to touch anything for fear of contracting a disease. In those days the police liked to show rookie reporters the black homosexuals jailed for the mere fact they were gay.

The police beat was where you learned that journalism was an unnatural act. You were called upon to abuse any civility you possessed, to thrust yourself into uncomfortable if not dangerous situations, to work ungodly hours—and all this for modest wages. Here you learned to argue with the *Plain Dealer*'s front office over cleaning bills for a suit that reeked of smoke after you covered a fire. You learned to be insensitive and brash. You also learned a distaste for editors. Most importantly, you learned whether this was what you wanted to do with your life.

And presiding over all this was a grinning bulldog of a man with a bald head and a lascivious laugh that almost always made you uneasy. This was the legendary Bob Tidyman, a combat veteran of the fierce battles waged to recapture France in World War II and the most jaded man I've ever met. He was the chief police reporter. His father, Ben, had held the same job for nearly a quarter of a century and had trained Bob and his brother, Ernest, in the vagaries of the beat when they were in their teens. Ernest, a seventh-grade dropout, became a novelist and screenwriter, creating the black detective John Shaft and winning an Academy Award for his *French Connection* screenplay.

All those years on the police beat can do things to a man, and Bob Tidyman was the recipient of every lesson the street could teach, maybe each a dozen times. The environment was enough to erode even the most virtuous soul. Tidyman had overseen the basic training of a generation of *Plain Dealer* reporters, making some and breaking others.

He liked to tell of the time he and his brother had witnessed a prisoner using knotted sheets to escape via a window in the Cuyahoga County Jail, visible from the police beat office. When they excitedly called the scene to the attention of their father, Ben Tidyman smiled and said, "Let him get away, boys, and then call the desk. It's a better story if he escapes."

The key to getting along and understanding how the beat operated was to know that Bob Tidyman did not work; he was an overseer. If you understood that, and accepted it the way you would the Gospels or the Constitution, things would be fine. If you did not, Tidyman would make your life so miserable you would pray for deliverance from the darkness of the place and become a librarian.

I received my draft notice the same day I received a memo that I was to report to the police beat. I was able to skirt the draft because of my childhood bout with polio, but there was nothing I could do about Tidyman except show up at the appointed hour and accept my fate.

I had spent most of my first few months at the paper on the rewrite desk, essentially writing shorts and taking notes from the police reporters and turning them into two-paragraph stories. The day John F. Kennedy was assassinated I manned the phones, taking calls from a mournful public seeking information. There was no cable news in those days.

The city room was in chaos as the bells on the Associated Press teletype machines announced bulletin after bulletin. Everyone labored in a strange slow motion, trying to contemplate the enormity of the event. There was so much discombobulation that the city desk had to hang a huge sign with the word A-S-S-A-S-S-I-N-A-T-I-O-N because so few of the staff could spell it.

That night I asked the city desk if I could have a byline in the paper for history's sake. I was embarrassed to do so, but I could not let the moment pass. An editor simply nodded yes.

Death was a strange but vital part of the paper. I learned about that from the obituary writer, G. David Vormelker, a thin man with wireless glasses, a string tie and a pleasant smile, who would softly express condolences to a bereaved family and then slam down the phone and mutter about his lunch hour. "People who die on my lunch hour get shorter obits," he told me one day. Vormelker had utter contempt for people who died on *Cleveland Press* time. He hated death on deadline, too. He advised me not to die on a Thursday, when space was always short because of the food pages. For the record, Vormelker died on our time and the afternoon rival gave him a good obit just to stick it to us.

There was a lot of death on the police beat, too. Shootings, stabbings, house fires, drownings, car crashes, suicides, airplane crashes and any number of other bizarre exits from this life were in the beat's purview. One afternoon Hil Black, the chief police reporter for the *Press* and a man known for his dignity and skill, grabbed me and said that a respected federal judge had just died. Black was going to phone the widow; he wanted me there so that the bereaved woman wouldn't be bothered by another call from the media. It was an uncommon and thoughtful gesture, one I never forgot.

There were plenty of those calls as well as visits to homes to collect pictures of the recently passed. If you got there before the *Press*, you tried to get all the pictures of the deceased, leaving the afternoon guys with nothing. They would do the same to us.

If you were truly unlucky, you would be the bearer of the ultimate bad news, announcing to a wife that she was a newly made widow because her husband had just been killed in some drunken accident on a nearby highway. Then there were calls to the coroner's office, where an indifferent voice would yawn and give you the cause of death or tell you to call back because the body was still on the slab and they hadn't finished counting entry and exit wounds.

Often we would go into the night and visit scenes of mayhem. I remember a shooting on the East Side where the victim lay dead on a tree lawn and a homicide detective bent over to examine the body, dripping mustard from his bologna sandwich. These stories helped fill awkward silences while out on a date, but the paper's editors couldn't have cared less about them.

In those days reporters could roam hospital emergency rooms like tourists, talking to police and doctors while patients were treated for their wounds. One night at Mount Sinai an ambulance brought in a man who had been shot five times in the back of his head. Not one bullet had penetrated the skull, and the man lived. It was a good story but a bad address—which was code for "black"—and it received scant attention deep in the paper.

I first set foot in the police beat office early in February at 6 p.m. I was wearing a blue blazer and a rep tie, pretty much standard dress for junior reporters. Studying me, Tidyman asked in a quiet but scary voice who the fuck I was.

I introduced myself and explained that I had been told by the city desk to report to the police beat. "Those assholes never told me they were sending another college boy down here," Tidyman growled. "We already have a guy from Princeton who can't find his way to the crapper and washes his hands every time he picks up a phone. He's worried about picking up some disease from all this filth. This place is too sick for that."

Oh, man, I thought, this is going to be joyful.

The beat was all about phones and we were on them constantly, calling rounds of all the suburban police departments every hour before deadline. Sometimes one department would cover for another and provide misleading information about a late-night episode. Other times, when there were bad feelings between suburbs, they would rat out the other department.

The first thing Bob Tidyman told new guys was never to answer a certain phone in the corner. This was the direct line from the city desk, and Tidyman did not want anyone but himself talking with editors. If that phone rang, you were to track down Tidyman as fast as you could and tell him. He could generally be found in one of the many bars across the street on Payne Avenue. Tidyman would call the desk back, explaining he was up in homicide—a place he never went, because the detectives there generally despised him for a decades-old story he had written on police brutality or some other injustice.

Where now stands Cleveland State University's manicured soccer field sat a row of shabby bars that served us late and often, providing respite from nonstop telephone rounds and endless patrols of Central Station. Tidyman held court in Lubeck's Casino and other bars along the street. Cops drank there, homeless persons from the street would cadge drinks, and a few tired whores would take a nightcap at the joints. Tourists from the city room would stop by to catch some grit and a beer after deadline.

One night near closing, a cop shot the clock off the wall when the bartender announced last call. The scene was surreal: the smell of cordite, the ringing in the ears, the floating dust backlit by neon beer signs. Across the street, the police station remained indifferent to the noise. Another night someone fired a pistol into a phone book just for laughs. Again, the loud report brought no response from Central Station.

At the beat you learned to assemble greasy facts like a crossword puzzle. You phoned these facts to a rewrite person who sat in the comfort of the *Plain Dealer* office and who had the authority to question your very existence. If you missed a fact, rewrite would tell you not to call back until you had them all.

Getting the facts often meant dealing with the homicide squad and being pinballed back and forth between the cops and the city desk. What was the victim's middle initial? What was the caliber of the gun? The model of the car? Sometimes detective Carl Roberts would clean his pistol and look at me through the barrel while I tried to pry information from him on a two-paragraph murder that the city desk was obsessing over. Running up the stairs to homicide and back down to the phone on deadline over and over again turned the perspiration pouring down your spine into a stream of tension that knotted every muscle. After a while, neophytes learned to ask the right questions quickly and effectively.

The relationship between the police and the *Plain Dealer* in those days was rocky. One summer afternoon Tidyman was across the street drinking with a detective who was supposedly on duty when a squirrel ran through the open door, leaped onto the bar, and bit the cop on the hand. Fearing rabies, the detective went to the emergency room at St. Vincent Charity Hospital and reported the incident as a dog bite obtained while investigating a break-in. Meanwhile, Tidyman turned in the story about the squirrel and it appeared in the next morning's paper. In return, all the police reporters' cars were ticketed.

Tidyman offered up plenty of other reasons for police animosity. One night, a brand-new police car was stolen. The car had been parked beneath the window of our beat room at Central Station. We often exited the building through the window, down onto a parking lot. The atmosphere on the beat that night felt strangely electric. And then Tidyman walked in and announced he had just got a tip that a new squad car was missing, maybe stolen.

While the police began a frantic search for the vehicle, several of us began to make calls. We received an anonymous tip as to where the car had been abandoned. The cops could see tomorrow's headline. They were furious and embarrassed by our story.

The number two man on the beat was Donald Leander Bean, a rumpled reporter who squinted through thick glasses. The mentor of many aspiring Cleveland journalists, he also loved practical jokes. One of his favorites involved sending young reporters to the war memorial on the Mall to interview the mother of the Unknown Soldier.

Bean would go to great lengths to create hoaxes that would draw a *Press* reporter to the scene of a crime that never took place. A veteran of the defunct INS news service, Bean was the one reporter that you wanted on deadline in a late-breaking story. He was respected by the police and had a certain tenacity that endeared him to editors. He complained from time to time about his lack of promotion, but the desk dared not elevate him. Without Bean's presence, the police beat would have been a mere shadow of itself.

Bean came up with a suspect in the case of the stolen police car. The suspect was Tidyman, and Bean swore us to secrecy. I suppose the police suspected too, but there was always that lingering doubt. Years later when I learned that during the war Tidyman had once stolen a jeep for a joyride (and was later punished for it), I couldn't help but remember that night.

One Christmas Eve, the town silent and the police beat slow, we got a tip from a suburban police department on the West Side. A widow with four children reported that the utility company had shut off the gas and her kids were freezing.

It so happened Tidyman was just passing through on his way home from a quick stop at Lubeck's when the call came in. Standard practice was to phone the utility company's public relations man and get a comment. Instead, Tidyman ordered me to call the company president at his home and disturb the family dinner.

"Wish him a Merry Christmas," Tidyman said.

I made the call and, of course, the president was angered, referring the call to his PR person. The day after Christmas all hell broke loose. Executive editor Phil Porter, who knew that the idea had been to embarrass the gas company for going Scrooge on Christmas, demanded a memo. I sweated over writing one. Tidyman just shrugged.

CHAPTER 5

A Bad Address and a Bit of Luck

Cleveland reporters spent a lot of time on the city's East Side. We saw a city that was never mentioned in the newspapers, other than in short reports that told of some crime or tragedy. Overcrowded apartment buildings were foreign territory to those of us who drove home to the suburbs. Sorrow and despair filled the night air, along with the smell of smoke and garbage.

Glass broke underfoot in trash-filled alleys where feral cats darted across your path. Dark shadows foretold of danger and abandoned cars dotted the roadways, stripped of tires and chrome. I saw my first colorful telephone, a pink Princess style, in the apartment of a woman whose boyfriend had been shot and killed earlier in the day. I didn't know that phones came in any color other than black and wondered why the phone company would sell them to people in such need.

The city had yet to be overwhelmed by drugs, however, and you could navigate those neighborhoods fairly at will. In 1964 narcotics detectives told me there were a half dozen heroin addicts in the city. In a matter of only four years, as drug dealers began to prey on the despairing, the streets became considerably meaner.

Those of us who witnessed this side of the city often told the newspaper's editors how bad things appeared. Perhaps the most concerned among us was Roldo Bartimole, a veteran reporter originally from Connecticut who had an abiding sympathy for the impoverished of the urban core. Bartimole would quit the newspaper twice in frustration and then go on to publish his own pamphlet, *Point of View*, addressing the city's ills for the next 32 years. He savaged Cleveland's established institutions and was uncompromising with his former colleagues in the media.

There was no middle ground with Bartimole. Supporters viewed him as the city's conscience and critics despised his attacks on the establishment. Bartimole hammered the *Plain Dealer* for decades with withering and unrelenting force.

To understand where the city was in the early 1960s requires examining the mass migration of African Americans that began in the early years of the 20th century. Cleveland was prospering, with jobs available for those who wanted to leave the poverty and racial climate of the South. By the time of World War I, the city's population counted some 10,000 blacks. The wartime industrial boom, and the lack of immigration from Europe during that period, made even more jobs available. By 1930 some 72,000 African Americans lived in Cleveland, mostly on the near East Side, creating ghetto-like conditions in the Central Avenue area.

Because of discrimination on the part of businesses and labor unions, blacks were forced to work in low-paying service jobs. The nation's first public housing projects were built here in the late 1930s, but they were largely occupied by whites. Construction of these projects displaced many blacks and further exacerbated the crowded living conditions.

At the start of World War II, Cleveland's black population numbered about 80,000. As before, the war industry attracted thousands of new workers from the South. By 1960 there were 251,000 African Americans squeezed into an urban area that lacked services and schools.

It was this combustible atmosphere that young reporters confronted every day. Meanwhile, their editors went about their work as if these gathering ills were a normal part of the city's life. We reported our findings about a world filled with eye-opening events and angry people to a city desk inured to the "race problem," with its numbers rackets and street beggars.

After all, the ghetto was a "bad address," and the papers didn't bother to write much about such places—not because they were deemed unnewsworthy, but because the news that emanated from them was universally bad. (As late as 1959, a page-one story in the *Cleveland Press* would quote a realtor and prominent civic figure as saying that he did not rent to blacks because they were too messy.) Hence, the reigning editorial policy was to not pay much attention to that area of the city.

This myopia would come back to haunt not only the newspapers, but the entire city. The town, enraptured by its ethnic politics, dealing more with the past than with the future, launched into an urban renewal project that managed to make housing conditions even worse for minorities.

No single event affected the future of the city as did the decision in the late 1950s to undertake Erieview, at that time the largest urban renewal project in America. Erieview was heavily promoted by the *Cleveland Press*, whose new building on Lakeside would be a keystone of the development project. The plan displaced thousands of persons, ruined retail traffic on Euclid Avenue, and was never completed. The vast acreage of parking lots in the vicinity of East 9th Street still testify to the folly of the project, which one federal official deemed the Vietnam of the U.S. Department of Housing and Urban Development.

The *Plain Dealer* stood mute on the issue as those who lost homes sought residence in the East Side's increasingly over-populated neighborhoods, one of the antecedents of the Hough riots. Years later, writing in his book *Cleveland: Confused City on a Seesaw*, Phil Porter would lament the newspaper's inaction on urban renewal.

Compounding this was the fact that Louis B. Seltzer, the editor of the *Press*, had discovered it was to the benefit of his newspaper to play to Cleveland's ethnic populations. In so doing he managed to cripple the city's two-party political system and replace it with the power of his paper. He did this over 30 years while the *Plain Dealer* watched haplessly, having neither the appetite nor the ability to engage Seltzer in the trenches. Now, as the city entered the 1960s, the city was on a precipice. Its bewildered establishment clung to the tired marketing slogan coined by the Illuminating Company: "Cleveland, the best location in the nation."

If you were an aspiring reporter in 1964, answers to all of this were beyond reach, yet the experience of being out in those streets left you with an uneasy feeling that something was wrong, and that something was going to happen.

We all dreaded the Saturday overnight. This was the shift where only one reporter was responsible for the city between the hours of midnight and 8 a.m. No other news organizations were on duty and even the *Press* relaxed its relentless vigil since it did not publish on Sunday. My trick for handling this lonely assignment was to hand-deliver an early edition of the Sunday paper to the police radio officers like some groveling supplicant, begging them to call me at the beat if something happened. One

Saturday night in November, overwhelmed at having responsibility for a whole city, I made my humble offering and then
returned to our shabby office and went to sleep.

About 3 a.m., the harsh ring of one of the phones woke me.
It was police radio and there were shots being fired on an East
Side street. Multiple shots, the officer said.

The best thing for me was to stay where I was and try to put
the story together by phone. I had an address and went to the
crisscross directory, the virtual bible of the beat, which listed
by address each street's occupants and their phone numbers.
A skillful reporter could deputize an entire street and ask what
neighbors had heard or seen, assembling a fair idea of what was
taking place without leaving the building.

The shooting had awakened nearly everyone on the street.
Residents reported that dozens of shots had been exchanged,
blowing out windows of parked cars, shattering picture
windows, and exploding streetlights. Stop signs were riddled
with bullet holes. The police estimated 40 shots had been fired
and reported that no one had seen a thing. This wasn't unusual
given the little rapport that existed between these neighborhoods and the authorities.

It took six hours to gather what facts I could, and I stayed
beyond my shift to work the story. This, I thought, would be
worth something for Monday's slow news hole. I was chagrined
when the desk asked me to boil it down to a paragraph, and that
paragraph didn't even make the paper. The frustration of seeing
stories like this one occur night after night made you question
yourself, the city, the system and the future of all the aforemen-
tioned.

Even worse was appearing on the scene of a breaking news
story on deadline. The first order of business: find a telephone.
There were plenty of pay phones across the city, but not nearly

enough when a murder, fire or some other form of mayhem was taking place and you had to report it. In the days before cell phones you always needed a pocketful of change to feed the phone while you talked to a panicked city desk that was freaking out for facts that would not be available for hours.

(One day a public relations man from the telephone company, a former reporter, stopped at my desk and gave me a sticker that read: PHONE IS OUT OF ORDER. "Use this to reserve a pay phone in a moment of need," he instructed.)

When faced with the confusion surrounding a breaking story, you also needed some luck. Actually, all the luck you could amass. Proper timing of your arrival was your first bit of fortune. When an accident or catastrophe takes place, the sense of shock that descends on witnesses and victims makes them particularly vulnerable to questioning. They talk easily and often provide the most dramatic accounts. Once the authorities arrive, the mood changes and gathering information becomes more difficult—in some cases, almost impossible.

Then comes the part where you sort out the information, judge the worthiness of your various interviews, and seek the best account of what occurred, all while keeping an eye on the opposition and an ear to the phone where the editors are in a state of conniption. By now the scene has changed, and the focus shifts to families, hospitals or the morgue.

All these factors came into play on the windy night of April 24, 1964. It was early on a Friday evening when we got a call that a Northwest Airlines plane had crash-landed at Cleveland Hopkins. It was a flight from Washington, DC, with 77 passengers. I was told to get to the airport immediately. That was all the information available at the moment. The drive felt interminable.

The luggage area was a mass of anxious humanity. I checked

the phone banks, all of them occupied. I then checked the crowd and noticed a tall man in a gray suit with a briefcase. Something about him attracted my attention.

"Excuse me, sir," I interrupted. "By any chance were you on that Northwest plane?"

"I was," he said. Great. A break, I thought.

The man went on to explain that the nose landing gear on the turboprop plane had collapsed 10 seconds after touchdown. The aircraft veered sharply to the right, the propeller blade on the right side snapping off and ripping into the fuselage.

"I expected that to happen," he said as I looked at him quizzically. The blade had punctured the aircraft in the midsection where the cloakroom was located. There were no seats in the space.

"The woman sitting across the aisle from me did not have her seatbelt fastened for the landing," he said. "She was eating and her tray flew from her lap and she began to slide down the aisle. I figured the other prop would break, and she was heading toward the spot where the blade would rip into the fuselage.

"That is when I grabbed her by the shoulder and held her until the plane came to a halt."

The man had saved the woman's life, and he was acting like he did this routinely.

I was writing all of this down as fast as I could. The TV crews were beginning to arrive and, as always, we were on deadline. My adrenaline level was reaching a rock-and-roll frenzy. I could see a phone open up nearby and I asked the gray-suited man to wait for me.

When I finally got through to the desk, the editors were in their usual state of restlessness. I related my story while a rewrite man typed it to paper as an editor assaulted me with question after question. "Young man," he asked, "who are we going to attribute all of this to? We can't let you make all of this up, you know."

I told him I'd be right back and hung up before the whole exchange became personal. A few minutes later I called him again. My mood was exultant.

"OK, who is the guy giving you all this information?" the editor asked, his voice filled with the usual city desk skepticism.

"His name is I. Irving Pinkel," I replied.

"Who the hell is I. Irving Pinkel?"

I paused, savoring what I was about to say next.

"Well, he happens to be NASA's leading expert on air crashes."

Supervising a federal investigation into post-crash fires and their prevention, Pinkel had organized and studied more than 50 remote-control crashes of actual aircraft. He would later serve as the director of NASA's Aerospace Safety Research and Data Institute.

There was a brief moment of silence, and then the grudging admission that the desk was offering the story for page one. We beat the *Press*. I was jubilant.

A few days later I received a memo ordering me to report to the city room for assignment.

He never knew it, but I. Irving Pinkel had plucked me from adversity the same way he had done for that woman. I was free of Tidyman's purgatory.

CHAPTER 6

The Great Leap

Despite my contempt for the police beat, I missed it in the first days of my assignment to the city room. My major complaint regarding the police beat was that reporters did no writing, but instead phoned information to rewrite men who put their own flair on stories. Rewrite men occupied a more exalted position at the *Press* given the nature of its deadlines. Many reporters on the afternoon newspaper did little or no writing. I wanted to be a writer.

My promotion turned out to be less than inspiring. I found myself assigned to covering speeches at the City Club, filling in on obits, and covering charity events, house sales, lost dogs, retirements and frog jumping contests. It was a frog jumping contest in Hardscrabble, Ohio, one Sunday afternoon in July that elevated my value to the city desk.

What I didn't know about this contest was its historic significance. It marked the return of Ohio to the realm of official frog jumping championships, with the winner going to the nationals in California. The state had been banned from competition due to an oversight on the part of former governor Michael DiSalle, who had foolishly allowed a turtle trot to be held alongside the frog jumping competition at the Ohio State Fair. The introduction of reptiles was a violation of protocol in amphibious competition.

This was no laughing matter among state officials. It had taken three years for the ban to be lifted on Ohio frogs.

The event that stole the day took place in the junior division when Susie Herbold of Valley City appeared with a very small frog just as judges were announcing the conclusion of that part of the competition. Clutching the entry fee of 25 cents in one hand and the diminutive frog called Oglethorpe in the other, Susie was granted one last jump. A total of 37 frogs had gone ahead, and it was unlikely that this tiny frog posed any threat.

Susie lifted her frog from a pail and set him on a white X painted on a dark canvas. Oglethorpe eyed the skeptical onlookers and their frogs. Susie leaned over and blew on his speckled back and the amphibian went ballistic. Oglethorpe sprang three times for a total of 8 feet, 7 inches, the best leap of the day. After that, he jumped into a crowd of women and children, causing a frightful scurry.

It was a nice story for a sleepy Sunday afternoon, and the editors gave it prominent display on page one. I felt very good about it until the next day when I arrived for work.

"You just screwed yourself forever," an agitated Don Robertson greeted me. "You keep that shit up and the next thing you know you'll be covering the zoo. Don't you know that the crazies [meaning the editors] love animal stories? If they had their way the whole damned paper would read like a menagerie."

Robertson was right. My next story was a cock-crowing event, followed by a piece on a former CIA employee's pet rabbit with the number 007 stenciled on his ear, then a draft horse competition at the county fair, some ducks who had survived food poisoning, and a homing pigeon who rather walk than fly.

And because I did such a good job, I was sent to cover the Ohio State Fair. I needed to pay more attention to Don Robertson, I really did.

Robertson was a curious person. An accomplished novelist, he wrote 18 of them over his lifetime. When the books were selling, he would quit the newspaper business, but when the inevitable need for money arose he would beg his way back onto the staff. The editors tolerated him the way you would excuse the bad behavior of a good athlete. The man was a facile writer who almost never needed editing and could produce lucid copy on the cusp of any deadline. He was furiously outspoken, opinionated and truculent. In those days he wore his hair in a brush cut, smoked, carried a slight paunch, and was forever giving up alcohol, Bushmills being his drink of choice.

He had always been an *enfant terrible*, having in junior high spent a summer riding every streetcar line in the city, timing its delays, and noting the work ethic, or lack thereof, of the conductors. When he finished the story he gave it to the *Cleveland News*, which published it much to the dismay of the Cleveland Transit System.

Don's grandfather had been the founder and editor of the *Cleveland Morning Recorder*. Don's father, Carl, an accomplished man in many fields—an explorer and a national bridge expert—had covered city hall for the *Plain Dealer* during the era of Mayor Tom L. Johnson. He had died in Morocco in 1935. Don's mother, Josephine, worked for many years as the paper's medical editor. Her sweet disposition was in sharp contrast to that of her mercurial son.

Robertson dropped out of Harvard and served in China with the U.S. Army in the years following World War II, just before the communist takeover. He never talked about that part of his life. Afterward, he lived in New York where he began a trilogy of

Civil War fiction and wrote television soap operas to subsidize his writing. There would be many trips back and forth between the *Plain Dealer* and New York as his literary career ebbed and flowed.

His personal life was catastrophic. His first wife ran off with a wind tunnel expert from NASA; his second with Ernest Tidyman, Bob Tidyman's brother and a screenwriter of some prominence; and his third with the captain of a cruise ship. Years later he found joy in a fourth marriage, his new wife describing herself as the "cleanup hitter."

In the spring of 1964, I came to notice that Robertson always insisted on working on Sundays. This was generally the slowest news day of the week, which suited him because he liked to write his novels on company time. The editors did not mind much since Robertson represented real insurance if something big occurred.

But for Robertson, nothing was big enough to warrant his attention. "Don, oh Don," an editor's chirpy voice would call out, "the beat says that something's developing over on East 55th. Want to run over there and take a look?"

"Whatever it is, it's not big enough," Robertson would respond. Then he'd return to his novel.

All this gave me the idea that I should work on Sundays. I figured that if I could get close to Robertson some of those assignments that he refused would come my way, and they did, letting me accumulate more experience and bylines, and getting the city desk to look my way. Robertson's new refrain was, "It's not big enough. Let Roberts do it."

CHAPTER 7

Death Does the Holidays

There came a day when Robertson finally found a story that was big enough for him. That story was the brutal murder of a 16-year-old girl on a quiet street in suburban Garfield Heights. It happened around 1 p.m., two days after Christmas.

Plenty of murders occur in every city, but very few are mysterious and most are solved almost immediately. Murder can be as routine as mailing a letter. Every so often, though, a few cases that make headlines cause legions of reporters to scurry about like an ant colony trying to find scraps of information that can be pieced together to advance the story.

The Beverly Jarosz murder was one of these.

The *Cleveland Press* had refined the coverage of murder to an art form. Its combined use of photos, colorful copy, layout and graphics such as maps organized a chilling experience for readers. I still remember the murder of 8-year-old Sheila Ann Tuley, who on New Year's Eve in 1947 was found stabbed to death on a neighbor's porch. The panes of glass on the front door were stained with her blood as she tried to paw for help.

A *Press* reporter actually identified the killer, who turned out to be psychopathic.

The hearts of generations of reporters still quicken at the name of Beverly Potts, a 10-year-old West Side girl who was never again seen after the evening of August 24, 1951. The search for the missing girl went on for decades, and even today the discovery of her destiny would warrant headlines. The *Press* offered a reward for any information that would lead to her whereabouts.

But the most celebrated case, the one that would make national news and ultimately scar the reputation of the *Press*, was Marilyn Sheppard's murder in Bay Village, Ohio, on July 4, 1954. Editor Louie Seltzer personally signed a set of page-one editorials condemning public officials for not arresting the slain woman's husband, Dr. Sam Sheppard. It was a mistake of historic proportion.

A decade later, the U.S. Appeals Court would rule that Sheppard's conviction and life sentence be overturned due to violation of his civil rights. A federal judge would call Sheppard's trials a mockery of justice. The *Press* would shoulder much of the blame based on its pretrial coverage.

Maybe it was the anticipation of another epic murder mystery or maybe he just needed a break from fiction, but Don Robertson was energized by the prospect of competing with the *Press* on the Beverly Jarosz story. But this time he told the city desk that the story was too big to be left to him alone. He insisted that I also be assigned to drive and to pick up the odds and ends, especially coffee.

Covering a murder of this magnitude meant long, empty hours staring at the opposition, badgering frustrated police officials over the lack of clues, and dealing with the off-the-wall characters who routinely made appearances in cases like this one. And then there was the *Plain Dealer*'s insatiable city desk, which lived in fear that the next edition of the afternoon paper would appear with headlines so damning and dynamic that we would forever suffer the torturous embarrassment of being beaten on the story.

One night when city editor Ted Princiotto got it into his head that I was not taking the competition seriously enough, he told me of the time when the *Press* had beaten the *Plain Dealer* on eight page-one stories in a single day, calling it the bleakest moment in the history of the paper. "We didn't even feel like men," he said. That year *Time* magazine had named the *Press* one of the 10 most influential newspapers in America.

The Jarosz case was enervating. Newspaper, television and radio reporters all huddled in the hallway of the Garfield Heights police station on Turney Road. Everyone eyed everyone else suspiciously or feigned they knew something that the others did not. Paul Sciria, the ubiquitous television reporter from KYW (later WKYC), constantly bummed cigarettes, and for days the sound of coins sliding into the Coke machine made for the only action. Curiously, competing newspaper reporters didn't fraternize much, so a murder case like this one provided a rare opportunity to get to know one another. Still, everyone was wary about who knew what. When the door to the detective room would open we would all leap up and try to glimpse who was inside. Oftentimes it was only a detective on his way to the men's room.

I don't know how Robertson pulled it off, but he talked the police into letting us see the crime scene in the house on Thornton Avenue. Something like this would be unheard of today. "When we get in there," Robertson said, "I don't want you to stand around like a tourist with your mouth open and gape at the blood. You write down everything you see, including the titles of the books she was reading."

This is what I recall: blood stains on the bed and the walls;

a large hole in one wall, presumably created during the death struggle; and a dresser with the artifacts any young girl would possess, like a mirror, stuffed animals and pictures. What I remember most was the eerie and evil feeling that permeated the room. This was the place where, as the county coroner later put it, the most brutal killing in the history of Cleveland had been committed.

One day as we paced the hallway of police headquarters, a man with a bloodhound arrived to offer the cops his services in tracking the killer through the neighborhood. All sorts of people typically wanted to be involved in helping to solve a case. Robertson looked over at the man and his dog, then muttered, "Christ, this guy looks like *he* could be a killer."

I put it down to the kind of black humor that manifests itself when there is so little to write about. But Robertson, convinced that the man had the creepy appearance of a child molester, later checked him out, and he indeed possessed a criminal record. Other volunteers who showed up at the station included a man with a Ouija board and another who claimed to be an extra-sensory sorcerer. The police were taking as many as 50 calls an hour. Nothing was working. We were all stir-crazy.

The police were burning up so much time on the case that one officer's wife taped the name "Garfield Heights Police Department" on their marriage certificate and left it on the kitchen table.

From the very beginning, the Garfield Heights police were coming up empty-handed. The investigation focused on Beverly's two boyfriends, both of whom passed lie-detector tests. Another line of inquiry dealt with suspicious neighbors, but there never was enough evidence to support the theories.

While the police never publicly announced the suspects' identities, I was able to learn the name of one of the boys who had dated Beverly. Ironically, I had known him years ago when I worked as a summer playground instructor. He was a nice kid from a good Catholic family.

I went to his house unannounced. When his father answered the door, I introduced myself and asked to see the boy. The father was courteous but unyielding, noting what a terrible trauma this was for his son and for the family. He told me to leave. I asked if I could talk to him off the record about his son's relationship with Beverly. He agreed, with the caveat that the boy's name not be included in anything I wrote. I promised confidentiality.

The man explained that his college-student son had dated Beverly, but that it was not serious. His son, he said, had been home with a cold on the day of the murder. It wasn't much but it was something, and the city desk was hungry for anything. The *Press* had announced a $5,000 reward for information leading to an arrest, a declaration designed to lure information from the public. The paper later upped the reward to $10,000.

Trust is paramount in journalism. It is not uncommon for a reporter to know more than he or she writes, because in order to get that information a bond of trust has to exist with the off-the-record source. Since an editor needs to know the source of unattributed information, a similar bond of trust has to exist between the reporter and his superior.

It was late, so I called in my story to the rewrite desk. The assistant city editor on duty at the time was Wilson Hirschfeld, a longtime reporter and editor who could be dismissive, brusque and demanding, and who was clearly uncomfortable with his responsibility that night. We were destined to clash many times in the ensuing years.

But on this night, he was handling my story on the Jarosz murder. He questioned me about my source and the reliability of the information. I emphasized that we could not name the family involved or attribute anything to them. I had no confidence that the boy was a serious suspect. Hirschfeld made no objections to my reasoning.

The next morning left me stunned and embarrassed. There on page one was my story naming the suspect. I confronted Hirschfeld, who looked at me with piercing eyes as he slowly shook his head. "I couldn't afford to let the *Press* get the name," he said in a ghostly voice.

I now knew why Robertson had such antipathy for the desk. For one reason or another, the editors were always running scared. Over time I would learn that this was part of the newspaper's culture. I would also learn that Hirschfeld had agendas that went beyond covering the news.

Later I tried to reach the boy's father, but he would not take my call.

I drew assignments to cover both the wake and then the funeral the following day. It was sorrowful duty and even the jaded media stood by in respectful silence. Beverly's classmates from Marymount High School, dressed in their gray-and-blue school uniforms, walked by the open casket, their eyes damp with sadness, some trembling in grief. Maybe a thousand people filed through the church. Off in the corners you could see the detectives studying the mourners, looking for something, anything.

The investigation dragged on, the case getting colder with each passing day. Both papers continued to pursue it. The one piece of evidence that the police focused on was a length of rope around Beverly's neck. The other weapon, thought to be a four-inch knife, was never found.

As soon as he learned of the murder, Theron V. Moss, who had been in the rope business for 42 years, knew the Garfield

Heights police would call him. Twenty-five years earlier, during the investigation of a series of murders committed by the unknown Head Hunter of Kingsbury Run, the police had regularly called Moss. Rope was involved in those murders, too.

Moss examined the rope in the Jarosz case and determined it to be a fairly common cord used in window sashes or for clotheslines. A piece of similar rope was found in the possession of a neighbor; for a moment the police thought they had a break in the case, but the lead went nowhere.

Over the next 50 years, generations of police officers in Garfield Heights chased countless tips to no avail. The case remains open. Not long ago I drove by the house on Thornton Avenue, and I could still feel a sense of evil.

CHAPTER 8

Changing of the Guard

If Cleveland was on the verge of major change in the early 1960s, so too was the state of journalism in the city. Radio news still had reporters on the street and, more importantly, television news was beginning to come into its own. Every major story became a media event.

Television news had a greater impact on the *Press* than on the *Plain Dealer*. The six o'clock news on the city's three TV stations bit heavily into the afternoon paper's dinnertime market. By 1965 the *Plain Dealer* had increased its circulation by 50,000 and was rapidly closing in on its adversary, long the town's beacon.

Television wasn't the only force impinging on the reign of the *Press*. The creation of a vast highway system undertaken after World War II had pushed population from the city out to the suburbs, making timely delivery of an afternoon newspaper increasingly difficult. None of us could predict the demise of this powerful institution, but in retrospect all the fatal symptoms were there. In 1960 the *Cleveland News*, an afternoon paper owned by the *Plain Dealer*, sold its assets to the *Press* after competing with it unsuccessfully for more than 30 years.

Another alignment was taking place in Cleveland journalism, and that was the arrival of a new editor and publisher for the *Plain Dealer* and the imminent exit of the fabled Louis B. Seltzer, who had made the *Press* more than just a newspaper. The *Press* had become the soul of the city, reaching the working class in a way unlike any other institution in town.

Seltzer wasn't just another newspaper executive. For the better part of the century, he was the most powerful man in Cleveland.

And intersecting with Seltzer's waning career was 37-year-old Thomas V. H. Vail, whose own newspaper career was mightily advanced by the fact that his family had owned the *Plain Dealer* since 1885. Princeton educated and by his own admission at a loss for a career, Vail was urged by his father, Herman, to take over the drab morning newspaper. Tom had worked on the *News*, becoming its political editor. In anticipation of better things, he had transferred to the morning paper and apprenticed in various departments on the business side.

Herman Vail had even sought Seltzer's advice on the matter and was rewarded with a robust endorsement of Tom's promotion.

One could envision the wily Seltzer sizing up Tom Vail as a competitor, and embracing the idea the way a prospector would grasp newfound gold. The two men had one thing in common: they were fastidious dressers. Otherwise, they could not have been greater opposites.

Tom's great-grandfather, Liberty Emery Holden, had purchased the paper late in the 19th century. Over the years, as the family tree he sired branched out, ownership of the newspaper became fragmented so that there were varied interests as to its future. Hardly anyone in the family had worked on the paper. Herman Vail wanted Tom to gain control of it.

Seltzer, on the other hand, had literally grown up on a news-paper, first working in a city room at age 12 and becoming editor of the *Press* in 1928. A nationally recognized figure, he was the subject of profiles in magazines and newspapers. His personality dominated the city.

But if Seltzer thought that Vail in his Savile Row pinstripes was going to be less than competitive, he was mistaken. The *Plain Dealer* had been dull and plodding for most of its life. Its staff was old, the paper had no retirement policy, and its pub-lication each day seemed to occur merely out of habit. It held some cachet with the business community, the major law firms and the rest of the civic establishment, a group often at odds with the feisty Seltzer. The paper had no verve.

In a bit of a break with tradition, one of the first things Vail did was gain control of the titles of both publisher and editor. Generally, the publisher of a paper devotes energies to the busi-ness side of the operation, while the news side is the provenance of the editor. By holding both titles, Vail reasoned he could more quickly interject change into the look of the product.

And the paper was in dire need of change. For years the Forest City Publishing Company had been held in trust for the various family members.

Vail chose as his executive editor Philip W. Porter, who had joined the newspaper in 1922 and worked his way through the ranks. While Vail retained the glory and prestige of the title, Porter shouldered the day-to-day scut work that went along with being the editor: dealing with piddling $2-a-week merit raises, the usual union unrest, dissatisfied readers, seething public officials, unpleasant utility executives, public relations poachers and a building filled with boundless egos. In addition, both men authored "snowflakes," brief congratulatory notes on tissue paper sent to reporters for a story well done.

I took the snowflakes too seriously. After accumulating a few that made it clear my future on the paper was no longer in jeopardy, I began to think—which turned out to be a mistake. My thought was that I no longer wanted to be known by my byline of Michael D. Roberts. The reporters on the *Press* were known as Bob or Dick or Sam, so why couldn't I just be Mike?

Summoning up an excess of hubris, I walked the long corridor of executive offices and asked to see Porter. Phil looked like a newspaper editor. He wore a bow tie, smoked a cigar, and had a bit of a pug face with one bad eye that orbed off as if focused on someone else in the room.

As I presented my petition to have my byline changed, Porter's face began to flush. This was not a good sign. He thought for a moment, took a puff on his noxious cigar, then lit into me.

"I'm sitting here worried about a whole goddamn city falling apart, and you come in talking about something as chickenshit as your byline," he said. "I'll tell you what. I can make it so you don't ever get a byline. I can make it so you will be working weekend obits. Now get the hell out of here."

I exited a shaken but wiser person. I think of that meeting every time I write a check or sign the American Express bill, because forever after that I was Michael D. Roberts. Years later, Porter would confide to me his bitterness of not being named editor of the paper. He had worked a lifetime to attain the title. Sadly, in 1985, years after his retirement, Phil and his wife were murdered during a robbery of their home in Shaker Heights.

Aside from my flight of ego, there was still the *Press* to deal with. And for all the talk in the executive offices and Vail's brimming enthusiasm—he had taken to passing through the newsroom and complimenting staff members for the "terrific" job they were doing—directing the day-to-day scrap for news fell to one man.

Olive-skinned, mustachioed, with thinning hair, Ted Princiotto was a careful, curious and thorough man sometimes criticized for his cautious manner. He examined facts the way you would finger the pieces of a picture puzzle. In the fall of 1963 he became the *Plain Dealer*'s newly named city editor. He had started at the paper in its Canton bureau in the early 1940s and over the years had become a most reliable reporter.

In those days the job of city editor was one of enormous responsibility and power. The position involved directing the dozens of reporters who covered politics, city hall, the courts, medicine, space, the waterfront and the police beat and, most important, heading the paper's investigative efforts.

Princiotto's strategy to combat the *Press* was to use investigative teams to focus on major stories and to devote the time necessary to break them. While the nature of all reporting is basically investigative, the idea behind the teams was to go beyond the daily coverage and develop stories that merited headlines— big, bold, blockbusting headlines. This was in preparation for a circulation assault on the rival *Press*.

Because the lack of a retirement policy had stagnated the staff, reporters often spent years on a single beat. For instance, Princiotto had spent seven years covering the federal beat. His predecessor on the city desk had been in the job for 33 years. Vail's arrival changed that. Retirements suddenly began to create vacancies on the staff that were filled by eager, if not experienced, youths like myself who looked upon the work not as a job, but as an adventurous crusade.

The newspaper began to transform itself, aided by an odd amalgam of young college graduates working for an editorial leadership dominated by demanding World War II veterans. The vets, however, were unyielding in their lack of acceptance of new concepts and were both puzzled by and suspicious of this youthful wave.

One day a few months into the job I arrived at the city

room to find the place buzzing with excitement. Dozens of burly, unshaven men in work clothes milled about. I was a bit bewildered.

Sam Marshall, the affable labor writer who struggled with a lame leg, had just landed a blockbuster story, a reporter's dream. He had convinced members of the longshoremen's union to sign affidavits attesting that they were forced to pay kickbacks to local union boss Danny Greene in order to work on the docks. It was one of the best stories the *Plain Dealer* ever published. It felt great to be working on a newspaper capable of that kind of reporting.

Marshall won many national awards for his story, but missed out on the one journalists prize the most: the Pulitzer. Many years later Marshall learned that Louie Seltzer had used his influence on the Pulitzer board to prevent him from winning it. Greene served time in jail. Years later he would kill the notorious numbers king Shondor Birns with a car bomb and then subsequently be dispatched himself by a similar pyrotechnic device.

Marshall's was the first of a number of stories that would begin to erode the grip that the *Press* had on the city.

CHAPTER 9

Bergen, Booze and Birns

One day I was assigned to fill in at the old criminal courts building at East 21st and Payne Avenue, one of the most important newsmaking places in the city. The famous Sam Sheppard trial of 1954 had been held there. The aging 13-story art deco structure was wonderful for a reporter. The courtrooms were arranged around an octagonal rotunda. From up there you could look down and see who was coming into the building and what was happening on the different floors below. The building also housed the prosecutor's office, the jail and the sheriff's headquarters.

I had been told to go to the newsroom on the building's second floor and check to see if anything significant was happening that day. It was about two o'clock in the afternoon when I opened the door onto a darkened room, fumbled for the light switch, and blinked as a bare bulb brightened the vista. There were some desks and chairs in the room, but the main feature before me was a bed.

And in the bed, with blankets pulled up over his head, appeared to be a man. A voice issued from beneath the covers.

"Who the hell are you? Shut the light off!"

I quickly turned the light back off and announced myself as a reporter from the *Plain Dealer*.

"You one of those new kids they're hiring over there? You assholes all look the same, and you all wear those Tom Vail ties."

The room was still dark and I asked the man in the bed who he was.

"I'm Bus Bergen of the *Press*," he snapped. "I'm a world-famous reporter so don't you be running around the building looking to beat me on something. You see, kid, they call *me* with the news. So why don't you sit down. There's a bottle in the desk. Have yourself a drink and don't work up a sweat."

When the light came back on, there before me was my childhood idol, an elderly man with a gray crewcut and a rumpled suit rubbing the sleep from his eyes. He pulled open a desk drawer and offered a whiskey bottle. After I declined, he took a healthy swig.

"Don't be coming around here trying to scoop old Bus."

Drinking was part of newspaper culture, and Bus Bergen's fondness for that particular activity was legendary. The *Press* had threatened to fire Bergen so many times that it was an institutional joke. Once they had even pulled him off the street and made him work in the newsroom.

The only problem was that Bergen couldn't write. All those great stories that had carried his byline, the ones I had delivered on my paper route in Garfield Heights, had been the work of the rewrite desk.

On the occasion of Bergen being shunted to the office for disciplinary reasons, a common pleas court judge mistakenly thought that the grizzled newsman had been promoted and threw a party for him. Bergen's "promotion" to the city room didn't last long. He was too good a reporter to be tethered to the desk. Besides, he was Seltzer's favorite.

Despite the occasional reprimand, a lot of drinking was tolerated. One day a front-page bulletin in the final edition of the *Press* noted that the morning newspaper's drama critic had suffered a heart attack on East 9th Street. The *Press* hadn't had time to check facts before deadline, but our guy had been seen lying prostrate on the pavement. However, when I looked back at the critic's desk he was typing like nothing had happened. He had just imbibed a little too much for lunch and temporarily passed out.

Once at a cocktail party, George Barmann, a veteran reporter who could both write and drink, explained that a rookie reporter like me needed to learn how to work one of these affairs. If a utility company—especially the gas company—is throwing the party, he said, the bar will shut down at seven o'clock, so make sure to stash extra drinks behind the curtains. He also advised striking early and often at the shrimp bowl, for that crustacean was a favorite of the newspaper crowd. In fact, one or two reporters were known to fill plastic bags with shrimp and stuff them into their pockets.

At the Headliner, a block away from the *PD*, Red the bartender arranged rows of shots for the printers and pressmen who raced down the street between editions to have their whiskey. It was not unheard of for copy editors on the late shift to have flasks handy to ease the tedium of handling so much bad prose. Most of the excess drinking done on city side was usually late in the evening when the paper was put to bed.

Around 1 a.m., reporters and editors drifted to Payne Avenue. Payne hosted a panorama of slop chutes where the police beat shifted operations to Shai's or Sarada's Silver Grill or maybe the 2300 Club where the pinball machine shook and shuddered well into the morning. One of the legendary drinking feats of the time involved a copyboy, a thin, dark-haired college student who was destined to become an ace himself, only in another field of endeavor.

The copyboy, Dennis J. Kucinich, studied the city room and the way it functioned so carefully that one thought he surely would become a future inhabitant himself. Instead, he opted to become the mayor of Cleveland and embark on one of the most tempestuous reigns in the city's history.

Kucinich's claim to fame in the city room was the day he drank 10 martinis within a half hour to win a $30 bet. The incredible fact is that he had never had a drink before taking on the wager. Six reporters put up $5 apiece and paid for the drinks at the Rockwell Inn. Dennis won the bet, had trouble retching at first, then spent the next few days in a semi-stupor. He wrote that he never drank hard liquor again.

The best place for drinking in those days was the Theatrical Grill on Short Vincent. It was the epicenter of the town's nightlife and a haven for characters, criminals and constituents of every stripe. Law enforcement was drawn to the long U-shaped bar simply out of necessity, for the remnants of the mob liked to pose and preen around it. The jazz was good, the food more than serviceable, and the place a mecca for celebrities. Shondor Birns would sip white wine at the corner of the bar facing the entrance. Across the bar the FBI agent we called Mr. Boston would lend the scene a bit of federal oversight.

But the Theatrical was too expensive for a reporter making $120 a week. The city's criminal attorneys, who regarded the Theatrical as the real bar association, were usually good for a drink or two, in their mind buying insurance for favorable coverage of professional matters that might occur in the future.

Birns was at his usual spot daily, well turned out with a fashionable ensemble, a hat and a cigar. His face was hatchet-like, his eyes asquint. He had thin lips and a boxer's bounce to his walk. It was only a matter of time before our paths would cross, and I wasn't looking forward to it. The man was a killer.

The year before I joined the paper Birns had been the subject of a sensational murder investigation. He was sought for the killing of Mervin Gold, a financier who had used stolen Canadian bonds to secure a loan. Gold left behind an affidavit stating that the bonds had belonged to Birns. The police arrested him in Toledo where he had surrendered.

To the surprise of law enforcement officials, Birns produced an alibi that involved a 24-year-old Garfield Heights teacher who testified that she had spent the night with him. The woman, Allene Leonards, had been a classmate of mine through 12 years of school. I used to walk home with her in the second grade. Quiet and demure, she was the perfect witness for Birns and most likely saved him from a life sentence. They married the following year. For the next 40 years I tried to reach her, but she would never respond to my inquiries.

Over his lifetime Birns had been involved in so many crimes and allied with so many criminals that he indeed was the prince of thieves. Yet he got along well with many reporters, judges and law enforcement officials, many of whom helped him, in one way or another, in his effort to maintain legitimate businesses and seek respectability.

I had known of Birns for years through stories in the *Press* that branded him public enemy number one. His name regularly appeared in print, associated with myriad crimes. He was often an unwilling trial witness, refusing to give an inch to any prosecutor regardless of the nature of the case.

It was during a noon recess hour in one of those court cases that I occasioned to meet him. We were up in the rotunda of the criminal courts building when I approached him with a question about testimony in the case. He was leaning over the banister looking downward when I introduced myself.

He glanced over at me, his eyes pinched in a penetrating

scan. "Don't worry, kid," he said. "I'm not going to hurt you. Just don't ever borrow money from me and we will get along fine." Among his many endeavors, Birns had a notorious reputation as a loan shark.

He must have read fright on my face to make a comment like that. We talked for a few minutes, him responding to my questions with grunts and shrugs, leaving my notebook blank, which meant there would be nothing of substance in tomorrow's paper. As we talked, judges, police and other officials passed on their way to lunch, many acknowledging him with a "Hi, Shon" greeting.

"Look at this, kid, and remember it," Birns said. "I'm supposed to be a public enemy and all these people want to be friendly with me. Especially the judges. I wouldn't vote for any of the bastards."

For the next decade or so, before he was killed, I would have brief encounters with Birns, always friendly but never revealing. Once I was in a barbershop when he walked in and pulled out a wad of money, looked at me, and then handed it to the barber for safekeeping while he got a haircut. The Internal Revenue Service had been confiscating his cars and money in public places.

Making small talk, I asked about his handball game. He was reputed to be an excellent player. "I'm slowing down, kid, getting old," he said.

It wasn't until Good Friday in 1975, when Danny Greene blew him to pieces just as church was letting out at St. Malachi's, that Shondor Birns finally did slow down.

CHAPTER 10

The Federal Rap

J. C. Dashbach was close to 75 years old when he relinquished the federal beat to me early in 1965. I don't think he was happy about it. He had worked for several Cleveland news-papers, most of them now defunct, and had covered the news for a half century. He wore high-top shoes and rimless glasses, grunted a lot, and moved slowly around the old federal court-house on Public Square. He could be a pain in the ass. He never bothered to knock, walked in on private legal conferences as if he were a judge, and showed no respect to anyone.

Despite his advanced age, Dashbach could report. His compe-tition at the *Press*, John Betchkal, figured the only way he could beat him was to gather news from agencies located beyond the reach of Dash's mobility.

On the day when Dashbach was introducing me around the courthouse, a civil trial was under way involving the billionaire industrialist Cyrus Eaton. Eaton was suing his former accoun-tant over an incident that had taken place in the early 1940s, alleging that the man had illegally appropriated several thou-sand dollars. Dashbach barged into the courtroom during testi-mony with me in tow and seated himself behind Eaton.

U.S. District Judge Frank J. Battisti was hearing the case.

Upon Dashbach's arrival he gaveled the court and ordered him
to stop making so much noise.

"That is all that is going on here anyway," Dashbach shot back.
This was incredibly rude behavior in front of a federal judge.
Spectators cringed, awaiting the order for U.S. marshals to eject
Dashbach from the premises. Instead, Battisti ignored him.

Eaton, then 82, had a long and controversial business career
stretching back to the days of John D. Rockefeller. Among his
achievements was the creation of Republic Steel out of the amal-
gamation of several small steel companies. In a case involving
the Youngstown Sheet and Tube Company, Eaton was criticized
in court by the famous attorney Newton D. Baker for using
money from small investors to promote himself as an industrialist. He also embittered many over his friendship with the
Russian government at the height of the Cold War. Dashbach
had no doubt clashed with Eaton at some point in their lives.

So as the trial resumed, Dash leaned forward and whispered
into Eaton's ear: "You are still a no-good son-of-a-bitch."

Only the whisper had all the delicacy of a bullhorn. The
courtroom recoiled, Battisti whacked his gavel furiously, and
Dashbach assumed an air of majestic insouciance. We got up
and left before a contempt charge could be levied or a mistrial
pronounced. Eaton lost the case.

The federal beat had the broadest reach when it came to
news sources. It included the U.S. Attorney's Office, the FBI,
the Secret Service, the IRS, the Small Business Administration,
bankruptcy court, tax court, the U.S. Marshal's Office and an
array of smaller federal agencies. The bulk of the news came out
of the U.S. Attorney's Office.

Merle M. McCurdy was the U.S. attorney for northern Ohio.
A trim, handsome black man with an engaging demeanor and
smooth, polished courtroom skills, McCurdy looked the part.

In 1965 he had eight assistants in offices on the fourth floor of Cleveland's federal courthouse. (To understand how the scope of law has broadened, in 2017 there were nearly 80 U.S. attorneys in the Northern District of Ohio, a region that has lost population.)

One good thing about the federal beat was that the courthouse didn't have the usual medicinal-municipal smell. It was a civilized, leisurely setting, with thoughtful decor (the place even had some rugs) and a clean, professional atmosphere. Reporters could roam freely throughout the building, visit offices unannounced, and learn personally from judges the arcane intricacies of bankruptcy law. It was a far cry from what reporters experience today, with locked offices, security devices and tight-lipped officials.

Of course, you still had to dig up stories that the U.S. Attorney's Office did not want to relinquish. That involved developing special techniques like learning to read upside down and timing the attorneys' visits to the men's room in order to get a good look at what was on their desks. It was good practice to stop in and chat about the Browns or Indians for a minute or two, casting your eyes about for some glimpse of an affidavit, FBI report or court document. All you needed was some kind of lead and you could eventually pick up a few tips and ferret out a story.

I would even check in with the blind man at the newsstand to learn if he had heard some idle chatter. Every now and then he would come up with something. Apparently people would talk in front of him as if he was also deaf.

One attorney with many newsworthy cases was Robert J. Rotatori. A graduate of John Adams High School and Western Reserve College, Rotatori had a sense for which cases would make news and get a mention in the paper. He did not like for me to learn about a case until the office released it. So we would play a cat-and-mouse game, with me acting like I knew more than I did.

One day I was in Rotatori's office distracting him with the fact that I had heard he held the NCAA record for the most errors—five—by a college baseball player on a single play. On his desk was a court document with a reference to Shondor Birns. Birns, as I've mentioned, was a name that would put the city desk on red alert, so I knew my discovery would be almost guaranteed to land on page one.

How could I find out the story? There was only one option: wait until Rotatori went to the men's room and then rifle the papers on his desk. There was the risk that I might be breaking the law or even get fired. Finally, after what seemed like an eternity, he left his desk.

I slipped into the open office. The document that I had seen was still on top of the desk. Now I could clearly read that the case was an embezzlement involving Capital National Bank and that Birns was connected to it in some way. Bingo!

There was one problem. I had forgotten my notebook. My heart was beating with both fear and excitement. I rolled up my left sleeve and wrote notes on my arm until there was no space left, escaping the office just in time.

About two hours later, just as Rotatori was going home, I approached him and asked if there was something going on with Shondor Birns. He said that if there was something, he couldn't talk about it.

Even though I had a sense of the story, I wasn't sure the *Plain Dealer* would go with a "we learned" article. On rare occasions you could go with that attribution, but you had to be very certain of the facts. Since there was a crime involved in this case, doing so raised serious legal questions of libel.

City editor Ted Princiotto was waiting for me when I got back to the office. He was nearly salivating over the prospects of this story. When I told him that I didn't have attributions, the look on his face turned to disappointment. And when he saw me refer to the notes on my arm, disappointment turned to suspicion.

"I'm not sure we can go with this story," he said. "Did you talk to the FBI?"

I told him I hadn't had the time to do so, and added that the FBI most likely was not going to say anything anyway. In those days the bureau never said anything. J. Edgar Hoover was a tyrannical boss and a micromanager. The agents feared him more than God. Plus, it was hard to get to know them. When I visited the FBI I was instructed to bring something with me—a clipping, a picture, anything—to make it appear as if I had some information for the agent.

That night Princiotto called the FBI himself. After his many years on the federal beat, he had accumulated some good contacts and one was in the bureau. Even then, he was allowed only one question. I sat next to him at the desk as he posed it.

"If we went with a story on the embezzlement at the Capital National Bank would we be correct in doing so?"

I was nervous, hoping to avoid the embarrassment that a negative answer would bring.

The answer was one word: yes.

"I don't know how in the hell you got this story," Princiotto said. "But in my seven years on the beat I never broke one like this."

An unhappy Merle McCurdy held a staff meeting to discuss how the Capital National Bank story had been leaked. I was sure Rotatori knew, but he never said anything. We scored on the *Press* and it took two days to clean the ink from my arm.

The one story that I didn't get involved the U.S. Secret Service.

It surely would have caused a scandal and cost careers. In those days Cleveland was an important printing town, employing many skilled workers in the craft. Because of its prominence in the graphic arts, the town attracted counterfeiters. They in turn drew the attention of the Secret Service, which at the time was under the purview of the U.S. Treasury Department.

One day as I made my rounds at the courthouse, a postal inspector drew me aside and asked if I had heard about the mess the Secret Service had gotten itself into here. I had not, so he related what he had heard from an FBI agent.

A Secret Service agent was tracking a suspected counterfeiter and had broken into the suspect's Shaker Heights apartment while the man was in the bathtub. The agent, who had no arrest warrant, confronted the naked man and held his head under the bathwater in an effort to make him reveal where the counterfeit engravings were hidden. In the ensuing struggle, the agent suddenly realized he was in the wrong apartment. He fled.

The story brought to mind a similar incident that was rumored in the federal community. In this tale, a counterfeiting suspect was to meet a conspirator on Public Square to deliver engraving plates in a brown-paper lunch bag. The Secret Service had received the tip too late to get an arrest warrant, so the agent decided to waylay the man and grab the plates. So at noon on a sunny spring day the agent walked up to a man on the square who was carrying a lunch bag, punched him in the face, snatched the bag and ran off. He later discovered that the bag contained a ham sandwich.

When I began to make inquiries into these stories, no one seemed to know anything. Rotatori was the U.S. attorney who handled Secret Service cases; he was shocked, he said, to hear accusations against the agency regarding such foul and dastardly acts. "It is an effort on the part of the criminal element to besmirch the good name of the government," he added. He sounded like he was running for public office.

Even though I had nothing strong to go on, I asked Wilmer K. Deckard, the Secret Service agent in charge of the office in Cleveland, if there was any truth to the matter. A veteran agent, Deckard had spent much of his career on the presidential detail guarding the wheelchair-bound Franklin D. Roosevelt. "I wish I had a nickel for every time I carried that old man up the stairs," he told me one afternoon.

Deckard did not like Roosevelt's dog, a celebrated Scottish terrier named Fala that traveled with the president. The dog would invariably leap into Deckard's train berth and urinate there. He once kicked the dog, and it did not forget. Fala would growl at the agent in Roosevelt's presence, and the president could never understand why.

"If the old man ever found out," Deckard said, "I would have been out on my ear in a second."

When I broached the question of the two alleged incidents involving his agents, Deckard simply said that there were always allegations made about the conduct of law enforcement. He said he had long ago stopped paying attention to such things and that it was preposterous to think the Secret Service would commit such acts.

Still, I wondered. Several months later I learned that the Shaker Heights man who claimed to have been accosted in his tub was an African American doctor. A source in the courthouse said that Merle McCurdy had ordered a lineup of agents to see if the doctor could identify his assailant. He was unable to do so. Years later, still puzzling over the case, I was told that one of the agents was on vacation when the lineup took place.

The beat produced a rich variety of news and stories involving embezzlement, racketeering, postal scandals, tax cases, even an illegal radio station in Maple Heights set up by a man who dreamed of being a rock-and-roll disc jockey. One of the most memorable involved the newspaper and its coverage of a cancer cure, a curious story that still troubles after some 50 years. We'll get to it later.

CHAPTER 11

The Forged Rembrandt

A story of intrigue involving Rembrandt van Rijn drew me from the federal beat and thrust me into the esoteric world of fine art. In May 1965, Baldwin-Wallace College proudly announced that it had acquired a painting by the celebrated Dutch master. The accompanying page-one news report estimated that the work could be worth as much as $2 million.

Before the announcement, I had learned of the acquisition from a friend, James D. Harvey, who was a vice president of the college. Located in Berea, a southwest suburb far from Cleveland's cultural core, Baldwin-Wallace was not a place of pretense. B-W alumni tended to be first-generation college graduates who went on to have solid careers in the arts, business, music and teaching.

Presiding over the college was Dr. Alfred B. Bonds, a Southerner who had taught at the American University in Cairo, Egypt. His mild manner was deceptive and his understanding of power admirable. He had arrived at B-W in the mid-1950s with the college trying to find its future. Bonds, largely through his personality, assembled a board of trustees consisting of some of the best names in town. This was unusual, since Western Reserve College, Case Institute of Technology and John Carroll

University, located on the East Side, generally had the first pick of prominent personages.

Candidly, A. B. Bonds was a sophisticated hustler. And that turned out to be part of the problem.

About a week after the page-one Rembrandt announcement, Ted Princiotto called me over to the city desk. He had a tip that there was something awry with the story. He wanted me to check with the FBI to see if the painting was stolen artwork. I said I was sure it wasn't and told him what I knew about it.

"We have good sources questioning the veracity of the painting," Princiotto said. "Get on it."

What I did not know for a long time was just who the source was. It turned out that the dime-dropper was the Cleveland Museum of Art. That venerable institution had immediately challenged the painting within its ranks, but instead of being a good citizen and alerting the college, it chose to embarrass Baldwin-Wallace through the paper. If a similar incident had occurred at Western Reserve or John Carroll, it would have played out differently. This was an East Side, West Side thing.

My call to Jim Harvey created a frenzy at B-W. I told him that we were going with a story that would challenge the painting's attribution. Helen Borsick, the paper's art critic, had been on the phone talking to Rembrandt experts all over the country. Even though they had not seen the painting, all of them expressed doubt about its authenticity.

There are only so many known Rembrandt paintings in the world, and any expert dealing with 17th-century Dutch master-pieces knows not only the paintings but where they reside. But the art world lived for the discovery of a lost work, surely part of the attraction the school had for the painting.

Bonds was beside himself with anger. He cursed me on the phone, using language most unbecoming of a college president.

Harvey was more practical. He brought the painting downtown to the paper's offices and pledged total transparency in determining its origin.

Princiotto and the other editors gazed at the picture of *Titus, Son of Rembrandt* and nodded their heads knowingly as if they had some recollection from a long-ago art history class. That night we went with a page-one story challenging the work's authenticity.

Our inquiry had unearthed an even more fascinating twist. The donor of the painting, Dr. Oscar K. Cosla, carried a questionable provenance as well. He had moved from New York City to Berea on the promise of a lifetime salary from the school and a house in which to reside. With him, he brought his wife and a collection of hundreds of reputed old masters.

Cosla, 72, was a native of Romania. Somehow A. B. Bonds had found Cosla living in Harlem, persuaded him to donate his art collection to Baldwin-Wallace, and in return offered him and his wife a comfortable retirement. As the story unraveled it became clear that Cosla had misrepresented himself to the munificent Dr. Bonds.

The day after the story ran, Harvey and I flew to New York with the painting. It was a hot day and the scholars we called upon were at first reluctant to render an opinion. When an expert at the Metropolitan Museum of Art agreed to an off-the-record comment, however, we heard sobering news. Not only was the painting not a Rembrandt, it was of little value. Dr. Julius Held, a celebrated Rembrandt expert and an art history professor at Barnard College, also examined the painting and said it could not be over 150 years old. Rembrandt had died in 1669. Since the painting was signed as a Rembrandt, Held deemed it a forgery.

The focus of the story now turned from the authenticity of the painting to that of the shadowy Dr. Cosla, a retired heart specialist. When I finally visited him in Berea I founded a wizened, slightly stooped man with a thick Middle European accent and a beret worn with a peasant's carelessness. He said he was ill and needed to lie down as we talked. The soft shuffle of Mrs. Cosla could be heard in another room.

The house provided by the college was filled with paintings, some on the walls but most in racks. Gloom permeated the rooms, along with a distinctive camphorous smell later identified as salamander oil. It was an uneasy setting.

Cosla insisted that the painting he identified as a Rembrandt was authentic and shrugged off the opinions of scholars who deemed it a worthless fake. He said that over the years many experts had seen the painting and had confirmed its provenance. In fact, he added, he owned works by other masters such as van Dyck and Rubens.

"Michael, they are all good," he said. "You bring an expert here to see, and if they are not what I say then I will give you the most valuable of the collection."

Cosla said he inherited the collection from his father in 1920, recalling that the Rembrandt had been brought to their home in Bucharest in 1909. At the onset of World War II, Cosla hid the collection, distinctly recalling that the Rembrandt had been secluded in a haystack. After the war, he and his wife, Rose, an American citizen, escaped the Russian advance and in 1947 came to New York. With the help of the American government, they were able to bring the collection with them.

In the United States, the collection had been exhibited at such places as the Maryhill Museum of Art in Washington state, Montclair State College, Brigham Young University, the American Bible Society and the University of the Ozarks. Not what you would call lofty realms of the art world.

I left the house on Front Street feeling conflicted. Was I dealing with an elderly man slipping into senility, or beneath this feeble facade was Cosla a first-rate con artist? The question bothered me for days. Then Baldwin-Wallace announced it was going to retain Cosla on an annual lifetime salary of $22,000 as curator of his collection of nearly a thousand works.

At that point we learned that at least eight colleges and universities had been trying to entice Cosla to their campuses.

The story was intriguing, but pursuing it would require time, and there was a question of whether the paper would invest in it or just let it go. Cosla and the collection had to be traced back to the turn of the century, a period of some 60 years; the provenance of the paintings had to be documented, as did the doctor's medical career. I was confident that federal records would establish his movement and citizenship, but the paintings represented an arcane world and tracing their origin would be difficult.

I presented my case for further investigation to Princiotto and to my surprise got no argument. A decided change had come over the *Plain Dealer*; its aggressiveness was being noticed in national publications like *Time* and *Newsweek*. The growing euphoria for the paper's new direction helped sell the story.

Over the next several months I would learn a lot, but the most important lesson was how the art world was governed by silence, mystery, uncertainty and deception. It is a world awash in culture and scholarship, but one that is treacherous to the naive and uninitiated. Cosla had woven a web of deceit around himself and his collection, a deceit that he may have ultimately come to believe himself. He lived a life of endless lies.

Originally, Cosla said he inherited a collection from his father, but actually he had used his wife's inheritance of some $200,000 to begin to collect art. Whether he knew it or not, most of what he was buying were second- and third-rate works; some could be classified as junk.

Cosla was quite active in showing his collection to noted authorities on European art and soliciting their written opinions as to the merit of the paintings. Most of these experts skirted the issue by making benign and polite remarks. After all, it is painful to crush the spirits of a man who has devoted both time and fortune to what he considers a noble pursuit. And here is where the deceit begins.

The doctor's tale told of hiding his collection from the Nazi invaders in Romania. Records revealed that German officials had indeed visited the collection, but during their plunder of Europe's finest art they had developed a fairly good eye and took a pass. There was some reason to believe that Cosla may have had a brush with Nazi collaboration.

Though Cosla at first denied it, he was involved in a growing number of transactions with art galleries after his arrival in New York. Here is where I tend to think he knew what he was doing. It is not uncommon for a museum to acquire a work of art, display it under the name of a particular artist, and then later, maybe even years later, find through new research that the attribution is wrong and the work is of little value.

However, the museum's catalog may have listed the original attribution for years before discovery of the error. Many of these misattributed works would be auctioned off for as little as several hundred dollars. But if you possessed a copy of the old catalog along with the painting, you could present the work to your audience as one created by a renowned artist. Only the most knowledgeable would know the difference. Cosla had catalogs that had been retired and the paintings that went with them.

I flew to New York and visited the apartment building where

the Coslas had lived in Harlem. It was a strange place staffed by a German custodian who was suspicious, sarcastic and sanctimonious. In the ceiling of his basement apartment in the brownstone the German had mounted a shotgun with a trip wire that was certain to discourage intruders. There appeared to be a need for such security; the building was a scandalous place.

A sex cult occupied several apartments, the endeavors of the membership accompanied by the beat of bongo drums. As the cult celebrated, marijuana smoke seeped through the ventilators into Cosla's former first-floor apartment. When I asked the custodian about the doctor's medical practice he said the clientele largely consisted of neighborhood prostitutes.

The Coslas had rented three apartments in the building to house their collection of paintings. The custodian was often called upon to move the paintings, work that he found tiring and annoying. One day Cosla showed him the Rembrandt, and the German dismissed it as a fake. When an art professor from Baldwin-Wallace visited the collection in New York, he also challenged the painting's authenticity. An indignant Cosla expressed his dismay and the professor quickly returned to Berea, fearing he had jeopardized the deal.

Part of the arrangement with B-W was a gift of 12 paintings in return for a lifetime income and housing. A competent appraiser had valued the pictures at a half-million dollars. The problem was, he had never seen them. Cosla had requested an appraisal for insurance purposes. He then used the document as proof to the college that the works were authentic. The appraiser was not happy to learn that none of the paintings were true to their attribution.

Over a period of time I wrote extensively about Dr. Cosla, each article advancing the web of his scheme until it became clear that he had exhausted his welcome in Berea. It was an intriguing story about the mysteries of the art world, and I was sorry to leave it behind for the more mundane.

The school settled with the good doctor and he quietly faded amid the embarrassment that he had cast.

But the story hadn't quite yet ended.

One afternoon I was languishing in the city room, watching everyone else work, when I got a phone call from a reporter on the *Miami Herald*. He was inquiring about a painting that a Dr. Oscar K. Cosla had just donated to the University of Miami. Did I know anything about him?

"You know what," I said. "I'll be right down there."

It was my sad duty to relate to the president of the university, Henry King Stanford, the saga of the Cosla collection.

CHAPTER 12

That Other Side of Town

In a way, Cleveland is more a village than a city. What it embraces the most—its ethnocentrism—hurts it the most. Its Middle European heritage, with its disdain of landlords, government and the wealthy, never allowed the formation of a true amalgam, the American dream of a melting pot. Cleveland never became the sum of its parts, but just remained parts.

Cleveland was never a city the way a city is supposed to be, one with focus and direction where people care for it the way you would a family or a good school or a prized possession. It is a hard town to truly love. Live here long enough and you accept it as you do a cellmate in jail. It is a place where the promise of tomorrow far outweighs the reality of today.

Cleveland is divided in several ways—by race, by culture and by location. Some claim that the East Side versus West Side dispute is just a myth. I contend that its roots can be found in the settling of the city in the late 1700s. The predominant landowners in the Western Reserve were Yale graduates from Connecticut. Horrified by the harsh winters along Lake Erie, they would return east before the bitterly cold months arrived.

Only a handful of settlers, along with the area's native tribes, stayed year round. Their leader was Lorenzo Carter, truly a man for all seasons, who settled along the river west of the town's public square. By all rights the city should bear Carter's name, not that of surveyor Moses Cleaveland (who came here once and never returned, some accusing him of making a bad real estate deal).

The fact that Carter stayed, prevailing against the natives, the weather and the uncertainty of it all, made him a legendary figure, which sparked jealousy among those later eastern settlers. This was the initial fissure in what is now the great East Side, West Side divide.

Still, there is a certain majesty to the town's history. It is a tough, serious place where celebrity is at a minimum and struggle is at a maximum. It was built on commerce, a hard, back-wrenching, blue-collar kind of commerce, the kind that killed men in their early 50s through either working conditions or alcohol, whichever doused the spirit first.

It generated enormous wealth for a few and hard work for most. If God wanted a blue-collar town, there was no better place than Cleveland. It was a place where a handshake was enough, a shot and a beer was communion, and football was more uniting than politics. The work ethic thrived during two World Wars, and helped to win them, and never flagged throughout the Korean War.

Given the nature of the town's composition, its politics were of the ethnic variety, marked by a desire to live in yesteryear and distrustful of new ideas, other nationalities and the civic establishment. Sustaining its lethargic spirit was a vast pool of political patronage that supported generation after generation of families who served as government workers and perpetuated the election of those who made certain little would change.

This political atmosphere, along with the dominance of the

Cleveland Press for four decades, left the city and the county without the benefit of a two-party system. By the 1960s, the local Republican Party basically existed in name only. All this created a fertile breeding ground for corruption, assorted acts of malfeasance and shoddy government.

It was this breach of public trust that the editors at the *Plain Dealer* sought to exploit in an effort to shake off the lassitude that for years had been the newspaper's hallmark. Shortly after Ted Princiotto became city editor, he got the ball rolling by hiring a reporter who would go on to become one of the respected names in contemporary American journalism.

Donald L. Barlett began his work for the *Plain Dealer* in a covert manner. In 1965 he got a job as an attendant at the Lima State Hospital for the Criminally Insane, where for seven weeks he worked to catalog the harsh conditions of the prison, the abuse of its inmates, and the failures of a criminal justice system that did little to rehabilitate. His series of articles generated reforms by the state government.

Barlett was a bespectacled, soft-spoken 29-year-old whose appearance and manners were disarming. A former U.S. Army counterintelligence operative, Barlett was intuitive, self-confident, patient and quietly driven. He was the perfect investigative reporter.

While such reporters had always existed in one form or another, the 1960s saw their emergence. Newspapers like the *Plain Dealer* may have had as many as a hundred or more reporters on its staff, but most were assigned to beats or areas of specialization like the arts or health care. Few had time to linger on a subject. A daily newspaper was just that, and the majority of its effort was aimed at covering that day's news.

At the same time, government and business practices were becoming more sophisticated, sometimes overwhelming young reporters. When it came to investigating corruption, the city room followed this axiom: If the target is smarter than the tracker, there's a good chance the story won't make print.

In many ways, investigative reporting could be boring, thankless and time-consuming work. But it also took you to places you'd never been and challenged you to think creatively. You had to learn to recover from stumbling down countless blind alleys without succumbing to discouragement.

The work was focused and insular. An investigative reporter had to constantly guard against adopting a "cop mentality" over a subject and altering the story to fit suspicions rather than facts. The work often required complete secrecy, even with colleagues.

The most effective way to go after big stories was in teams; two heads were always better than one. The team approach also offered a witness to sensitive interviews, many of which were conducted off the record.

At first Princiotto teamed Barlett with Doris O'Donnell, a veteran of the defunct *Cleveland News*, where she had established herself as the city's most prominent woman journalist. Among other stories, she had covered the first Sam Sheppard trial in 1954. But O'Donnell and Barlett had different reporting styles. She relied heavily on former contacts, while he took a more *a priori* approach.

When Princiotto saw that the collaboration between the two reporters was not going well, I was assigned to work with Barlett. That journalistic partnership would be one of my most valued experiences. Barlett would go on to co-author eight books and win two Pulitzer Prizes, two National Magazine Awards and six George Polk Awards.

But in the summer of 1966, Barlett's attention was focused on Cuyahoga County Sheriff James J. McGettrick. Over the years the county sheriff's office had become a citadel of corruption and corrosive management, and McGettrick, the prototype Democratic party hack, was running a famously corrupt operation. He drank throughout the day, using tanks of oxygen in his office to relieve the suffering brought on by lingering hangovers. He also drew profits from a candy cart that sold overpriced confections to prisoners in the county jail.

Barlett discovered that things were so bad that an inmate dressed as a deputy routinely walked McGettrick's German shepherd, Sandy. One day the inmate simply tied Sandy to a tree and escaped with two pistols from the jail's gun room. The prisoner's father was waiting in a car behind the jail.

When the escapee was arrested in a West Side restaurant three days later, a deputy shot and wounded him with no apparent provocation. Sheriff's deputies did not allow Cleveland police to investigate the matter, fearing disclosure of lax jail practices. The prisoner, whom the sheriff clearly would have preferred dead rather than alive, was sentenced to nine to 62 years for charges involving the jailbreak. It soon became apparent that the incident was far from isolated. McGettrick was running a rogue operation on an inflated budget (the highest ever for the office), the payroll larded with patronage, his chief deputy operating a business that sold food to the jail. Not only that, his deputies conducted their official duties in violation of the law.

Barlett uncovered the fact that two bail-bond jumpers had fled from Cleveland to New York City, pursued by a bail bondsman's bounty hunter and one of McGettrick's deputies. It is illegal for a law enforcement agent to accompany a bounty hunter who is seeking to return an escapee from another state. The escapees in this case were 31-year-old Sheridan Nesbitt and his 23-year-old girlfriend, Delores Jones. He was charged with armed robbery and she with possession of narcotics.

While a bounty hunter can legally capture and return bond jumpers, a law enforcement officer must go through a cumbersome, costly and time-consuming extradition process. For McGettrick's deputies, due process meant capturing the bond jumpers, drugging them, throwing them into the back of a car, and driving through the night back to Cleveland.

We interviewed Nesbitt and Jones in prison, and their separate versions of the kidnapping were identical. The only problem in terms of their credibility was the fact that both were felons. Princiotto insisted that Barlett and I trace their movements in New York. That meant visiting the Wilthom Hotel in Harlem.

The Wilthom offered rooms with a television for $6.50 a night, or $6.25 with just a radio. The hotel was well situated amid a cluster of bars, among which Larry's Love Cottage stood out, and was not far from the Gotham City Loan Company, which conducted a lively business with the hotel's clientele, many of whom were junkies who hocked items to support their habit.

The hotel housed a diverse group of drug dealers, prostitutes and street people who began their day in the establishment's bar with stiff eye-openers. The place was so dangerously uncomfortable at 10 a.m. that it was difficult to imagine what it must be like at midnight.

Barlett and I were two white guys wearing trench coats. When we first walked into the Wilthom, half the toilets in the place flushed as residents rushed to discard their drug stashes. Hattie Thomas, who ran the place with her husband, Jimmy, scolded us and said that we had cost her guests a considerable amount of money.

Despite our intrusion, Mrs. Thomas was helpful in confirming that the two bond jumpers had indeed been at the Wilthom and had been taken by four men, two of whom were New York

City police officers. The local police, she said, were frequent visitors to her hotel, but an inquiry to New York's 28th Precinct was met with a denial of even knowing of the Wilthom. This added another dimension to the story.

"If that dog could talk, he could tell you a lot," Mrs. Thomas said, nodding toward Leo, a bulldog sleeping next to the staircase. Every guest, whether coming or going, had to pass him. The dog had been stolen three times, but always managed to escape his captors and return to the hotel. Leo looked the worse for wear. He had been hit by an oil truck, broken two legs, and lost an eye.

We wrote a series of articles detailing every aspect of the case, including the fact that Sheriff McGettrick was doing his best to hide documents, stifle interviews, and cover for the rogue operation. The county prosecutor, a former law partner of McGettrick's, took no substantive action. It was an example of how Cuyahoga County operated. McGettrick was voted out of office in 1968, but four years later a myopic public elected him to the common pleas court. In 1985 he was convicted of taking a bribe in a murder case and died in prison a few months later.

As for Barlett and me, we simply moved on to another example of how the county operated, this time the probate court, a cesspool of patronage, cronyism and legal thievery. A busy place, the probate court makes death an orderly and legal event, administers proceedings in cases of dispute, and performs sundry other duties. But we were mainly interested in the court's efforts to locate missing heirs.

When Barlett first proposed the story idea, it seemed like a daunting task. How were we going to find missing heirs when the court with all of its power and resources couldn't locate them? Intuition is what made Barlett such a great reporter. He sensed that the whole county government system was rotten, so why should the probate court be any different? Going into the story we had no leads. We found the list of the intestate cases, people who had died and left estates but with no known heirs to claim them.

In these cases, the court appointed a lawyer to launch a search. The lawyer would be paid out of the estate for what could be a time-consuming effort. If no heirs were found, the estate's remaining monies would revert to the state.

In the era before computers, court record searches could be maddening. We spent six months haunting the courthouse and the Cleveland Public Library, paying frequent visits to city hall to review death certificates and to funeral homes to check records. The work was tiring and uninspiring. It seemed like we got less done with each passing day.

We would come to work around 10 a.m. and leave around 9 p.m., then return to the paper at 3 a.m. when Princiotto finally could break from his daily duties to go over developments in the investigation. We would chart the search for heirs on a blackboard and walk through every aspect of the hunt to make sure of our facts. Nobody worked harder than Princiotto.

But then we got lucky. During the Depression the federal government had created a lot of jobs to pump money into the economy. One of them involved the clipping and filing on cards of death notices that appeared in the newspapers. The Cleveland Public Library continued the practice after the federal program ended. It was a godsend.

These notices listed the deceased's survivors, and by crossreferencing the family members over a given period of time you could trace several generations of relatives. The cards were in a room near the front of the library, their existence not well known. They became an invaluable reference source for us and an embarrassment to the court.

For example, attorney Ernest Abram had been assigned by the probate court to find the heirs of one Hyde J. Stewart. After four years of searching, including a trip to Dublin, Ireland, Abram billed the estate for 150 hours of legal work, totaling $7,500. He failed to find any heirs.

It took us three days to find Stewart's heirs, and the only travel we did was between the library and the courthouse. U.S. Representative Robert E. Sweeney was assigned a case by the court with an estate worth $22,864. After Sweeney located no heirs and charged nearly $10,000 to the estate, we were able to find relatives in a week.

The court was a morass of questionable practices. One probate court bailiff inherited $40,000, claiming he was a friend of the deceased. In another case, accusations of a forged will were not thoroughly investigated. In a case where assets were listed as more than $4 million, the court approved lawyer's fees of $250,000 and failed to make public that the mortgage business involved in the estate was a financial fraud.

That summer Barlett left the paper and took a job with the *Chicago Daily News*. Geraldine Javor, an Ohio State journalism graduate, joined me in the probate probe, and we labored on the project well into the fall. When we finished, it was clear that there were not enough reporters on staff to adequately cover the court's corrupt practices. Its shady operation had become a way of life.

CHAPTER 13

The Really Big Story

In the days before social media's ubiquitous reach, newspapers harbored the ominous fear of missing "the big one." The big one was a story of global magnitude that suddenly occurred on your watch or on your beat. An inability to handle it rained shame and embarrassment on the paper and its staff.

According to *Plain Dealer* lore in those days, the worst gaffe in the history of the paper had been its failure to cover the end of the Civil War. How in the hell do you miss the end of a war, particularly that one, went the refrain. This would prove not to be true, but the rumor in the city room in 1965 was that the paper had not reported Lee's surrender.

The newspaper's coverage of the Civil War had been interrupted in 1865 by a change in editors that altered the paper's position on the war. The new editor stood for peace at any cost, while those on the staff maintained a strong anti-slavery position. The paper temporarily closed over this controversy and was not publishing at war's end.

Had it not been for the big one a hundred years later in the summer of 1965, the Civil War story would have continued on as the most mythical embarrassing moment in *Plain Dealer* history. There would be no such myth attached to the saga of Robert Manry.

Manry was a 47-year-old copy editor on the paper's city side. There was a certain remoteness to the copy-editing community. They tended to be older, more seasoned journalists who were removed from the reporters and worked different hours. They generally regarded the younger writers with suspicion, having to endure their deficient prose and dismissive attitudes. In turn, the writers looked upon the copy editors as obstacles to their literary greatness.

If you were one of the young writers, an aspiring ace, chances are you didn't know the names of the copy editors let alone their personalities or interests. That's how it was with Bob Manry, who to some of us just seemed to be a sketchy figure in the back of the city room. Only those close to him had any idea of his plan for the next few months.

It was a simple plan, but daunting. Manry wanted to sail across the Atlantic Ocean with a friend in a 13.5-foot sailboat.

There are many accounts of the Manry saga in *Plain Dealer* lore, and many of them have been challenged. All of the principals in the drama have died, so there will probably be no absolute account of what took place. Even Manry's book does not thoroughly deal with all the elements that went into the making of the big one. I personally had little to do with the Manry story, other than driving his family to the airport for their flight to England. But the Manry story affected me and the rest of the staff. It shamed us and drove us to drink.

The year before, Manry had written to executive editor Philip Porter asking for a leave of absence to sail his boat from Falmouth, Massachusetts, to Falmouth, England, with a friend. Porter granted the request. Sometime afterward, the friend got cold feet and begged out of the trip. At first Manry was crest-fallen, but after some consideration he resolved to sail solo.

Manry did not tell his colleagues at the paper that he had decided to make the trip alone until June 1, the day of his departure, when he mailed letters from Massachusetts to Porter and the copy desk. His story now took on a different dimension.

Upon learning of the solo voyage, the newspaper launched coverage of Manry and his small boat, *Tinkerbelle*. Word of Manry's progress came after he encountered ships at sea, including a U.S. submarine that came upon him in the middle of a war game. After that, following Coast Guard reports, his progress was charted regularly, and he encountered several ships that sent reports to the *Plain Dealer*.

Overnight, Manry became international news. The paper was inundated with calls concerning him. Readers were hungry for reports. He was the story of the summer, and this is where it began to go bad.

Anticipating Manry's arrival in England (where he would be greeted by a crowd of 50,000), the paper dispatched a team consisting of reporter George Barmann, photographer William Ashbolt and promotion director Russ Kane. The trio relaxed, planning their coverage of what promised to be a leisurely and festive story.

Unbeknownst to them, they were about to be scooped. A trawler had been searching for Manry for 35 hours; on board were a cameraman and an enterprising Channel 5 TV newsman named Bill Jorgensen.

Later Manry would admit that he had undervalued the news-worthiness of his story, largely because before his departure he had tried to sell it to a few publications, including the *Plain Dealer Sunday Magazine*. There was only lukewarm interest, and he had made no agreements regarding his personal story of the voyage.

With that reasoning, Manry essentially gave the whole story of his 78-day adventure to Jorgensen on camera. The three-and-a-half-hour televised interview was a major coup. Ironically, just as Jorgensen was departing in the trawler to begin the search, a Royal Air Force search plane located Manry and dropped canisters of fruit, along with another canister containing a note from Barmann, Ashbolt and Kane saying they were in Falmouth with Manry's wife and children. Also rumored to be in that canister was a sweatshirt with the words PLAIN DEALER emblazoned on its front. According to that story, Manry refused to wear it.

The *Plain Dealer* paid for the family's trip, restored Manry to the payroll, and prepared a homecoming celebration.

Manry would later write of the excitement he felt over seeing his family again, but added that he found the presence of PR man Russ Kane troubling. He feared that the paper might use his trip as a promotion, something he would not let happen.

Channel 5 was the property of Scripps-Howard, which also owned the *Cleveland Press*. Nevertheless, the television station offered the *Plain Dealer* the opportunity to view the Jorgensen interview prior to broadcast and use the content for a series of stories. Given the competitive nature of the media, it was a thoughtful and generous offer.

But in a disastrous decision, Phil Porter declined. The ever-vigilant Louie Seltzer then turned the interview into a week's worth of page-one headlines in the *Press*. We got beat twice on our own story! Some said that Porter had a personal animosity toward Jorgensen. Apparently, at some point in the past Jorgensen had televised news about Porter's divorce, which Phil considered unfair.

In the city room, Porter's decision was devastating to morale. The embarrassment it brought down on us was palpable. Wanting to avoid the ridicule of my *Press* counterparts on the federal beat, I simply did not report in, leaving the beat uncovered for that week. Other reporters did the same. The opposition would laugh in your face if they found you hiding in a bar. In attempts to blunt the impact of the television interview, editors sought any story idea that concerned the Manry family and its history. They wanted me to interview the family dog. I refused.

What had started out as a wonderful adventure story for a slow summer turned into a tale of mistrust and bitterness. In many ways, things were never the same at the *Plain Dealer*. Bob Manry would not return to the newspaper, and the mere mention of his name would provoke arguments and accusations over the coverage of his story. In the city room, a lack of confidence in senior management began to grow. *Esquire* magazine added insult when it gave the paper its Dubious Achievement Award.

There was anger, too—sometimes emanating from unexpected places. One afternoon in 1969, I was in a bar across from the Knesset in Jerusalem with a reporter from the *Chicago Daily News*, who introduced me to some of the other foreign correspondents. Suddenly, an elderly man rose from his chair and pointed at me.

"Are you from the *Plain Dealer*?" His accent was British.

"Yes," I said, reaching for his hand. He withdrew it in a gesture of contempt.

"I hate that newspaper with all my passion," he retorted, flushed with anger. I was totally bewildered that a Brit in Israel would even know of the *Plain Dealer*, let alone hate it.

The man's wife calmed him, and he went on to relate the source of his ire. He had been the photo editor of the *London Daily Mirror*, which had partnered with the *Plain Dealer* in hiring a trawler to take the Manry family out to meet Bob. It was an effort by the *PD* to recover from the Jorgensen scoop.

The idea was that the *Daily Mirror* would get exclusive photos of the reunion, and it advertised them as such. There was only one problem. A *Plain Dealer* staffer had secretly allowed an Associated Press photographer aboard, and the wire service provided every paper in London with the same photos. The man was humiliated.

The Manry experience had a destructive impact on the spirit of the *Plain Dealer*, stigmatizing the paper. The favorable coverage of the *PD* by national news magazines, our growing number of daily triumphs over the dreaded *Press*, and the influx of talent that invigorated the city room all went for naught because of bone-headed editorial decisions regarding the story.

Bob Manry faded away, and in the wake of his disappearance came rumors of his unhappiness with the paper. He was too much of a gentleman to go on record about what had taken place. But his silence fed rumors and distorted facts such that the true story may never be known.

I greatly admired Phil Porter, but it was clear he had made a series of bad decisions in not recognizing the importance of the story and how deeply readers were engaged in Manry's quest that summer. None of us were privy to the front-office reaction to the blunder, but it appeared as if nothing had happened. No one was fired or demoted. In fact, some were promoted. In his 1976 book on Cleveland, Porter mentions Manry only once.

CHAPTER 14

The Sheppard Case, Part 2

During my childhood, my family revered our doctor, a man who had performed back surgery on my mother and relieved the suffering that had rendered her almost bedridden. When we spoke of him it was with veneration and thanks. No doubt others felt the same, for from time to time short articles in the newspapers would note that the doctor had saved a man's life when coming upon an automobile accident or had revived a heart-attack victim in some crowded public place. Dr. Samuel H. Sheppard was a hero of sorts in our house.

I remember reading the newspaper the day after the July 4, 1954, murder of Dr. Sheppard's wife, Marilyn. It was shocking news; it was as if, my mother said, something terrible had happened to someone in our family. The case would become the most famous and controversial murder in the history of Cleveland. It provoked headlines for more than a decade, provided grist for a long-running television series, and stoked countless conspiracy theories. In December 1954, after a media circus of a trial, Sheppard was convicted of killing his wife. Later, ironically, I would play a small role in the case.

If the *Cleveland Press* had taken pleasure in the *Plain Dealer*'s bizarre debacle regarding Robert Manry's sea voyage, the sentiment was returned when it came to how the afternoon newspaper dealt with Marilyn Sheppard's murder. On June 6, 1966, the U.S. Supreme Court ruled that Sam Sheppard had not received a fair trial based on the publicity preceding it and the carnival atmosphere during it. The order meant that Sheppard would go free unless the Cuyahoga County prosecutor decided to retry the case.

While the Supreme Court's order was in a sense a blanket indictment of the media's conduct during the trial, a series of signed editorials by *Press* editor Louie Seltzer urging Sheppard's arrest constituted the soul of the case. It was a different world in 1954. Newspapers still held sway, while television was just getting off the ground. Court reporting of major trials was an art form, and readers savored the details of a good murder case, preferably one involving sex, high society and savagery. The Sheppard case had it all.

Twelve years later, much had changed. The civil rights movement had instilled a new sensitivity across the nation, not only toward minorities but toward the rule of law itself. The media now reconsidered its sometimes lurid ways when it came to handling delicate legal issues.

After the 1966 court order was handed down, county prosecutor John T. Corrigan decided to retry Sam Sheppard. The media had to prepare for a reprise of the most sensational murder case of the century.

At the *Plain Dealer*, the decision was to bulk up the coverage with sidebars, shorter articles dealing with the mood and character of events surrounding the day-to-day conduct of the trial. This involved assigning several reporters to the story.

Given the era's competitive, ego-fueled atmosphere, the

reporter who drew the main story became the key figure in the newsroom. With that assignment, one could count on plenty of space in the paper and lots of page-one bylines.

Even so, John Rees, the paper's day city editor and a respected journalist, cautioned us about excessive hubris. "Boys, bylines don't buy groceries," he would say while we fought to see who would be the ace of the day. At that time, a byline above the front-page fold was more nourishing than a steak dinner.

As I recall, there were two reporters vying to cover the Sheppard trial: the paper's star woman reporter, Doris O'Donnell, who had covered the original 1954 trial for the late *Cleveland News*; and the idiosyncratic Terence P. Sheridan, who had moved from the paper's Akron bureau to cover criminal court.

O'Donnell had been consumed by the Sheppard case, breaking important stories during its early investigation. Over the years she had collected everything she could about the murder. Some felt she was obsessed with it. Should anyone raise the question of Sheppard's possible innocence, O'Donnell would respond with a litany of facts that rejected the mere thought of such reasoning.

Sheridan's presence at the *Plain Dealer* would harden into legend. He was among the best reporters on the paper, with an incisive mind, a gifted street sense and writing skills of some dimension. But he was insolent, mercurial, rebellious, intolerant of authority, easily provoked and generally dismissive of the greater portion of his colleagues.

Sheridan turned the ace race into a cut-throat competition. In his efforts to gain an edge in the game, he allegedly seduced one of the secretaries who passed story assignments from the front office to the city desk. Intercepting these memos allowed Sheridan himself to propose the story idea to the city editor and thus likely garner the assignment.

There was a bit of mystery about him, as well. His age was uncertain, his military career was vague, and his resumé had a fictional ring to it.

There was no mystery about his ability in a bar fight. It did not exist.

I'd first met Sheridan a year or so earlier. I was at my desk typing a story when a voice behind me announced that its bearer had been assigned the adjoining desk. I turned to greet a man in his 30s with glasses, an angular face set off by pursed lips, and a know-everything nod.

"I want you to remember one thing," Sheridan said. "I'm the best reporter in this place, and don't forget it." I shrugged it off, mentally noting the arrival of another aspiring ace in a roomful of aspirants.

Years later Sheridan would write, "There were a half-dozen of us, journalistic gun fighters walking around with egos tied low on the hip, too dumb to realize we were merely by-line freaks riding shotgun on a stagecoach going nowhere." Management never quite knew how to deal with him and never appreciated the positives that he represented, particularly his keenness for calling out lazy and indifferent reporters in bars and even in front of the whole city room.

I'm not sure how it was decided that Sheridan would get the key coverage of the trial, but he did. And I'm sure O'Donnell didn't like it. The *Plain Dealer* was allotted two seats in the courtroom, with the second reporter providing the sidebars.

One day during the trial Sheridan and Ken Huzar were at the city desk briefing Ted Princiotto. Huzar, who had been assigned the color story that day, said there really wasn't anything of significance to report. Sheridan suddenly took affront.

"There were all kinds of stories," Sheridan said. "You just didn't see them." The ensuing argument grew more heated and the two retired to the men's room. Huzar proceeded to smack Sheridan around, leaving him bleeding on the floor.

The day managing editor, an unassertive man whose chief function was to monitor expense accounts, walked in to see Sheridan rising from the floor, clearly injured. Before the editor could even ask what had happened, Sheridan pointed to the door on the toilet stall.

"It snapped back and hit me in the face," he said. "You better get that fixed before someone really gets hurt." The custodian was summoned, who after examining the door scratched his head.

I was assigned to the trial for several days and was surprised by Sam Sheppard's condition. The decade in jail weighed heavily on him. He seemed remote and confused. I saw him stuff a candy bar into his mouth, wrapper and all, while he autographed a Bible for an elderly woman. He shuffled his loafers as he walked. It was clear that his strange behavior was the result of alcohol or drugs or maybe both.

The trial was far from the dramatic event that the first proceeding offered, although many of the national reporters who had attended in 1954 were on hand. The prosecution's case was as flat as the mood in the courtroom. Some of the witnesses were dead, the facts of the case had a tiresome ring to them, and time had drained much of the suspense from the proceedings.

Still, it was a surprise when the jury returned a not guilty verdict. When word reached the inmates in the county jail above the courtrooms, they responded with wild cheering—as much out of scorn for the legal system as for support of Sheppard.

I remembered that scene years later while covering a congressional hearing in Washington on the treatment of jailed prisoners. Sheppard was scheduled to testify in a room largely populated by ex-convicts who expected the former doctor to be their spokesman and present the evils of prison life. He failed completely, babbling incoherently until the crowd booed him from the witness stand. It was sad.

Anyone I met who had anything to do with the original investigation or trial felt that Sheppard was guilty. But over time, various theories surfaced regarding the "real" killer until it became a pastime to search for the conspiracy that had implicated an innocent Sam Sheppard.

One of the popular figures in these theories was a man named Richard G. Eberling, who at one time had in fact been a suspect in the case. Former *Plain Dealer* reporter James Neff wrote a book on the Sheppard case entitled *The Wrong Man* in which he makes a case for Eberling as the murderer. Several years after the second trial, I had encountered Eberling in the strangest manner.

One night Don Bean called from the beat to report that the police had arrested a man on a murder charge after seeking him for 10 years. It was a slow news night, so I went to the newspaper's library to see if I could find the original story of the murder. As I was going through old microfilm, I came across a different story about a window washer who had been arrested for jewel theft. In fact, some of Marilyn Sheppard's jewelry had been found in his possession. I recognized the name immediately. Richard Eberling was my wife's interior decorator.

Things proceeded to get weirder. When I got home that night, Eberling was sitting at the kitchen table discussing fabrics with my wife. A few months later, she discovered that some of her jewelry was missing.

While Eberling's link to the Sheppard case was fraught with uncertainty, he in fact would be proven to be a killer, and may also have murdered his stepmother.

The night he was at our apartment, Eberling announced that

he had just been selected as the interior decorator for Mayor Ralph Perk at Cleveland City Hall. I didn't quite know what to say, but warned that anyone who went public with a city hall job would be subject to scrutiny. Eberling shrugged his shoulders.

I decided to let the *Press* have this story. Eberling's roommate, Obie Henderson, was a clerk at the *Plain Dealer*. Henderson had befriended Wilson Hirschfeld, who was then the paper's managing editor. Henderson knew how to play office politics and I'd already had several brushes with Hirschfeld, so a battle with him over Eberling was not worth it. It took a few days, but the *Press* finally reported the story as a breathless exposé. A few years later, Eberling would resurface—and once again it would be about murder.

CHAPTER 15

A Summer with Art Modell

At the *Plain Dealer*, the aces over on city side looked upon their colleagues in the sports department with curiosity, envy and suspicion. Outside of an occasional drink at the Headliner, the two groups rarely interacted. The only thing they had in common was the paper itself, for their work and their culture were completely different.

The same held for the features department, which the aces preferred to call the women's department, if they acknowledged its existence at all. To them it was at best an obstacle on the way to the city room. That department housed such endeavors as food, radio and television, film, theater and fashion. Since the aces were busy saving humanity, it never occurred to them that it was the revenues generated by the features department that allowed them to engage in flights of fancy.

During football season there was some animosity toward the sports department over Monday's paper when a Browns story occupied the eight columns across the top of page one. That precious part of the paper, the aces thought, should rightfully be reserved for serious news and not a recounting of something everyone who cared already knew. But as fans, city side reporters were always curious about the real story behind a player or a team. The problem with sports coverage in those days centered on the limitations as to what was reported. Many of the escapades of Jim Brown and others were never published.

Sports reporters no longer had to spend a year on the police beat as they once had. And that, the aces believed, was where real reporting was learned.

In reality, the culture surrounding a team is what made sports reporting difficult. A reporter on that beat was almost a captive of each sports organization and had to be mindful of unwritten rules that governed the locker room. Otherwise, he would be frozen out and of no value to the newspaper. Nobody liked it, but that was the reality of the situation and the price you paid to cover the teams.

There were a few instances of sportswriters involved in businesses with team owners. One prominent writer, for example, had urged several Indians players to invest in a mortgage company. When the principal of the company suddenly died it was discovered that he had been running a Ponzi scheme, shifting monies from one account to another in a con that bilked investors out of thousands of dollars.

In college I wanted to be a sportswriter and devoted far more time to that endeavor than to my studies. I was the sports editor of the school paper for four years, worked at the *Plain Dealer* sports department on weekends, and covered all the Baldwin-Wallace teams. Later I would learn that covering sports was a limiting pursuit. I believe that most fans, given the opportunity to cover pro sports, would never again view the games or the players with admiration.

There were unhappy aspects to being a sports reporter, things that could pitch you into a dark and cynical depression. Things like the Cleveland Indians' decades-long losing record. When the talented Danny Coughlin, the emerging ace of the sports department, covered the team in the 1970s, years reminiscent of the Dark Ages, he yearned for his final day on the beat. On that day, he promised, he would piss on home plate. He never did so, but he felt a sense of joy at the end of his assignment almost as if he had been freed from prison.

The spirit of competition between the city's two newspapers was never more intense than it was on the Indians beat back then. The team may have been lousy, but the fierceness of the coverage of its meandering ways was such that the *Press* reporter and his *Plain Dealer* counterpart barely spoke to each other for the rest of their lives.

Maybe it was the town's sports culture in general, or maybe it was some suspicion about Cleveland Browns owner Art Modell held by the paper's front office, that caused me to be summoned up the long executive hallway, the same one I had trod in embarrassment after my byline encounter with Phil Porter. This time my meeting with him was interesting.

Porter got to the point. It seemed there were many questions regarding Modell. There were even rumors that the money he had used to purchase the Browns in 1961 was tainted by the mob.

Porter said he did not want to turn the Modell story over to the sports department. Certain members of the department's staff, he thought, were too close to the Browns owner. A few of them had even advised Modell to fire coach Paul Brown during a newspaper strike in order to avoid coverage.

"Essentially we want you to look into Modell's life," Porter said. "Profile him and where he got his money and whether he has ties to any unsavory characters. And I don't want you to go through our sports department in any way."

It was a challenging and troublesome assignment. I worried

a bit that I was being turned into a hatchet man. I didn't know Modell, but I was aware of the suspicions about him—especially after his firing of coach Paul Brown, one of the city's all-time sports icons, in January 1963.

Brown had been the driving force behind the Cleveland team ever since its inception in 1946. Founded by Arthur B. "Mickey" McBride, a marginal character in town who owned a gambling wire and a taxicab company, who associated with mob members, and who knew nothing about football, the Browns became a legend.

McBride relied on his son's former college roommate, Creighton Miller, who had been an All-American halfback at Notre Dame, to fashion the embryonic beginning of a Cleveland team. Miller made the single most important decision in the history of the franchise. He hired Paul Brown away from Ohio State, which had won a national championship in 1942. With that single stroke, a football dynasty was born.

From 1946 until Modell's arrival in 1961, Paul Brown had a free hand in running the Browns both on and off the field. Even when ownership of the team changed, Brown was relied upon to manage the team's affairs as he saw fit. In retrospect, there was no way that Art Modell and Paul Brown could coexist.

Brown had never dealt with someone like Modell, and likely felt that the new owner—whose background was in advertising—had nothing to offer except perhaps some marketing ideas. For Modell's part, the purchase of the team represented how he was going to make a living. In order to make that work, he had to control the organization. The two men were on a collision course.

John Minco, the team's former sales and marketing director and Modell's longtime confidant, told me that Brown dismissed Modell from the beginning. "Art would ask for a meeting at say

3 p.m., and Paul would never show up," Minco said. "It was only a matter of time before it all blew up."

The last straw, according to Minco, was the late 1961 trade of halfback Bobby Mitchell to the Washington Redskins for the league's first draft choice—the ill-fated Ernie Davis, who shortly thereafter died of leukemia without ever playing a game for the Browns. Modell found out about the trade during a phone call from Preston Marshall, owner of the Redskins. Modell was outraged.

In the midst of a lengthy newspaper strike, Brown was fired on January 7, 1963, a move that shook the Cleveland sports community and attached a permanent stigma to Modell's persona. Obviously, that stigma had prompted my assignment.

I met Modell at the Theatrical Grill one spring evening in 1966. He'd had a good couple of years. The Browns had won the National Football League championship in 1964, and in 1965 the team's record was 11–3, the best in the NFL, though it lost the championship that year to the Green Bay Packers. That night, however, Modell wasn't celebrating. His mood was tinged with suspicion.

"Look, I don't know what your intention is for this story," he began, "but I know what some people think of me. I'm a New York Jew who came to Cleveland and fired its legendary football coach. I don't like that thinking, but I understand it."

I was taken aback by his remarks, which had come minutes into our first meeting. He then laughed and asked what I'd like to drink. It was clear that he was primed for the meeting and was studying my reaction to his assertion. I told him there was more to his story than rumor and that I was going to try to tell readers who he was.

That night we set the ground rules. I could travel with Modell daily to summer practice in Hiram, sit in on meetings, interview friends, talk to his banker and even to women he was dating. In all, there really were no rules connected with the story.

It was a strange and uncertain summer. Jim Brown had undertaken a second career as an actor and was in the UK filming *The Dirty Dozen*. It was becoming evident that he might not return before the season started. The rest of the players were preparing for another successful run, but I could sense an undercurrent of racial problems. The black players mostly ate by themselves on one side of the cafeteria, the whites on the other side. There was no sense of camaraderie, and a sullen atmosphere prevailed.

But there was nothing sullen about Art Modell. His mercurial mood shifts could dance between jocular hilarity and face-flushing anger. He was a complex man, confident in his ways, eager to control, sensitive in terms of ego. He was entertaining, with a quick wit and a self-deprecating manner. My sense was that he was a hard man to work for, but generous to a fault when someone asked for help. He was good company.

He had bought the team for $4 million, he said, borrowing all but $50,000. The loans were from Union Commerce Bank and Rudy Schaefer of the Schaefer Brewing Company. Modell made his money in the advertising business and prided himself on his marketing instincts. Years later, when the very mention of his name would provoke the meanest retorts, it struck me that Modell never really had money, lived in constant debt, and lent too much trust to his instincts.

His overriding temperament was marked by a need to be in control. Maybe it was a sense of insecurity or a strain of defiance in his DNA, but it was an attitude that would come into play in his dealings with Paul Brown and Jimmy Brown, in his meddling with coaches, and ultimately in his lack of business prowess. He also displayed a lack of judgment when seeking advice from those around him.

One quickly learned that Modell did not like to hear bad news. The best way to gain his confidence was to agree with him at all times. Three decades later all these qualities would play a major role in the darkest moment of his life—and the darkest moment in the history of Cleveland sports—when he moved the Browns to Baltimore.

Despite the anxiety over Jim Brown, the summer of 1966 was bright with promise for Modell. At 41, he was a sought-after bachelor who could be seen breezing about the city in a convertible and talking football with fans at places like the Theatrical, the Statler Hotel and the Pewter Mug. In those days he was the most accessible sports owner in town, and he could charm the most caustic critic.

Modell dated various attractive women in town, but never for long. His mother, who lived in New York, insisted that he marry a Jewish girl. Art used this as an excuse to avoid serious romantic entanglements.

I remember sitting in his office at the old Municipal Stadium one afternoon when a phone call came from one of the principals involved in filming *The Dirty Dozen*. At first Modell was courteous, but I could hear his voice harden as his face formed a frown.

"What do you mean you can't tell me when the movie will be finished?" he blurted. "I've got to sell tickets, and to do that I've got to know if Jimmy is coming back."

I couldn't hear the caller's response but I could see the anger welling in Modell's face. "Look," he said, "remember this. Anytime I can fuck you I will." With that he slammed down the receiver and muttered some obscenities about Hollywood.

I have often reflected on that moment. I was never sure that Modell really wanted Brown back. I knew he went to great lengths to keep Jim out of trouble. And there was racial strife on the team that was said to be generated in part by Brown. Some of these ingredients may have been involved in the firing of Paul Brown. Writers who interviewed Jim Brown about that summer say that he chafed at Modell's attempts to control him and decided to quit.

The great fullback never again played for the Browns. I wrote a lengthy profile of Modell for the *Plain Dealer Sunday Magazine* that fall that essentially discounted the suspicions surrounding him. Little did I know that 30 years later he would become the scourge of the city, a man destined to live in infamy in the minds of Clevelanders. A true prisoner of posterity.

While I would run across Modell from time to time over the years, I rarely dealt with him professionally. In the eyes of the fans, I don't think he ever recovered from firing Paul Brown, and this must have influenced public attitudes when it came to proposals for a new stadium. The convoluted story behind the failure of the city and the county to come forward with a stadium for him matches Modell's own financial miscalculations. That all this led to the team's move is surely the city's saddest chapter in sports history.

Over time, Modell confided to friends that he thought Cleveland's corporate community was turning against him, as he received little support for his efforts to remodel Municipal Stadium. That suspicion is probably correct. In 1978 *Plain Dealer* executive editor David Hopcraft ordered that the reporter covering the Browns be replaced by a more aggressive journalist; he sensed that the paper was too soft on Modell. Essentially, it was the same order that had been expressed to me 13 years earlier. Hopcraft later joined the Browns as a public relations counsel and said that he had been ordered to make the reportorial change by a higher authority at the paper. The only higher authority was publisher Tom Vail.

The twists of fate involved in Modell's financial demise are legion; they are recorded in *Fumble*, a book by Mike Popular, who worked for Modell for 21 years. But there was another element to the story, a figure who seemed to come out of nowhere to cast a long shadow over Modell's fortunes. His name was Dick Jacobs.

Jacobs and his brother, David, were from Akron and succeeded in making millions of dollars as mall developers around the nation. The general public and a large part of the business community had never heard of them, so when they purchased the Cleveland Indians in 1986 the move came as a huge surprise.

Former city council president George Forbes remembers meeting Jacobs for the first time and the shock of being told that Jacobs was interested in buying the Indians in a cash deal. Politicians had feared the day when they would awake to learn that the team was moving. A move had been rumored for years as the team's ownership passed from one wealthy Clevelander to the next in charitable life support. Everyone knew it could not go on forever. For a politician to lose the Indians on their watch was akin to political suicide.

"The first thing I did was call George Voinovich on the phone," Forbes told me. "I said, Mayor, get down here. There is a guy in my office who wants to buy the Indians and he is going to do it with cash."

So began a remarkable era in Cleveland sports history. It was also the moment when the bell began to toll on the reign of Art Modell as the city's sports impresario. Never were two men so different in personality and in action.

Whereas Modell was emotional, Jacobs was cold and calculating; whereas Modell was warm and congenial, Jacobs was courteous and aloof; whereas Modell lived on borrowed money, Jacobs had a reservoir of assets; whereas Modell shunned advice and relied on instincts, Jacobs sought information from anyone he deemed knowledgeable; and whereas Modell had awkward relations with city hall, Jacobs quickly developed political allies.

Perhaps the most telling meeting between the two men took place when Jacobs asked whether more of the advertising revenues from the scoreboard and signage at the old stadium should be directed toward the Indians since they played many more games there than the Browns. Modell refused to consider the request.

Jacobs looked at him and said laconically, "Then why don't you let me buy the Browns from you?" The truth was, Jacobs really would have preferred to own the football team.

This offer and its delivery must have stunned Modell. After all, he had spent decades as the symbol of Cleveland sports. Now in front of him was a man the town hardly knew proposing to buy the iconic football franchise on the spot. Modell had to sense the seriousness of the proposal.

I never thought Jacobs wished ill will toward Modell, but the events that followed propelled one man into nearly legendary status and dealt the other an ignominious blow.

In the early summer of 1966, however, all of that was unimaginable to Cleveland sports fans looking forward to an autumn of Sunday football. And neither Art Modell nor the rest of us realized we were living in a city about to explode into violence.

CHAPTER 16

A Bad Day at the Café

Monday, July 18, 1966, was scorching hot. I was hoping to slip from work early and get a beer around the corner at the Rockwell Inn. I wanted to cover my exit with the return of reporters from their beats, which always created commotion and congregation around the city desk. Over the past year, racial relations in Cleveland had grown in intensity, and news from city hall and the education beat was drawing the primary attention.

The Rockwell Inn was the favored location for a surreptitious escape from the newsroom. The backstairs at the *Plain Dealer* were easily reached, lightly traveled and emptied about a block from the bar. Conversely, the route to the Headliner held little cover.

I had been sitting on a barstool for only a few minutes when a breathless copyboy named Truby rushed in, exclaiming that the city desk wanted to see me immediately. Not good news. Moments like this created a ping-pong of uncertainty. Was I in for an ass-chewing, or was something up?

The summons turned out to be an invitation to the night

that changed Cleveland forever. It was a historic waypoint, the first violent rejection of a bitter past that had held half the town hostage for so many years.

"The police beat is reporting a disturbance in Hough," Ted Princiotto said. "Take a photographer and get out there."

This was not surprising. Racial incidents had increased on the East Side, most of them revolving around the state of the city's schools in that area of town. African Americans were protesting segregation efforts and the lack of facilities.

A dramatic sign of what was to come had occurred on April 7, 1964, when Reverend Bruce Klunder, a 26-year-old minister with the Student Christian Union, was accidentally crushed by a bulldozer during a protest over the building of the Stephen E. Howe Elementary School. Angry protesters viewed the school's construction as an effort to avoid integration of students in two other new schools.

Klunder laid down behind the bulldozer; the equipment operator, trying to avoid three other protesters who had positioned themselves in front of him, and unaware of the minister's presence behind him, put the earthmover into reverse. *Plain Dealer* photographer Dudley Brumbach took one of the most haunting pictures of the civil rights movement in Cleveland, showing the dead Klunder sprawled face down.

That night, in what was reported as the worst civil rights violence in the city's history thus far, 300 police officers were called on to restore order, using teargas and arresting some 50 people. In a page-one editorial, the paper pleaded for rational leadership on all sides. Government had spent decades ignoring the crowded and squalid conditions infecting the inner city. Those of us in the city room that evening felt a sense of descending dread.

As the unrest and demonstrations mounted, tension seemed

to grip Cleveland's soul—especially on the East Side where Italian and black neighborhoods abutted and area schools were under consideration for integration. The tensions manifested in sporadic and spontaneous gatherings at school sites that drew the police.

I remember one cold morning at Collinwood High School when a group of students assembled outside the school, refusing to go to class. A pickup truck pulled into their midst and out got a man wearing overalls and an Indians cap. "You get in that school or I'll kick your ass right now in front of the TV cameras," he shouted at his son. With that, he grabbed the boy by an arm and turned him over to a nearby teacher. "Hold him while I get the other kid." His actions broke up the querulous assembly and the academic day proceeded uneventfully.

Murray Hill in Little Italy was a territory forbidden to African Americans. Not only were passersby not tolerated, the threatening nature of the neighborhood was such that black people would drive for miles to avoid the place. Unsuspecting outsiders who wandered into the neighborhood were beaten and on more than one occasion found dead.

One freezing night with Murray Hill in turmoil over an investigation of one such deaths, I remember huddling for warmth and safety in the car of a *Press* photographer outside a church while an angry crowd milled about, loud and threatening. The city desk wanted comments from the protesters, but there was no way I was going to announce that I was a reporter.

So as I drove out to the Hough neighborhood in the fading light that sweltering July evening, I expected more confrontation and simmering anger that would stop short of violence. The scene on Hough Avenue was bizarre. The street was filled with people pushing racks of clothes, carrying boxes of looted goods, and drinking liberated liquor. The crowd was in a festive mood and for the moment there was no sense of danger. Some of the merrymakers were hawking their stolen wares.

Back behind a bowling alley a merchandise mart of sorts had been set up. Men's suits were selling for $10, liquor $3 a fifth, wine 50 cents a bottle, prime beef $1.25 a pound. As I moved through the neighborhood, several people offered me deals on neckties, shirts and a huge pot roast. The only thing the police could do was take photographs of the frolicking looters for later investigation. I didn't feel threatened, but was quite aware that the mood could change at any moment and when it did, I'd better be in a safer place.

In the midst of all this, I found a working pay phone. The booth had been battered, its glass broken and its interior smelling of warm urine. It was always a treat to call the city desk in these situations.

The hardest thing for the desk on a story like this was to grasp its magnitude and assign enough people to cover the basics while keeping an eye on inviolable deadlines. But the somewhat cynical desk often wasted time by treating the initial description of events with suspicion. The editors figured that an overzealous reporter was trying to wrest space from them. Several reporters had been dispatched from downtown, but because of the vast chaos of the disturbance none could be readily located.

I was glad to find Bob Daniels on the other end of the phone line. He was on rewrite, thank god. Daniels was quick, accurate and understanding, as good as it got. He comprehended that during a race riot the city desk could not afford to ask for the participants' middle initials.

Daniels stayed with the story all week and accumulated a massive amount of overtime, so much so that reporter Don Bean, ever the prankster, cautioned that the paper did not have that kind of money and would probably have to pay it off over a year's time. Editors in the city room were so focused on the developing story that they ignored the string of firecrackers that copyboy Dennis Kucinich set off in an effort to simulate riot conditions inside the newspaper's offices.

As I described the scene to Daniels, a little boy pressed his face to the fractured glass of the phone booth, his eyes wide with a mixture of excitement and fear. I told Daniels that fires were being lit and that the police were doing nothing to prevent the looting.

"Bob, this one is for real," I said. "Tell the desk that they are going to need more people out here." With deadlines pressing, it was clear that we would only be able to present a bare-bones, just-the-facts story in the morning.

We reported that one woman had been killed, numerous people injured, and a series of fires set throughout the neighborhood. As the evening progressed so did the violence, forcing some firemen to abandon the flaming buildings in order to protect themselves. The crowds grew in size and vehemence. Sporadic shooting was taking place and the police were reporting sniper fire. By midnight, it was too dangerous for us to move freely among the ruins of a once-vibrant neighborhood. Even while standing amid the destruction, it was hard to believe this was happening.

Daylight brought some relief from the shooting and arson. Shopkeepers returned to witness their livelihoods trashed by looting and fire. Much of the desecration had taken place right in front of the police, who seemed helpless to prevent it.

In the morning I stood there as Joe Berman surveyed his grocery store, which surprisingly had not sustained severe damage. He tried to secure the door with six-inch spikes, but they didn't hold. Looters sacked his place in broad daylight along with Larry's Meat Market, which had served the neighborhood for 19 years. Earl Gamer, the market's owner, stood distraught outside the business he had worked so hard to maintain.

"I'm ruined," Gamer said. "That is it. They just put me out of business. They even went into the basement and broke open the safe. I'm broke, flat broke. I can't and won't reopen again." Gamer was bitter, noting that when he first opened in Hough very few African Americans lived there. "They say we are capitalizing on them," he said. "That's not true. They came to me, I didn't come to them." Next door, Vincent LiBassi, owner of Larry's Fruitland, surveyed his devastated store and estimated his losses at $20,000. He just shook his head.

As the men poked through what was left of their businesses, a crowd composed mostly of black youths gathered and laughed gleefully. They mimicked the store owners, and someone threw a rock that spider-webbed the windshield of Berman's station wagon. It was hot, and Berman's brow gleamed with perspiration. His hands shook. Defeated, he slumped into his car and asked the police to do their best.

"You know how it is," one policeman said.

"Nobody appreciates the job you are doing, nobody but me," Gamer responded. "Look, watch the store for me, but if it's your life forget about it."

I asked Berman how long he had been in business here.

"No time to talk," he said. "Twelve years here, that's how many. The family wants me out. Huh, you know what the trouble is, don't ask me."

The crowd, which had grown to 40, called his name and jeered. Berman drove off, squinting through the shattered windshield.

No sooner was Berman out of sight when an elderly black woman named Tillie angrily confronted the youthful taunters. "What we gonna do now?" she said. "What we all gonna do for food now after you damn people drove him out? Shame, I say shame, shame, shame on all of you."

A few in the crowd teased Tillie and accused Berman of ripping off the neighborhood with his high prices and poor-quality food. Tillie went on her way, mumbling that young people had so much to learn about the world.

Up the street, Herman Dixon, a black man, painted the window of his market with a sign that proclaimed SOUL BROTHER: BLACK OWNER. "If I'm hit tonight it's going to be hard to come back," Dixon said. "There is so much tension on the street, too much, and that is going to draw crowds." His market was not spared.

Meanwhile, downtown at city hall, Mayor Ralph Locher was the captain of a city totally out of control. With every available police officer working 12-hour shifts, there was no sign that the rioters could be subdued by local authority alone. By noon on that second day, Locher had summoned the Ohio National Guard to retake the neighborhood.

There is nothing more ominous than armored vehicles, heavy weapons, and men in battle dress roving a city neighborhood. The firepower represented by this invading force provokes an empty and fearful feeling. One mistake or hostile move could result in numerous casualties.

The National Guard, however, did not arrive until 11 p.m. that second night—and in its absence the rioting and looting continued, along with sniping. One man who was helping to board up a black-owned store was shot in the head, killed by what police called a stray round. The Guard quickly intimidated the riotous crowds.

Over the next few days the violence slowly receded, although sporadic shooting continued in the night and three more people were killed by unknown assailants. By Friday, some semblance of peace had returned to the trashed-and-burned neighborhood. Downtown, the city's civic and political leaders were trying to recover from the shock of the devastation and the concomitant national news coverage. The *New York Times* had its best civil rights reporters at work here.

The Cleveland newspapers were interested in determining the immediate cause of the riots. The focus of inquiry was the 79er's Café, where the events that triggered the conflagration had taken place on that hot Monday afternoon. The café, a squat building occupying the southeast corner of East 79th Street and Hough Avenue, was a social hub in a neighborhood where cheap whiskey and wine helped blunt the prospect of an aimless, empty future. There were a lot of these hopeless havens in the ghetto.

On Friday morning I walked into the place. It was quiet. There were no customers, and one of the two Jewish brothers who owned it, Dave Feigenbaum, was working behind the bar, readying for business. The café was long and narrow, with 20 stools, a couple of booths, and a troublesome cigarette machine that patrons had to pound to get their change. After a couple of drinks, a frustrated customer might beat on the machine until all of the change spilled out, much to the disgust and anger of the Feigenbaums.

In situations like this one, reporters often hesitate to introduce themselves. People may react with either hostility or helpfulness. I walked to the end of the bar while considering how to tell Feigenbaum I was from the *Plain Dealer*. That was a mistake.

Right then a black man rushed through the door and attempted to vault the bar. Feigenbaum reacted instantly, grabbing a baseball bat. The man tried to scramble over the bar and reach behind it, shouting "I'm going to kill the son of a bitch!"

Feigenbaum's bat struck the man on the wrist, making a snapping sound and sending the intruder to the floor recoiling in pain. The bar owner cursed and pulled out a shotgun. It all happened so fast that I had no avenue of escape. I had walked to the end of the bar away from the door. There was no telling what would have happened had the other man reached the gun first.

That split second told me more about life in Hough than any interview. If I ever taught journalism, I thought, there would be at least one lecture on how to navigate hostile taverns.

The next morning we went with a page-one story detailing the incidents that had triggered the riots. The story was important in that it belied the conspiracy charges that the authorities would weave over the next few months.

Abe and Dave Feigenbaum were not well thought of by their customers. Earlier in the year someone had tried to set their car on fire. Someone had flushed a lighted cherry bomb in the men's room toilet. There was an attempt to burn down the bar. A year and a half earlier, their uncle, Benjamin Feigenbaum, had been shot to death in his car not far from the café.

Maintaining peace was no easy matter for the brothers. The drinking often led to a contentious atmosphere that invited trouble. There were muggings in the men's room, many in the crowd had lengthy criminal records, and the clientele was under the impression that the Feigenbaums were taking advantage of them.

That Monday a number of patrons in the 79'ers Café were in mourning for Margaret Sullivan, an African American woman who had died on Saturday night. Sullivan was a prostitute who had been arrested a dozen times and at age 16 had given birth to a child. People liked her, and 120 attended her funeral.

Her friend Louise, another prostitute, showed up at the café on late Monday afternoon with a greasy cigar box. Both Louise and Margaret Sullivan had been banned from the 79'er after Abe Feigenbaum labeled them undesirable characters. But Louise was intent on collecting money for Sullivan's family and wanted to pass the box among the bar's patrons. Dave Feigenbaum was dubious about the collection.

"I didn't know where the money was going to go," he said. "And we had another collection going on at the same time." The other collection was for a man who had faced charges of 99 to 140 years but got off with a sentence of only two to 15 years. It was a celebratory gift to the prisoner.

The trouble began when Dave Feigenbaum ordered Louise to take her cigar box and leave. She refused. Feigenbaum was insistent. They began to curse at each other, each retort more vulgar than the last. Some customers later claimed that an angry Feigenbaum had uttered something derogatory about blacks. Regardless, the incident with Louise had created uneasiness and touched a collective nerve.

So when a man walked in and bought a pint of cheap wine, tensions in the café were already high. They peaked when Feigenbaum refused to give the man a glass of ice water. The wine was a takeout item and because of that, Feigenbaum reasoned, the purchaser did not deserve anything extra.

Angry, the thirsty man turned to the crowd of drinkers and loudly proclaimed that he had been denied a glass of water. He made his way outside, scribbled the words NO WATER FOR NIGGERS on the paper bag that had held his wine, and placed the homemade sign on the bar's front door.

By now a crowd had gathered outside the 79'er; word of mouth soon embellished Feigenbaum's actions, creating an infectious fury. The jeering crowd around the now-embattled café quickly swelled to almost 300. The brothers called the police four times with no response. When someone in the crowd attempted to ignite the building, the fire department was summoned, but the trucks quickly left when no fire was found. Angered, the brothers resorted to contacting local television stations in hopes of embarrassing city hall.

The ensuing riot turned into an unchecked rampage. When police finally did arrive, it was too late. The inability to restrain what was originally defiance emboldened the crowd. It also brought out snipers who throughout the night exchanged gunfire with police.

Later the Feigenbaum brothers would blame the riot on police inaction. Armed with a rifle and a pistol, they had returned to the bar that evening, threatening the crowd and fending off arson attempts.

The impact of the Hough riots was enormous, casting a pall of fear, uncertainty and suspicion over the city. Downtown workers who lived on the East Side did not linger after 5 p.m. Drivers sped along Chester Avenue or took circuitous routes home, and pedestrians both black and white avoided eye contact while crossing downtown streets. It felt like we had all stepped into an alternate reality.

The riots had shamed the city, disrupted business, and clearly were about to alter the political status quo. For reporters like me who had graduated from the grit and grief of the police beat, there was little doubt as to what had led to the eruption of violence on that hot July day. But Cleveland's civic, political and business leaders, who had been caught off guard by the ferocity of events, appeared clueless. They immediately sought to place blame elsewhere. The violence had to have been perpetrated by outsiders, went one line of reasoning, while another held forth that the riots had been planned and executed by subversives, communists perhaps.

Cleveland's newspapers editorialized for calm and collective thought in the wake of the riots, but they were also clueless in their insensitivity to the true conditions in the community. The papers had played a role in perpetuating the myth that all was well in the city and that occasional stories of black concerns were simply part of urban life.

CHAPTER 17

The Nigerian Ambassador

In the early 1960s the *Plain Dealer* was starting to understand that race relations would become an important story, but there was no thought that it would become *the* story for the rest of the 20th century. In 1963 the paper had hired its first African American reporter, Robert G. McGruder, who had been the first black editor of Kent State University's student newspaper. But almost immediately upon his arrival he was drafted into the Army.

McGruder was tall, thoughtful and quiet, with a sense of dignified leadership that eventually would gain him the executive editorship of the *Detroit Free Press*, a position he held with much acclaim. His absence to military service in those critical years leading up to the Hough riots was unfortunate.

Cleveland's African American community was viewed by the newspapers as an entity apart from the rest of the city. Members of the black community were mentioned mainly in criminal stories or in stories about the welfare budget. The few black councilmen were sometimes quoted when they complained about the poor city services in their wards. Black obituaries were rare.

There had been protests in the past. In 1946, for example, African Americans had organized to desegregate the dance hall and other facilities at the Euclid Beach amusement park. But it was not until the early 1960s, when it became apparent that blacks were being shortchanged in educational opportunity, that Cleveland's African American community rose in sustained protest. This resulted in incidents that the news media could not ignore. Suddenly, it became important to hire black reporters.

Identifying with the various communities that inhabited a city was part of a newspaper's mission. Editor Louie Seltzer at the *Press* was brilliant at courting Cleveland's European ethnic blocs, dedicating at least one reporter to cover the various cultures and the personalities within them. He even sent reporters abroad to stir memories of the old country. Using this tactic Seltzer not only built his newspaper's circulation, he also built a bond between the paper and Cleveland's ethnic groups that for three decades gave him the power to essentially run the city.

The *Plain Dealer* was weak at this kind of interaction with readers. It made some attempts, but for the most part the paper concentrated on suburban readers. It particularly shunned stories about African Americans unless crime was involved. *Plain Dealer* editors did not regard themselves as racists. To them the black community inhabited a remote place that held little news interest. Therefore, they had no interest in educating themselves about the African American experience.

Others felt differently. In the mid-1960s, the paper had instituted a summer intern program for college students, after which the participants were asked to evaluate their experience. One year the interns united to write a scathing report about the degree of racism they felt existed in the newsroom.

Jim Cox, a reporter at the paper for five years before going into television news, once observed that the *Plain Dealer* seemed to be caught in a time warp, struggling to get out of the 1950s. This culture may have been linked to the fact that for many years the newspaper had been held in a trust administered by the Cleveland Trust bank, historically one of the city's most conservative institutions. In many ways the paper reflected the town, which had to be dragged into the future despite itself.

At the *Press*, even given Seltzer's keen understanding of the city's ethnic dynamics, coverage did not extend much into the African American community, either. He did have a few black reporters on his staff, one being the seasoned veteran Hil Black, the chief police reporter. The *Press* reported frequently and elaborately on Shondor Birns' illegal numbers racket that permeated the East Side. All of this meant that Cleveland's black community had little voice other than its own *Call & Post*, which published weekly under adverse economic circumstances and spoke to no one outside its limited subscription reach.

Because the black community was viewed as something alien and even fearful, there was a sudden need for someone at the *Plain Dealer* to interpret this culture—its workings and its issues—so the newspaper could better understand what to write about it. In 1965 the paper had launched a series of articles by Doris O'Donnell, who lived with an African American family for a few weeks. It may have been a naive approach, but it was as much an effort to tell what life was like for black people in Cleveland as it was a primer to give editors an understanding of the dawning racial era.

The best solution, of course, was to recruit African American reporters, but there were few to be found. Black activists had begun to ask, almost as a challenge, how many reporters of color did the *Plain Dealer* have on staff? Once Bob McGruder had been drafted by the Army, we had none.

That was about to change.

One summer day I came to work to find a fresh face occupying the desk behind mine. William S. Davis, a young African American man wearing horn-rimmed glasses who had attended Hiram College, barely looked old enough to have graduated from high school.

I asked Davis what he was going to be doing.

"I'll be covering the inner city," he said.

"When are you going down to the police beat?" I had visions of Bob Tidyman running this poor kid's ass around the cop house like some bird trying to find its way to freedom.

"Oh, I won't be doing anything like that," Davis said in a manner that suggested I had insulted him. "I'm on the reporting staff."

This was quite unusual, if not puzzling. The police beat was as much a ritual for young, inexperienced reporters as any of life's passages. You hated it, yet you needed it. It wasn't long before all of us were wondering what kind of special dispensation the paper had granted Davis. It turned out to be a lot.

Since most of the aces were out there skimming off page-one stories like whipped cream, the heavy day-to-day lifting on the paper fell to others, those who tracked city hall's bond rating, the expenditure of tax dollars, the vicissitudes of the bureaucracy, and other inert pursuits. Few were more relentlessly engaged in these matters than Roldo Bartimole. Bartimole felt concern over the nature of urban life and its abject realities. He was a serious man engaged in serious work on a newspaper that had yet to get serious about the looming urban problems.

Ted Princiotto assigned Bartimole to act as a sort of mentor to Davis. The two were to work together on stories that focused on the impact of urban renewal on the city's social fabric. Bartimole had experience in this area from his days as a reporter in Connecticut.

Davis and Bartimole were conflicting personalities. Davis was a gadfly around the city room, an extrovert who liked to gossip and drop hints about how the *Plain Dealer* had recruited him. The paper, he claimed, had loaned him money, given him an American Express card, and located an apartment for him. The young man's intention clearly was to impress everyone, but the result was back-biting and resentment.

By contrast, Bartimole was a withdrawn soul who spoke in a rasp, and who went about his work diligently and methodically. If Davis was ostentatious in personality, Bartimole was frugal. Davis was an office politician, Bartimole the office provocateur, constantly challenging editors to reach deeper into stories.

Years later Bartimole would recall that Davis didn't actually work as a reporter. He was more of a facilitator, organizing interviews with African American groups and providing the coffee and sweet rolls. The two shared bylines on stories, but Bartimole did most of the reporting and all of the writing. How was Davis going to learn, Bartimole would ask Princiotto, if he didn't do some of the stories himself? No real answer was given.

As time went by, there would always be more questions than answers.

One day Davis tapped me on the shoulder and said that he was sorry, but I couldn't go with his group on its upcoming trip. I had no idea what he was talking about, nor did I care. Davis didn't like me because I ignored his attempts to extract office tattle.

It seems that Davis had gone around the city room and invited about 20 people to accompany him on a weekend trip to New York and Washington to celebrate the anniversary of the independence of Nigeria. President Lyndon Johnson was to appear at a formal ball. According to Davis, his uncle was the Nigerian ambassador to the United States. The trip would be paid for by the embassy.

Almost from the beginning, things began to go awry. The special reception at the United Nations on Friday turned out to be a routine tour. Some people went back to the Americana Hotel, where Paul Anka was performing that evening.

Most of the group, however, flew to Washington that night for the ball and the appearance of President Johnson at the embassy. The men donned tuxedos and the women, mostly wives, wore evening gowns. They had been promised by Davis that they would be conveyed by limousine, but no cars were waiting at the airport when the travelers arrived. Davis hastily arranged for a convoy of taxis to take everyone to an obscure apartment building that had seen better days. They were greeted by a very confused man and his pregnant wife.

It was then that Davis announced that serious developments in Vietnam had prompted the president to cancel his appearance and the embassy to postpone the celebration. However, Davis had arranged for coffee and sandwiches to be served at his friend's place, which turned out to be a three-story walk-up.

Davis' tuxedoed coworkers demanded to know what was happening. His reply was evasive and a bit incoherent. The women in the group announced they were leaving, fearing that they were traveling with a disturbed soul. Several others decided to abandon Davis and take a train back to New York rather than fly.

Sometime in the next day or two, Davis disappeared. The disgruntled travelers returned to work on Monday and at first were reluctant to tell their story, which at best was embarrassing. Finally, the ridiculous details of the trip began to emerge and took the form of a mysterious fraud. The outing had resulted in costly airline and hotel bills for which the *Plain Dealer* was ultimately responsible. Over the next few months the paper paid off Eastern Airlines, United Airlines and the Americana Hotel with free advertising.

Meanwhile, Davis was still at large with the newspaper's American Express card. Higher-ups at the paper were strangely silent about the Davis affair. Executive editor Bill Ware never acknowledged a five-page memorandum outlining the apparent scam, sent to him by reporter and trip participant Jim Cox.

A few days later, Don Barlett and I were talking to Princiotto at the city desk when a copyboy said there was a call from Travelers Aid in San Francisco. Davis was trying to charge a flight to Hawaii, using Princiotto's name to authorize the purchase.

Princiotto asked that Davis be put on the line and took the call in his office. The copyboy remained on the line and overheard a conversation in which the city editor authorized a ticket to Cleveland and ordered Davis to return. We never saw Davis again.

Like the Robert Manry saga, the Bill Davis tale was simply added to the *Plain Dealer*'s trove of idiosyncratic lore. But to the observant, the Davis episode represented another incredibly naive attempt to somehow connect with Cleveland's African American community, a part of the city it had ignored for the past century.

Even the shock of the Hough riots failed to awaken the town's slumbering political and civic leaders, who had trouble fathoming what had gone wrong. The business community was in denial and the politicos were casting seeds of blame, hoping that something would sprout and take hold to exonerate them.

A hastily assembled grand jury, chaired by the recently retired Louie Seltzer, met for a few days and returned a verdict. The riots had been inspired and instigated by the communists!

But to those of us who covered those fiery nights it was obvious that the rampage and violence had been spontaneous, a reaction in sweltering weather to decades of frustration and poverty.

In the coming weeks, the grand jury report would be denounced by no less than the U.S. attorney general, the FBI, civil rights organizations, church groups and others. Only the local political leaders applauded the report. Terrified that the situation would recur, perhaps even enveloping downtown, business leaders opened a dialogue with the black community.

That wasn't the only result of the riots. With the emergence of Carl B. Stokes as a candidate for mayor the following year, Cleveland's political scene was about to change forever. Hough had offered the opportunity for American history to bless the beleaguered town. Hough had also ensured my place on the newspaper and put me in the running for ace.

CHAPTER 18

The Day the Paper Cured Cancer

On a Friday morning in August 1966 a headline across the front page of the *Plain Dealer* trumpeted: "Stock Jumps on Cancer Cure Rumor." The story was written by John E. Bryan, the paper's financial editor, and carried a copyright. The most important local revelations in the *Plain Dealer* were often copyrighted, mostly to force competitors to give credit to the paper if they sought to pursue the story. There was also a bit of pomposity attached to the display of a copyright.

But there was something curious about this story, the way it was played on page one and the abandon that its appearance projected. First of all, stories about cancer cures were generally approached with the utmost care, lest the announcement be false, a fraud or some figment of medical impropriety. A cure for cancer is what almost everyone wanted to read, but such declarations often proved to be more rumor than reality.

The story that August morning, while being couched with some disclaimer, carried a lead that read: "A cure for cancer, long hoped for, may be imminent." Stock in the Rand Development Corporation, a local research company, had jumped from $7 to $18 per share almost overnight following a magazine article that appeared a few months before.

Many of us in the city room sat up when we read the story. There was something about it that rang hollow, like an empty barrel. And sure enough, the federal government (in the form of the Food and Drug Administration, and the Securities and Exchange Commission) instituted legal proceedings against Rand, asking for a permanent injunction against the distribution of the serum and the sale of the company's stock.

The action took place in the midst of a 12-week vaccination program that was being administered to some 100 critically and terminally ill cancer patients. Many of these patients had come to believe that the serum had helped them and would save their lives. The federal court had issued a temporary order to stop the program until a full hearing took place. Representing the government in the hearing were U.S. attorney Merle McCurdy and assistant U.S. attorney Robert Rotatori.

During the hearing, cancer patients in the program and others began to line the hallways of the federal courthouse on Public Square. It was a pitiful sight, with frail and obviously ill people of all ages sitting on the hallway floors looking at passersby with empty, frightened eyes. McCurdy and Rotatori were picking apart Rand's careless and improperly applied research and proving to the court that the serum was not what it advertised. The dying looked on, hope fleeing with each argument.

Company president H. James Rand was a bit of an oddball. When the Academy of Medicine of Cleveland asked him why he didn't use animals in his research experiments, he replied, "Aren't people animals?"

The hearings were held in February 1967. I had just been transferred from the federal beat, which was fine with me given what was occurring in the ornate courthouse. You could only write so many stories with sad endings before empathy hardened to cynicism simply out of the need for emotional survival.

So I was surprised one morning to get a call from McCurdy. He told me to get down to his office; he wanted to talk about something that had just come up. I took the Number 3 bus down Superior Avenue to the courthouse and made my way through the thicket of sick people who lined the halls to McCurdy's fourth-floor office.

The moment I saw him, I could tell he was angry. Really angry. McCurdy was always suave and cool, never emotional. My relationship with him fluctuated with the degree of annoyance caused by my presence in his office.

"You see those people out there?" he began. "Your damn newspaper caused this."

This was an old refrain often heard in situations that created stress for public officials, and I steeled myself for the next blast. He asked me if I knew what he meant. I told him I wasn't sure.

"Well, I'll tell you," McCurdy said. "There are people on your paper involved with this story who own stock in Rand. We think the story was an effort to inflate the stock and make a killing before the whole thing was revealed for what it is."

Then McCurdy suddenly caught himself and would not comment further.

I was stunned, but I remembered the buzz in the city room when the story broke. There was something suspicious about it.

McCurdy looked at me. "You get back to the paper," he said, "and tell Tom Vail we are going to indict some people from the paper, and he better be prepared to write about that, too."

Wow!

I returned to the *Plain Dealer* offices and relayed the message to one of Vail's two male secretaries. Then I disappeared, figuring that a wave of turmoil would soon issue forth from the executive hallway. I waited and waited, and then nothing happened. It never did.

I've often wondered about that case. The court issued a permanent injunction against Rand's cancer cure, but there was no follow-up to McCurdy's accusations against the paper. It wasn't the only time that a controversial situation would evaporate into silence in the executive offices.

Years later I was having lunch at Johnny's and saw Rotatori at the bar. I seized the opportunity to ask him what had transpired in the Rand case. "Mike," Rotatori said, "I can't remember all the details, but I do know that a lot of prominent East Siders were involved. Some were politically connected. I'm not certain, but I'm sure Merle dealt with them."

The case was an example of another level on which the town functioned. Whatever the endeavor—business, sports, politics, crime—there was always more to the story than one could possibly fathom let alone unearth, unless you developed a special instinct for the way Cleveland worked. And that could only come with time.

CHAPTER 19

Carl Stokes and the Changing City

In 1967 James M. Naughton was the top political writer at the *Plain Dealer*. He occupied the position with skill, his personality radiating humor, friendliness and, above all, confidence. He had worked on the *Painesville Telegraph* even before graduating with honors from Notre Dame University, then served as an officer in the U.S. Marine Corps just before Vietnam turned ugly.

Apart from his journalistic acumen, Naughton was a delightful prankster. One day the irritable Roy Adams found his desk on the elevator. Naughton was the prime suspect. He would make his election predictions at the City Club wearing a swami's turban. He once appeared at a presidential press conference wearing a chicken head.

Naughton was universally respected in the city room and active in the newspaper's union affairs. Of all us reporters, he was clearly an ace on the rise. In two years he would leave to become White House correspondent for the *New York Times*. Later he was part of the executive team on the *Philadelphia Inquirer* when it won 12 Pulitzer Prizes. He should have been the editor of the *Plain Dealer*. He would have threatened the status quo, his personality and ability overshadowing everyone else in the front office.

But in the summer of 1967 Naughton was the principal writer covering an election in Cleveland that would make history. This was a story that any self-respecting ace wanted a piece of, and I did my best to become part of the team.

The mounting racial unrest that culminated in the Hough riots had politically coalesced Cleveland's black community. In 1965 an African American state legislator, a Democrat by the name of Carl B. Stokes, had run for mayor as an Independent and lost by only 2,143 votes to the incumbent Ralph S. Locher. To appease his angry constituency, Stokes requested a recount and picked up 219 votes.

In those days the mayor served a two-year term, and by the time the 1967 election campaign loomed it was clear that Locher was in trouble. In many ways Locher was unsuited as a politician. Reserved and scholarly, he had been the law director under Mayor Anthony J. Celebrezze, who in the middle of his fifth term in 1962 was named secretary of the U.S. Department of Health, Education and Welfare by President Kennedy.

By ordinance, the law director was elevated to the position of mayor if a vacancy occurred midterm. For Locher, the promotion could not have come at a worse time. The city's vast and failing urban renewal project, which had uprooted thousands of people—many of them black—was a constant irritant; the racial situation was confounding and alarming; industry was leaving the city in droves; and the business community was near panic. The newspapers were losing confidence in Locher's leadership.

I remember being in the mayor's office late one afternoon shortly after the Hough riots. Locher had his feet up on his desk, his tie loosened, a distant look in his eye. He was clearly overwhelmed by the events of the previous days. It was his 51st birthday.

"I'll be blamed for this forever," he said, not directing his words to anyone in particular. It was hard not to feel for him. Locher was a decent man caught in turmoil that had been festering for years.

If the city was on the brink of change, so too was the newspaper business. The year 1966 marked the end of an era with the retirement of Louie Seltzer, the celebrated editor of the *Cleveland Press* and the most powerful figure in town during his 38-year reign. It wasn't long before the afternoon paper began its downward spiral.

And the following year, on March 1, 1967, the *Plain Dealer*, family owned ever since Liberty Holden's purchase of it in 1885, was sold for $55 million to the Newhouse newspaper chain, headquartered in New Jersey. *Plain Dealer* editors intentionally omitted the dollar amount of the transaction from the paper's story announcing the sale, only to have the rival *Press* provide the figure the next day. It was one of those embarrassing moments relished by the afternoon paper.

That March morning Bill Ware, who had just replaced Phil Porter as executive editor, stood on a desk in the *Plain Dealer* city room and announced the sale to a stunned staff. The Newhouses were known to be tough on labor unions, and the leaders of the Newspaper Guild immediately seized on that fact. Everyone was anxious.

Everything had appeared to be going well for the paper. Circulation and ad sales were up, we'd received favorable notices in the national media, and publisher Tom Vail had recently announced plans for a new building to be constructed near the lake to facilitate the delivery of newsprint. Vail wanted to create a regional newspaper, one that possessed national clout in addition to local impact. The building project was budgeted at $25 million, but Porter later reported that inflation had driven the price up to $40 million, an unattainable sum.

What really drove the sale was the fact that various branches of the Holden family wanted to cash out. They had let it be known that the paper was for sale. Part of this desire to sell may have centered on the promotion of Tom Vail (Liberty Holden's great-grandson) to the position of publisher, largely at the behest of his father, Herman. The elevation of young Vail bypassed at least one other family member who had aspired to a career in the news business, possibly creating some hard feelings.

What the staff feared about the new ownership never materialized. The sale did, however, put Vail in a different position. While he held the titles of both editor and publisher, his principal duties shifted to running the paper's news side. His dream of creating a publishing empire vanished when his family sold the paper out from under him, and I felt sorry for him. It was a blow to the city, too.

By early 1967 the powers that be—the newspapers and the business and civic communities—had turned away from Ralph Locher and begun to consider options for the upcoming election. Given the city's volatile environment, there seemed to be only one choice. Privately, the establishment weighed the risk of supporting Carl Stokes, a black man, for mayor.

Inside the *Plain Dealer*, sentiments about Stokes were mixed. Doris O'Donnell and several other veteran reporters raised suspicions about Stokes' former career as a state liquor agent. O'Donnell was close to the police department, where many believed that Stokes had taken bribes in the course of his work. She was pushing for the paper to launch an investigation into his past.

Others of us found something compelling and refreshing about Stokes. Throughout the Democratic primary race I was with him on many autumn nights, particularly during his campaign ventures on the city's largely white West Side, where racial epithets said behind his back were common. But the arrival of a black man in an Irish home to speak with the neighbors about running for public office was more than just a novelty. It was damn near revolutionary.

A political campaign of this magnitude allows you to peer into the soul of the community. I covered it every day that fall, starting with the candidates in the morning and writing until the 11:20 p.m. deadline. We traveled all over the city, visiting churches, clubs, schools, restaurants, weddings and even funerals. It was exhausting but educational.

There were different speeches for different neighborhoods, and we reporters would smile as the message was adjusted to fit a particular ethnic group or modified to include street talk. You could sense that when people met Carl Stokes in person, they liked him. His charm could dissipate the hostility he encountered in those early meetings in private homes. His only allusion to race came in the form of an earnest request to just give him a chance.

Stokes looked like a mayor. He moved through crowds with grace, flashed a smile with a fraternal glow, and spoke with a reassuring tone. His well-trimmed mustache and natty appearance lent authority to his persona. He gained the sympathy of many West Side women.

But behind the charm was another side to Stokes that over time would surface. He was thin skinned and could be ill tempered. While covering a meeting at the U.S. Department of Housing and Urban Development in Washington, I saw him nearly come to blows with a member of the Northeastern Ohio

Coordinating Agency. Stokes, who in his youth had learned how to box at a Cleveland recreation center, had to be restrained by an assistant secretary of HUD. I didn't make much of the incident in the story, but was taken aback by his sudden volatility. His internal anger was understandable, given that he had been raised in poverty and essentially fought for everything he had, but he could not afford public displays.

In the primary Stokes again faced Locher along with the former mayor of Lakewood, Frank Celeste, who felt certain he would gain the endorsement of the *Cleveland Press* and ride to victory like other ethnic politicians in the past. I labeled him Fast Frank, for he could pass through multitudes of voters like no other candidate. He loved food and campaigning.

Locher moved through the primary as if undergoing painful rehabilitation after surgery. Early that summer he had lost any chance of regaining the mayoralty when Cleveland police chief Richard R. Wagner testified in defense of the death penalty before an Ohio House committee in Columbus. "In Cleveland," Wagner said, ". . . we have people saying they intend to overthrow the government of the United States and, incidentally, shoot all the Caucasians. One of those groups is RAM." RAM referred to the Revolutionary Action Movement, a militant black organization.

With racial tensions at a fever pitch, Wagner's remarks ignited a response from the African American community that stunned Locher. The United Freedom Movement, a civil rights organization, demanded that Locher explain the police chief's words. The mayor refused to meet with the group, brushing them off on his safety director. What followed was a seven-day demonstration during which civil rights groups conducted a "wait-in" in the mayor's office and picketed his home. Some 32,000 people signed a petition calling for Locher's recall; about 47,000 signatures were needed. Stokes quashed the movement and handily won the primary.

The national media, first attracted by the bleeding in Cleveland, now reacted to the growing possibility that a black man might run a major American city. It was the height of the civil rights movement, and the whole world watched as our nation struggled with an issue that had plagued it from its very beginnings.

So Jim Naughton and I presented Bill Ware with an idea. We wanted to devote an entire *Sunday Magazine*, some 50 pages, to a behind-the-scenes account of the historic campaign. We knew the city desk would brush off the idea. Anything over 600 words dealing with politics was a paralyzing thought, a strenuous effort that would make the desk's editors move their lips as they read. We were talking upward of 5,000 words. Ware, who over the years had run various aspects of the Sunday features department, better understood the logistics and signed off on the proposal.

The 1967 mayor's race was the most exciting, memorable and important election ever held in Cleveland. It gave a reporter something to write about other than the decades-old issue of whether or not to sell the Municipal Light Plant to the Cleveland Electric Illuminating Company.

Adding to the story's interest was Carl Stokes' opponent, a man whose life in almost every way was the diametric opposite. First, he was white, the grandson of a U.S. president, a Yale graduate. His clothes had a drip-dry hang on his slight frame, and he exuded little warmth and almost no humor. Second, he was a Republican, an endangered species in Cuyahoga County.

Seth Taft had moved into the city from the upper-class suburb of Pepper Pike, the kind of move that assured Republicans of losing an election in Cleveland. He was 44, an attorney at the prestigious law firm of Jones, Day, Cockley & Reavis, and an advocate of county government reform. He later served as a county commissioner. Taft was, as Phil Porter once categorized him, a do-gooder.

But above all, Taft was a classy and respectful politician, and it was this quality that helped the city avoid an inflammatory election that could have even further divided it.

Anticipation of the race reached global proportions, with journalists from throughout the world arriving in Cleveland. An endless parade of reporters with foreign accents questioned us about the candidates. I was once interviewed by Dutch television in the men's room of a restaurant. No one was more grateful for help than Japanese television, whose reporters bowed in thanks. The *New York Times* took a desk in the corner of our newsroom.

While each candidate pledged to keep the issue of race out of the campaign, it was clear from the outset that race would indeed be the key issue. How could it not? That issue was exactly why the rest of the world was watching.

The election would be close, so the margin of victory could hinge on which way the newspapers threw their support. Both campaigns sought endorsements. At the *Press*, Tom Boardman had succeeded Louie Seltzer, but in title only. A conscious decision had been made to change the role of the city's afternoon newspaper from one that fiercely drove issues to one that simply reported the news. The *Press* delivered such a wishy-washy endorsement of Stokes that the candidate wondered why it had even bothered to make an effort.

Meanwhile, everyone wondered what the *Plain Dealer* would do. Behind the scenes the business community, spearheaded by the leadership of the city's two most prominent law firms, Jones Day and Squire, Sanders & Dempsey, lobbied Tom Vail to support Stokes. The leaders of these firms had supplanted Seltzer as the town's power brokers.

On September 3, the *Plain Dealer* endorsed Stokes. His response: "Hot dog, now we are legitimate." It was a remark he would later regret.

There was always a bit of controversy over the endorsement. Vail looked upon it as a bold achievement, perhaps his proudest moment. Years later Stokes would write that the business community and Jack Reavis of Jones Day were the decisive players behind the endorsement.

Vail was a loner, aloof and not totally engaged with the community or the newspaper's staff, a man who found social discourse uncomfortable. Later in his life he would tell me that he had never been part of the city's establishment, and it was only then that I understood the fragile nature of his position. In the 1960s, most of us had assumed that the wealthy Vail was as much a part of the establishment as anyone in town.

His resumé didn't fit the job description of a publisher and editor of a paper the size of the *Plain Dealer*. A newspaper is a place of such diverse personalities, intellects and interests that conflict is routine and in many ways inevitable and healthy. Leadership in that environment has to be smart and flexible. It needs to possess a thick skin, harbor a healthy skepticism about nearly everything, and make hard decisions. Vail was smart, but he shied away from painful decisions and situations, preferring to delegate or avoid them. His view of the city room was filtered by editors eager to please him.

As election day approached, citizens girded themselves for events that threatened to further divide their ranks. On the schedule were four major debates, which pundits predicted would constitute the crux of the campaign. The debates would cover crime, unemployment, neighborhood decay and an unresponsive city hall. Throughout the campaign, both candidates had tried not to open the combustible Pandora's box of race, but its specter hovered.

Taft had warned his campaign workers that any reference to race in their political efforts would be met with expulsion. But two campaigns were being waged against Stokes: one by Taft and the other by dissident Democrats who trod through neighborhoods that fall cautioning voters against the installation of a black man (using a racial epithet) in the mayor's office. Taft could not stop this insidious endorsement, and the Stokes campaign seethed at its rhetoric.

Television ratings would show that each debate drew 100,000 viewers. In the city's barbershops, discussion of the fortunes of the Cleveland Browns gave way to speculation about those of Carl Stokes.

For Seth Taft, the first debate was a disaster. The moderator introduced the Republican candidate to a full house at Alexander Hamilton Junior High School while Carl Stokes cleaned his fingernails. Later in the evening, when Taft turned to his opponent and said, "It was about time somebody pulled you from your high horse, Carl," Stokes laughed uproariously. His scorn was evident.

Taft's evening only worsened. Stokes ridiculed life in Pepper Pike compared to that in Hough. He chided Taft for his seven-bedroom home and patrician lifestyle. Taft tried to laugh it off, but there was more pain than humor in his reaction. The evening shattered the morale of Taft's workers.

The second debate was a virtual reversal. It was held at John Marshall High School on the West Side, clearly partisan territory for Taft. In fact, during his introduction Stokes was met with a smattering of boos. But that was nothing compared to what followed when he reiterated his attack on Taft's heritage and Pepper Pike address. An unrelenting crescendo of anger, thick with hostility, left him stunned. Stokes had overplayed his hand with this particular crowd, displaying a characteristic that would haunt him throughout his political career: annoying hubris. What he said next indicated just how off balance he was.

"Seth Taft may win the November 7th election for only one reason. That reason is that his skin happens to be white."

"The auditorium fairly exploded in a backwash of noise, a surge that came like an angry sea, a bellowing roar that jerked Taft's head up from his notes, his eyes dilated in surprise," I wrote when describing that moment in the debate. "The wave of noise caught the former boxer with his guard down. He stood there for a moment trying to regroup, looking out into an angry crowd that rose to him, an immense cacophony of sound."

Still Stokes continued, unburdening himself of a deep-seated ache that he generally tried to conceal, but only further antagonizing the crowd. "Seth Taft is not a racist, he is not a bigot," he said. "But he does not believe that the people of Cleveland can rise above this issue."

This led to Taft's finest moment of the campaign. Taking his place on the podium he held up a full-page newspaper ad that read: "DON'T VOTE FOR A NEGRO. Vote for a man."

It was part of a Stokes ad campaign using race as its theme that had run throughout the primary and now into the general election. In a matter of minutes, Stokes' blunder had given Taft's faltering campaign new life. Taft's claim that Stokes had no good government programs to offer had gained traction. This night would not be forgotten by the huge television audience. Financial contributions to Taft increased and the race tightened.

The third debate, advertised by the media as the rubber match, turned out to be anticlimactic. Seth Taft turned attacker and jabbed at his opponent, searching for vulnerabilities through barbs and quips. For his part, a humbler Carl Stokes turned into a policy wonk, detailing his proposals for city hall. The volatility of the campaign slowed, settled and sputtered a bit.

The final debate, held the Saturday before the election, was the traditional City Club engagement. Taft had momentum, his staff no longer believing that Stokes was invincible. A *Plain Dealer* poll showed Stokes slightly ahead, which indicated that Taft had come a long way in the race.

A large crowd at the Hotel Sheraton-Cleveland waited in anticipation for the two candidates to square off. Both appeared tired. In an effort to restore energy to his campaign, Taft went after Stokes, calling him an absentee Democrat, an absentee legislator and an absentee landlord. The obvious implication was that he would be an absentee mayor.

Throughout the debate, Stokes kept his cool, refraining from emotional responses and focusing on his plan for city hall. The final question posed to him dealt with his time as a legislator. Taft had repeatedly challenged his attendance record at the statehouse. After slowly withdrawing a folded letter from his pocket, Stokes read it to the audience:

> Dear Carl,
> The reports I hear of your performance in Columbus are excellent and I congratulate you on the job.
> Seth Taft

You could feel the air go out of the room, and for a moment there was stunned silence. Those of us who had covered the campaign from the beginning felt we had witnessed the decisive moment in the most historic mayoral election of our time. If nothing else, the election engaged people with the city once more. It also gave Cleveland a feeling of pride that it had not enjoyed since before the Great Depression.

On Tuesday night, following a cold day replete with snow flurries, the polls closed after a healthy turnout. Then the arduous job of counting the ballots began, with Taft taking an early lead and holding it until midnight, when the East Side vote began to trickle in. Just before 3 a.m., Stokes passed Taft by 2,000 votes and continued to build the lead. Ten minutes later, he was proclaimed victor.

Cleveland had become an international story. The African American community celebrated; some thought the city—and the nation—would never again be the same, and they were right. Cleveland had met the future.

CHAPTER 20

Glenville

There was one man at the Rockefeller Building campaign headquarters that night who did not make an appearance. Martin Luther King Jr. was asked by the Stokes campaign to exempt himself from the celebration. Years later, former city council president George Forbes told me that King's appearance would have been a distraction. Stokes wanted this to be his moment.

The newly elected mayor's relationship with the media was quickly established. We were barred from the mayor's office, a stunning announcement that portended an acrimonious relationship not only with reporters but also with the organizations they represented. The office had generally been open to reporters, who often sat with the mayor at the end of the day and exchanged views. These informal sessions generally gave you some insight as to what was happening in the city.

This would not be the case with Stokes. In his book *Promises of Power*, he tells of lecturing a *Cleveland Press* reporter on why the mayor's office would no longer be a place where political gossip led to back-stabbing scenarios that played out in the media. Stokes branded many of us as racists.

It is true that a handful of writers and editors at the *Plain Dealer* did not like or trust the mayor. They were wary of rumors regarding his past, and for a time there was an ongoing investigative effort to verify them. Many of these rumors were fed to the paper by the police department. Stokes was angered by all of it.

But for the most part, the newspaper staff was pleased with the outcome of the election. It was the dawning of a new day in Cleveland.

I would not get to know Carl Stokes very well as mayor. Throughout most of his time in office I would be elsewhere on different assignments. More than any other mayor during my time as a journalist—from Anthony Celebrezze to the present—Stokes challenged the city to be better. He attempted to hire the best people available for his cabinet, engaged the police department in a bitter struggle, and paved the way for African Americans to hold city jobs and gain recognition from the business community. He tried in vain to break away from the old ethnic politics of stagnation and cronyism.

Many hoped that Stokes could alleviate racial tensions in Cleveland, but that rift was too wide for one man to bridge. He endured significant racial contempt and in the end saw his political career crumble. Part of that was his own doing, for he was a proud, prickly man of quick temper and little forgiveness.

Much of Stokes' personality is reflected in his book. For all his dislike of the media, he was naive about the way it functioned. He tells the story of accepting an offer from Tom Vail to find a way the *Plain Dealer* could be helpful. Stokes was at war with the police department, which he considered racist, incompetent and unresponsive to his reforms. He suggested that the newspaper launch a series on how the police force was run. Vail heartily agreed.

While the idea of a newspaper trying to be helpful might sound innocent and maybe even worthwhile, it was fraught with unanticipated consequences. In a way, the offer was Vail attempting to be Louie Seltzer, and Stokes trying to get at his nemesis through the paper. Making an arrangement like this is always a bad idea, because you can never be sure what course a story will take. Besides, Stokes saw the story one way and the paper quite another.

The series, heavily influenced by Doris O'Donnell and her police contacts, painted a picture of a hard-working, dedicated law enforcement organization responsive to the city's needs, not the rogue force that Stokes was trying to subdue. When the angry mayor called Vail and charged that the story that appeared was not the one they had agreed on, the publisher stood behind the story.

Stokes was at the pinnacle of his popularity on July 23, 1968, when his political career began its steep descent. That was the night of the Glenville shoot-out. Three policemen along with a civilian and three suspects were killed and 15 others wounded in a gunfight whose origins remain murky. The official determination was that the police were ambushed by black militants, but many believe that the police incited the event.

I learned of the story while sitting in a helicopter awaiting liftoff for an assault on a Viet Cong stronghold. Someone had a copy of the Army newspaper *Stars & Stripes* with a headline about a massacre in Cleveland. I wondered what I was doing in Vietnam when the story was at home.

But as things turned out, I was better off where I was. Glenville proved fateful not only to Carl Stokes but to the *Plain Dealer* as well. The paper assigned a group of reporters to conduct an in-depth study of the shooting. The official line was that the police had been ambushed in a carefully planned attack.

The reporters challenged this assertion, then were rebuked by editors who claimed that they were not qualified to draw conclusions. The story was killed and the reporters' notes confiscated. A few days later the *New York Times* would print a story that raised the same question that the *Plain Dealer* team had been pursuing: had overzealous police provoked the shoot-out in a moment of spontaneous confrontation?

Challenging the assertion that the militants had planned an ambush directly countered the official story from downtown. As during the Hough riots, an aura of denial permeated the city's upper reaches.

The quashing of the Glenville story profoundly affected city room morale. It furthered the decline of the staff's confidence in the senior editors, and in turn shook the editors' belief in key members of the reportorial staff. This feeling would fester amid the growing turmoil that engulfed our society.

CHAPTER 21

The Ace Race

I sometimes would buy a copy of the *New York Herald Tribune* at Schroeder's Bookstore on Public Square and clip a column or story, then tack it to the city room bulletin board with an annotation: *Why can't we do this?* It was a plea for a more creative approach to our journalism.

Down the street at the *Press*, Dick Feagler wrote a regular column that was probably the most-read piece in the paper, if not the city. Feagler was a rare talent in two ways. First, he could write, and second, he had an uncanny sense about what Clevelanders wanted to read. We had nothing to match him.

Then one day, pinned to that same board was a note announcing a monthly writing contest, with a $25 prize for the best piece. By *Plain Dealer* standards, $25 was a princely sum. A $2 merit raise was given grudgingly and disappeared with the next Newspaper Guild increase.

The important thing, though, was that the announcement invited us to tell different stories and to experiment a bit in writing them. The aces were pushing the envelope.

Even better, I won the first several contests. One prizewinner was inspired by my discovery that the guards of a Brink's truck parked outside the *Plain Dealer* building had locked themselves out of the armored vehicle and were using a bent coat hanger to unlock it through a gunport. Then there was the guy who returned from vacation to find his driveway turned into a railroad siding. I won another $25 for my grim account of the midair collision of an airliner and a small plane near Dayton. Body parts decorated tree limbs, swaying in the breeze in a macabre dance. The top of a man's skull, its hair perfectly parted, rested on a fence post, and the body of a pregnant woman had burst among rows of corn. The scene haunts me to this day.

The Stokes election had consumed the greater part of a year, and when it was over I looked to return to a sense of normalcy. Phil Porter's departure as executive editor had brought changes in the paper's leadership. Bill Ware was named as Porter's replacement, and Ted Princiotto became night managing editor. Russ Kane was the new city editor, a change that had a marked effect on the direction of the city room.

Kane was a smart, personable man who had been captured by the Germans in the fighting near the end of World War II. He was laid-back, thoughtful and oriented to a softer approach to the news. Princiotto had run a tight ship, stressing investigative pieces and basic hard-nose journalism to thwart the nemesis *Press*. Kane was more casual.

Kane's sensibilities appealed to some of us. He embraced the kinds of stories that gave the city a different flavor. This was well and good, as long as the basic discipline of running the news operation was maintained. Over time, that didn't happen.

Meanwhile, the Vietnam War, racial tensions, and the spawning of a youth drug culture were creating a strange new chapter in American life, one that fomented hostilities between the generations. It was a world made for a reporter.

The war in Vietnam had been creeping up on the nation and

on the paper since 1962. With each troop deployment the war's measure of column inches grew, as did public anger and protest. By 1965 Vietnam and civil rights were the two major stories dominating the national news. The war became a local story when caskets from Southeast Asia began to arrive at Cleveland Hopkins International Airport.

Early each week, the government would release the casualty list. The Associated Press would wire the list and the city desk would quickly scan it for anyone local killed in action. If you were unlucky, you drew the assignment of visiting the bereaved and offering condolences while asking for a picture and a few details about the son or husband. After a few of these missions, you made sure you weren't around when the AP list arrived.

Even worse were the funerals. The soldiers accompanying the body would respond to questions with clipped, uninformative answers, staring over your shoulder and making you feel like the ghoul you were. War stories were easier to write than to report, and you knew readers paid attention to them.

The war also manifested itself in the increasing number of protests on local college campuses. The military draft threatened young men who did not want to fight. Here you could witness genuine frustration and anger, and the emotion made for graphic stories. One afternoon at Western Reserve University a former college classmate of mine was beaten and arrested for disobeying a police order to disperse.

The world seemed to be coming apart. And to make things worse, someone else won the monthly writing contest.

The winner that month would become the real ace of aces. Pipe smoking, possessed of a youthful countenance, shod in Frye boots, and jacketed in rumpled corduroy, Joe Eszterhas projected the misgivings of a displaced person, which as a Hungarian immigrant, he once was. He was 22 when he joined the *Plain Dealer*. At Ohio University he had won an award proclaiming him the best collegiate journalist of the year. The White House gave him a gold medal.

Eszterhas was a product of his refugee past and fit into the growing wave of discontent with the establishment. He could write and had boundless energy. He had the confidence and talent that make a man careless. He took risks in a culture that was averse to such, and in time that paradigm would come to haunt him.

Eszterhas would eventually out-ace us all. One website estimates his current net worth at around $18 million—most of it made during his years as the highest-paid screenwriter in Hollywood. All that would come later, but at the time I begrudged him the $25 prize money.

Russ Kane wanted stories that dealt with the changing times. I found myself frequenting bars in University Circle to learn about the drug culture. Drugs made a dramatic entrance into Cleveland in the late 1960s. Somewhere in the back of my memory I recall a narcotics detective telling me in 1964 that only a handful of heroin addicts lived in Cleveland. Just a few years later the city found itself so overwhelmed by drugs that federal narcotics agents opened an office here and began to go undercover.

The growing antiwar fervor, the hopelessness in the ghetto, and a swelling rejection of authority all contributed to what became known as the turned-on generation. Another factor, although difficult to measure, was organized crime's role in the distribution of drugs, an activity it had eschewed in the past. But now there was just too much illicit money to be made.

The use of drugs spread beyond the ghetto and into prosperous white communities, where a youth culture of "hippies" challenged the establishment's every norm. Anyone over 30 was not to be trusted; ponytails and facial hair replaced the crewcuts of the 1950s. LSD, a newly popular hallucinogen, became the drug of choice for many, including university intellectuals.

While New York, Chicago and San Francisco were centers of dissent, Cleveland had its own measure of discontent. The combination of drugs and the insurgent attitude of young people confused and confounded the authorities, who found themselves mounting an increasing number of drug raids and confronting demonstrators almost daily. For many of us on the paper, the decade had gone from the hope and glamour of the Kennedy years to the dark disillusionment of a brave new world.

The local protest movement was headquartered on the East Side in several bars on Euclid Avenue near University Circle. To get the story behind the street-talk rhetoric, I tried to meet with some of the movement's leaders. Late at night, I'd often look across a bar and see federal narcotics agents whom I knew nursing drinks and attempting to do much the same.

There was one figure who symbolized the movement here, a wispy, soulful-looking street poet who went by the lowercase name of d. a. levy. His poetry spoke of revolution. Some of it was laced with pornographic interludes. He made outrageous statements about putting LSD into the city's water supply. All of this gained the attention of the police department, which was frustrated by its inability to quell the discontent.

Ever since 1919 the town had been somewhat paranoid about communists, who were thought to have played a role in organizing labor unions and strikes over the years. The feeling was fueled by the Cold War and the prevailing attitude among Cleveland's Eastern European immigrant communities whose families back home were suffering under the oppression of communist dictators.

As late as 1962 the House Un-American Activities Committee was holding hearings on communist activity in Cleveland that dated back to the 1930s. The concern was such that the police department had created a "subversive squad," a spooky unit that searched for anyone thought to be undermining the community. Any deviation from the norm caught the squad's attention. In time it would shift its focus from communists to black militants.

Levy's unsettling poetry, confiscated from the few bookstores that sold it, made him a subversive miscreant in the eyes of law enforcement officials. He was jailed after being charged with five counts of reading his poems to teenagers and thereby contributing to their delinquency. According to George J. Moscarino, an assistant county prosecutor, this was a very serious matter indeed.

"Our office has been interested in having a decent community for our children," Moscarino told me. The righteousness of the prosecutor's office under the estimable John T. Corrigan always rang with an unyielding peal.

Police had also confiscated all of Levy's bumper stickers proclaiming BOMB CLEVELAND AND NOT HANOI. A *Plain Dealer* editorial concluded that police harassment of the poet was making Cleveland look like a backwater province.

When I visited Levy in his sixth-floor cell in county jail, he claimed to be a political prisoner who was entitled to reading materials. A fellow poet, Robert J. Sigmund, who had also been arrested, wrote a message to the guards on toilet paper proclaiming a hunger strike. He also did not want to be disturbed during moments of meditation.

Some referred to the 26-year-old Levy as the king of hippies, and for a while he was idolized and featured now and then in the daily media. He had been discharged from the Navy as a manic-depressive. There was something gentle and mystical about him, as if he were from a faraway place.

Levy's girlfriend, who went by the name dagmar R, lived with him in a $75-a-month apartment in East Cleveland. She supported him since, according to Levy, his job as a poet brought in only 89 cents a day. The charges against him were finally dropped, but the stress of it all must have strained his already frayed psyche.

On Sunday, November 24, 1968, Levy put a .22-caliber rifle to his forehead and shot himself. Friends had noticed something wrong during the last week of his life. He had burned all of his poetry, borrowed a suitcase for a trip that he said would be out of this world, and ordered Dagmar from the apartment. Sigmund compared his friend's death to that of Hemingway, noting that Levy went out a legend. I sometimes think of him. It was such a strange time and he was such a peaceful soul.

CHAPTER 22

Charger Charley

Not everyone who hung out in Euclid Avenue's drinking establishments possessed d. a. levy's gentleness, particularly Charger Charley and his band of mind-blowing motorcycle thugs who could often be seen at Adele's Lounge Bar mingling with the poets. Charger Charley's and my paths would cross for nearly 30 years. My appearance in his life would always signify bad karma.

In 1967 motorcycle gangs had reached a new popularity thanks to a book called *The Hell's Angels* by Hunter S. Thompson, who would become a New Journalism idol. People were fascinated with the outlaw cult, another expression of anti-establishment behavior in a world that had gone restrictive and rudimentary.

Thompson's motorcycle gang was the real thing, made up of men who had abandoned society to become outlaws and even killers. Other gangs were less radical but still carried a sense of danger and a desire for freedom from societal norms. Cleveland was a perfect place for that kind of bonding.

It was one of those nights at Adele's, hippie central. I was doing my usual prospecting for an angle on a story dealing with the decline and fall of decency. Among the fashionably bedraggled—denim, leather and chains—I stood out in a blazer and a rep tie. I looked like a lost encyclopedia salesman. I was sitting by myself at a table when a group of unshaven men sporting black leather jackets and bad attitudes strode in and looked at my near-empty table. It was evening, but they all wore sunglasses.

"Move over, asshole," one of them said, followed by a menacing belch. Adrenaline ran a warning alert down my spine. There were five of them, and they filled the table with a lot of chair scraping and grunts.

They introduced themselves and I had the pleasure of meeting Charger Charley, Umm, the Hulk and Blinky. The fifth just mumbled. All were festooned in Nazi regalia, with swastikas, Iron Cross earrings, and the trademark German helmets favored by motorcycle gang members. Blinky's jacket displayed a badge that read "Please be kind or I'll kill you," and they all wore "100% Sin" patches. Various medals commemorated such events as the summer afternoon when they terrified the town of Geneva-on-the-Lake or a sexual escapade that started out as a myth and ended up a legend.

All five boasted of minor scrapes with the "fuzz" and bragged about having their own bail bondsman. They liked to harass ordinary citizens; Charger Charley's favorite sport was scaring old ladies. They hated peace marchers.

Charley said he once was ticketed for going 150 in a 50-mph speed zone. He asked the cop for three copies of the ticket so he could prove it to the rest of the gang.

Their appearance belied their true being. They dressed and acted demonic in order to "blow people's minds," an axiom they enjoyed using in their profane repartee. They liked to portray themselves as the hard cases, society's outcasts. Few of them worked. What they did best was simply hang out and sneer at people. They were living a dream in a world that had turned upside-down. They were street actors.

The gang members looked upon me as an oddity—bespectacled, bookish, somebody from the other side, a tourist of sorts lost among society's underbelly. They urged me to pierce my ears and wear a swastika to work to blow my editors' minds. They wanted to meet them, but I said it wouldn't be a good idea because editors were a lot like cops. They seemed to understand and sympathized with me for having to endure them. I liked that.

When word got around the paper that I was working on a motorcycle gang story, one of the editors from the features department wanted to run a piece about the women that the gang members dated. These guys didn't date, I said. They just picked up suburban girls at bars.

Regardless, the editor wanted me to escort one of his women reporters and introduce her to the gang. I didn't think this was a good idea, but against my better judgment I agreed. The reporter, Jeannie, was young and attractive, which should have been another tip-off that the paper was making a mistake.

The night the two of us walked into Adele's, everything stopped. Charley and the boys stared rudely. Jeannie wore a pained expression. I wore one of fear. The gang became animated, pushing and shoving one other to reach us. I held a chair for Jeannie and she sat down at a table. Just as I was about to sit, I heard the thunk of a long, ugly knife blade striking the tabletop. The blade quivered like a telephone line in a summer storm.

"Mine," said Charley, signaling to the spot next to Jeannie.

"We have to go," I said, grabbing Jeannie by the arm and pulling her toward the door.

"Hey, come on, man," Charley pleaded. "Stick around. We haven't even started drinking."

That was the point. Alcohol would only fuel a scene that could easily get out of control and into the police blotter. The best thing was to leave, and as quickly as possible. We were outside the bar when Jeannie looked down and picked up a $20 bill from the sidewalk.

"Oh, shouldn't we go back in and see if we can find out who lost it?" she asked. Believing that she had suddenly gone crazy, I simply took the bill from her and put it in my pocket.

My page-one story on the gang ran a few days later along with a page of pictures taken by Michael Evans. Evans would later become the White House photographer for Ronald Reagan.

In response, police department officials called to scold me for romanticizing guys who were basically street bums. A woman from the West Side wondered why we had wasted time and space on scum. Charley called and suggested that I not come around Adele's for a while.

With the gang story behind me, I settled down to the usual routine of murders, funerals, parades, fires, speeches at chicken dinners—stories hardly worthy of ace status. Then one Monday morning about a month later there was a call from the Euclid police. It was about Charley.

Over the weekend Charley and Blinky had used their chains to break a jewelry-store window and steal rings for a couple of girls they knew. They were caught and brought before a municipal court judge who gave them a choice. He would either bind them over to the grand jury on felony charges or they could join the Marine Corps.

They chose the greater of two evils—the Marines.

It took me about 10 minutes to get in touch with the Marine Corps major in Cleveland in charge of recruiting. Yes, he said, the two miscreants were scheduled to leave for Parris Island in South Carolina. I marveled at the irony of Charley in the Marine Corps. So did the city desk; they dispatched photographer Ray Matjasic to go with me.

Matjasic was perfect for the assignment. He had been a Marine in World War II and still carried a load of shrapnel in his legs from combat on a once-obscure Pacific island.

Parris Island is an iconic place where since World War I hundreds of thousands of young American boys have made the transition to manhood—a process accomplished in a matter of eight weeks. This is where Marine Corps recruits receive basic training. The cadence of marching men is the island's melody.

"There isn't anything wrong with American youth that we can't cure in eight weeks here," one Marine officer told me. "If we can reverse 18 years of fiddle-faddle in that time, there can't be anything really that wrong."

In 1967 Parris Island still carried vestiges of World War II. Aging Quonset huts were still in use, and the mantra was still the same: God wasn't dead, morality was no laughing matter, and patriotism and professionalism were sacred entities. The solemnity of the place was often broken by the noise and thunder of the drill instructors, whose job was to strip naked the souls of the recruits and reconstitute them with discipline and motivation.

The war was reaching its apex and the Marines were fighting fierce battles in the northern reaches of South Vietnam, adjacent to the demilitarized zone. Every day brought casualties, and graduates of Parris Island were almost certain to serve a tour in Southeast Asia. That year 3,000 Marines died in Vietnam.

One afternoon during a break, a drill instructor took me aside as he field-stripped a cigarette and let the breeze carry away its remains. He looked at me from beneath his campaign hat, which sat inches from his nose, and spoke soberly. "Don't get misled by what you are seeing here," he said, referring to the behavior of the DIs. "This is no show that we are putting on. These men are going to a place where they may die. We are doing everything here to avoid that happening. Death is a serious business, and so are we."

For Charger Charley, this experience had to be more than traumatic. For someone who bragged about throwing mud at old ladies, who flexed his forearm to make a tattoo of Sidney the Snake dance, and who slept until noon, Parris Island had to be a descent into hell itself.

But for the Marines, Charley was hardly an annoyance; in fact, he was a welcome addition to the island. The people there liked diversity. When the commanding officer of the base, Major General Rathvon McClure Tompkins, saw the pictures of Charley and Blinky in their motorcycle garb, his stern visage suddenly softened.

"What great 'before' pictures," he exclaimed. "When we get through, the after pictures will really tell a story." I had no doubt, but that afternoon I had no idea just how far and how long that story would last.

I watched Charley for a few days. My presence meant that he received special attention, the drill instructors screaming at him to run faster, jump higher, shout louder and crawl lower under barbed wire in a muddy obstacle course. Move your ass, lady.

Finally, I couldn't take it any longer. I wanted to know what was going through Charley's mind. There was no such thing as a spare moment at Parris Island in those days. The basic training course had been cut to eight weeks because of the demand in Vietnam, and recruits were being marshaled through it in record time.

When I asked Charley's DI if I could speak with him, he said

I could only have a few minutes. He didn't want to disrupt the platoon from its march.

He called over to Charley, who was in the back of the ranks.

"You have someone here to see you. Do you know that man there?"

"Sir, I can't see. I forgot my glasses."

"You ain't supposed to see," the DI yelled. "Now get over here."

And then, there he was in front of me. Charley's once long and unruly hair was shorn close, his facial hair was barely stubble, and gone were the patches and medals that had been such important symbols of his lifestyle.

Now he looked like everyone else around him, a nondescript government-issue grunt in plain unadorned green fatigues.

"Charley, how are you?" I greeted.

"Terrible," he replied. "This is the baddest place in the world. People are always screaming. It's painful. But don't get me wrong. I thought motorcycle outlaws were bad. They are sissies compared to the Marines. Quote me on that. Tell them the Marines are a bigger gang. Most of the gang members in Cleveland couldn't make it here."

During our brief conversation, Charley showed total remorse. The Marines, he said, were trying to take a stupid kid and make him into a sensible man. It was a moving reincarnation.

The last time I saw Charley at Parris Island, the drill instructor was screaming at him: "Sweetpea, this rifle of yours better be clean enough to eat offa!" Although I would look for him now and then, it would be 21 years before I found him. And when I did, I dared not tell him of my odyssey.

CHAPTER 23

We Need You to Look
In On the War

It was Thursday, November 9, 1967, and I had just come
back from a greasy cheeseburger lunch at the Rockwell Inn.
A quickly consumed beer and burger was standard fare, as a
reporter's schedule could be unpredictable as well as unending.
There was something exciting about coming to work and having
no idea where the day would take you. It wasn't always fun, but
it was different. This day was slow. The mayoral election was
over and the town began to settle in for the coming holidays and
the bad weather to follow.

I was sitting at my desk watching George Barmann read the
Press. He would read a page, rip it out, then cast it to the floor
in unending repetition until the litter around him created a fire
hazard. The discarded pages had indeed caught fire more than
once as a result of an errant cigarette. Late at night I watched
the Polish cleaning women deal with Barmann's trash and wondered what they thought of us.

Barmann was in the midst of his mess when Bill Ware's secretary, Mary Jo, stopped by to say that when I had a minute

Bill wanted to see me. That long walk up the executive corridor made me apprehensive. A summons almost always meant something was up, and that was not always a good thing.

Ware motioned for me to sit down. He smiled and leaned back in his chair. "Mike," he said, "we are sending you to Vietnam. We need you to look in on the war. How soon can you be ready?"

I was stunned. While much of the country did not want to have anything to do with Vietnam, most journalists secretly yearned to go. Besides the war, the place offered mystery and adventure, and many reporters had emerged from it as notable personalities.

And we had all read Hemingway.

As for me, I had thought about covering the war, but had never really considered it a possibility. Of course, I had followed the events in Vietnam closely and had interviewed or talked to many who had been there. Earlier in the year I spent an evening with Peter Arnett, who had just won a Pulitzer Prize for his war reporting for the Associated Press. Arnett said to look him up if I ever got to Saigon.

So as Ware continued, I couldn't believe my good fortune. The assignment would be open ended, and I would need to spend a week in Washington being briefed at the Pentagon and State Department. I would need to be vaccinated against typhoid, cholera, the plague, tetanus and other assorted illnesses, 15 inoculations in all. I was to begin making travel arrangements immediately.

I walked out of Ware's office with two people on my mind: my mother and Terry Sheridan. Unbeknownst to me, when I had received my draft notice my mother took it upon herself to personally visit the draft board with the medical records from my bout with polio. Her argument was so persuasive that the board declared me unfit for service. She had gone to great lengths to protect her son, and now he was about to embark on what she would think a both foolish and dangerous venture.

As for Sheridan, it was common knowledge that, in the spirit of the great ace race, he had submitted a fictitious resumé carefully crafted to meet a search for a potential war correspondent. He cataloged his military experience (Airborne qualified), his bountiful language skills (excellent French), and his abilities to navigate hostile situations (Special Forces resourceful). He didn't feature his reporting skills, for he considered them unparalleled. The best on the paper.

The question was, how could I deliver the news of my Vietnam assignment in the most ace-like manner to get the biggest reaction from Sheridan? For this I needed collaboration from the aces of aces, Joe Eszterhas.

Within minutes, Eszterhas moved into action. "Hey, Sheridan," he said, "did you hear they're sending Roberts to Vietnam?"

With that, Sheridan bolted from his chair and charged down the corridor to Ware's office. I'm sure he explained how cowardly and unequipped I was for an assignment that was something he could do far better than anyone. Ware never said a word to me about the meeting, but I didn't need to know. It was all part of the competitive game.

As for my mother, all she said was to be careful.

The last time the *Plain Dealer* had sent anyone off to war was during WWII. Gordon Cobbledick, whose fame was as a sportswriter and editor, traveled to the Pacific, and Roelif Loveland, one of the paper's most legendary reporters, went to the European Theater. Both men had long retired, leaving no institutional memory for this kind of reporting.

As I prepared for the trip, I figured I'd be excused from the daily grind, and for the most part I was—that is, until a cold Friday night, the 15th of December. I was on a date at an obscure pizza place on the West Side. The place was so remote it only had four tables. It was about seven o'clock when who should come through the door but Truby, the troll of a copyboy who specialized in locating reporters in the oddest of places at the most inopportune of times.

"Hey, they want you downtown," Truby said. "There's been a bridge collapse on the Ohio River. A plane is waiting for you at Lakefront Airport."

My date just rolled her eyes, She did not look happy even when I said she could take the uneaten pizza home.

The Silver Bridge, on the river at Point Pleasant, West Virginia, had collapsed at 4:15 p.m., taking with it some 100 persons; 46 had died and two were missing. The plane ride seemed like forever and Eszterhas already was on his way. I was wearing a thin raincoat and loafers on a night that was cold, the riverbank thick with mud.

When I arrived, a barge in the middle of the river held rescue workers pulling bodies from the water, a gruesome sight reflected by harsh floodlights that cast eerie shadows over the dark water. The resourceful Eszterhas had managed to pose as one of the rescuers and was on the barge, no doubt already developing a page-one story.

A milling crowd had gathered on the bank near the fallen bridge. Women were sobbing and crying out while men searched among the bodies for friends or family members. It was a bad scene. A *New York Times* reporter complained that his desk had ordered him to find a drugstore and buy a thermometer to take the temperature of the water. That was a new one. Our desk hadn't fallen that low yet.

I found the last people to have made it off the bridge before it crashed. They were Buck Hayman and his wife, Barbara. They were driving across the bridge when it collapsed; their car was hoisted on one of the broken girders and miraculously carried to shore and safety. Buck, a good old boy, saved a truck driver from the wreckage and then went to have four whiskeys.

The Silver Bridge would prove to be somewhat of a disaster for the *Plain Dealer* as well, one that was decided by the U.S. Supreme Court. Several months after the collapse, Eszterhas returned to the scene and wrote a piece on the family of Melvin Cantrell, who was killed in the disaster. Joe interviewed the children of the victim, but their mother was not present. Subsequently, she sued the paper and won $60,000 in an invasion of privacy suit. The paper appealed the decision and it was reversed. The family then challenged the appeal and the case was finally heard by the U.S. Supreme Court, which upheld the original verdict. The case would play a role in later events on the paper involving Eszterhas.

Cold and muddy, I returned to Cleveland and did not linger anywhere near the city desk. I prepared for my departure to Southeast Asia, where I knew I could at least count on better weather.

I was on my own to figure out how and what to cover in Vietnam, a place a half a world away, a strange land full of hazard and hardship. A reporter could not have asked for a greater challenge that fall.

While there were a lot of questions and protests about the war, there was also optimism as 1967 entered its last months. General William Westmoreland, the commander of U.S. forces in Vietnam, addressed the National Press Club and stated that there was light at the end of the tunnel, that the war was nearing an end. So it appeared I would be on hand for this historic moment.

Personally, I had developed no strong feelings for or against the war. I was exercising the journalist's privilege of objectivity, always a dubious position considering that human frailty is a big part of life. The reports were mixed on the war's progress, and you could not gather a consensus by simply following the news.

I applied for my passport, began to get my shots, some of which needed time to take effect, and ordered my airline tickets from the Pan American office on Public Square. The ticket manager came out to meet me when he learned I was flying to Saigon. He had just returned from managing Pan Am's Saigon office.

He looked at my coach-class ticket and advised that I switch to first class, regardless of the cost. "It is one hell of a long flight there," he said. The trip was 30 hours in the air. First class was $931.17, nearly double that of coach class. I took it, figuring that I'd be gone before the accountants found out. Besides, Cleveland was 8,778 miles from Saigon.

Expenses would be a consideration on the assignment, especially after I was told to limit my cablegrams. The cost per word was expensive. I had to rely on the mail for most of my articles, but that turned out to be surprisingly fast—three days to Cleveland via the Military Postal Service, which correspondents were authorized to use.

Anyway, I had not intended to cover much breaking news. I marvel when I think of the Internet and the ability today to send a story from virtually anywhere for next to nothing in cost. As for living expenses, I would be living almost totally on an expense account. I was earning a salary of $11,000 and the paper would bank that in my account at Cleveland Trust.

Another consideration was what to wear to a war. In those days people dressed up when they flew. I was reading Graham Greene's *The Quiet American*, the classic novel about Vietnam, and on the cover was a rendering of a man in a tropical business suit. It was the middle of winter and the only place I could find a tropical suit was at Hauck's Menswear in Berea. I bought a blue suit and then wore it only once, on the flight to Saigon. The suit languished for almost a year in a hotel closet, the humidity turning it a luminescent green and imparting a strange odor. I discarded it. For years afterward, friends chided me about showing up for a war looking like I was seeking a mortgage at a savings and loan.

I worried about my fitness and jogged daily for five weeks. I could feel a difference in my wind and legs. I had no idea what to expect so I read everything I could find about Vietnam, which at the time wasn't much. South Vietnam's I Corps was in the north where the Marines were fighting. If Charley and Blinky were in Vietnam, it was likely that the boys would be engaged in battle.

My week in Washington was hectic, confusing and daunting. The U.S. effort in Vietnam was complex and extensive, and a great deal of it had nothing to do with military operations. I had 14 briefings from various governmental organizations operating a variety of programs. The briefing about IR8 rice, a high-yield variety of the grain, was long and boring. You could tell who had been in-country by the number of acronyms they could rattle off: MACV, CORDS, DRAC, AWADS, ARPA, OSAFO, OPCON, WHAM, SOTAS, CONUS, PAVAN, ICC, CINCPAC and at least a hundred more. Finally, I visited the South Vietnamese embassy for a visa.

The paper asked for help from the Associated Press bureau in Saigon, and to arrange it I flew to New York to meet with the wire service. Wes Gallagher, then AP's general manager, offered advice about covering a war. During World War II he had reported from Denmark, North Africa, Greece, the Balkans and Austria. Covering a war, he said, is serious and challenging work. You will have to take chances, but know your physical and mental limitations and don't overextend yourself. Risk only when you must.

It was good and sobering advice that would prove true.

Before I left, Gallagher gave me an Associated Press medical kit with a set of basic medicines. It also had a dissertation on dysentery, a condition one was sure to encounter. Several occasions would arise when I popped tetracycline pills from the kit like peanuts.

On Friday, January 26, at 6 p.m., I boarded a Boeing 707 at Cleveland Hopkins to begin my journey. As the jet lifted off and circled the city before heading into the western skies, I was struck by a transitional feeling of both excitement and loneliness. I felt that somehow life would never again be the same, that where I was going and what I would see would change something in me.

CHAPTER 24

You Would Be a Fool to Go

We landed in San Francisco around 9 p.m. California time and I checked in at the Mark Hopkins Hotel. I had been advised to order a drink at the Top of the Mark before bed. When I got to the bar, two Marine sergeants were having their last beers in the U.S. before spending their second 13-month tours in Vietnam.

I was glad for their company and eager to learn their thoughts on the situation into which I was about to venture. They could not have been more alarming. They questioned my sanity and said the fighting was becoming more intense around a place they expected to be assigned: Khe Sanh.

In the coming month the siege of the remote Marine combat base at Khe Sanh would become a haunting headline, and as dangerous a place as there was in Vietnam. One Marine spoke of tigers and snakes that added to the fearsome nature of the North Vietnamese infantry, considered to be among the best in the world, a match for the Corps.

"I wouldn't take you anywhere near the place," the Marine said. "And you would be a fool to go." His tone and manner were both chilling and sustaining.

I never saw those Marines again, but I never forgot what they said.

The next morning I flew to Honolulu where there was a layover for a couple of hours before the next and longest leg of the trip, this time to Manila. This was where you got an idea of the vast reach of the Pacific Ocean. The hypnotic drone of the 707's engines cast a spell in which time and space ceased. On the seemingly endless flight—well beyond any immediate reach of land—we were a speck suspended over nature's sea.

By the time we landed, I was unsteady with jet fatigue and uncertain in the crowd of travelers at the airport. After many hours in the air my suit had lost its shape, and I had the uncomfortable feeling that comes with wearing the same clothes for days. Manila's tropical heat forecast what was ahead. I already regretted my choice of clothing.

Newspaper people used to be able to identify a colleague by appearance. It was not necessarily the clothes, but the way they were worn. Baggy and rumpled, a loosened tie pulled to the side, a notepad jammed in the jacket pocket, a half-tucked shirt and a manner somewhere between nonchalance and disdain.

That is what the man standing next to me looked like as we boarded the flight to Saigon. I took him for a reporter and he was. His name was John Riddick and he worked for the *Tucson Daily Citizen*.

I had never met anyone as inquisitive, and during the final hop into Vietnam he asked me dozens of questions about what I thought of the war, America, its strident youth culture, and the nature of journalism. He made the time pass, so there was no dwelling on my growing apprehension of what lay ahead.

Riddick and I became friends. Having financed the trip himself, he had no deadlines or appointed destinations. He darted around Southeast Asia as if he were some cartographer checking on longitudes and latitudes to make sure they were in order. We spent many a night atop the Caravelle Hotel in Saigon drinking beer, watching the war, and questioning the sanity of it all.

Vietnam was perilous in unimaginable ways. Ten years after leaving the embattled land and returning home to Arizona, Riddick died of a mysterious blood disease that doctors said he had contracted in Southeast Asia. The place had an insidious way of reaching out and killing.

It took only three hours to reach Vietnam and begin our descent into Tan Son Nhut, the country's main airport outside Saigon. The sky was a sullen pewter and below was a game board of silvery rice paddies. Patches of raw red soil contrasted with the verdant jungle. The pilot warned that we should tighten our seatbelts because we were going to have a hard landing.

Then a surreal scene came into view. Off the port wing an air strike was in progress. A jet fighter was making a bombing run on a jungle redoubt. The bombs exploded in a flash followed by a cloud of greasy gray smoke. It was like watching a movie.

The 707 was not in a standard, slow landing pattern. It was not unusual for commercial aircraft to take ground fire, and there was no percentage in being in a hanging descent, making a fine target for some ambitious guerrilla fighter. A commercial carrier would disembark its passengers as quickly as possible, then take off for some safe overnight destination. Tan Son Nhut, which also served as the main military airfield, was subject to nightly mortar attacks.

As we struck the runway with a jarring thump and the engines reversed, I had the first of many you-bet-your-life moments when the mouth goes dry, adrenaline explodes, and motion slows and shifts into such high definition that all the senses rev into a vivid awareness. This sensation would visit me many times in the next year.

Somewhat shaken by the manner of arrival, I slowly made my way up the aisle for my first steps in-country. I have been to Vietnam three times, and my initial reaction was always repeated. As the cabin door opens, a fetid smell like vegetables decaying in the sun overwhelms. Then follows a blast of smothering humidity that momentarily stuns. A paltry reward for a long journey.

CHAPTER 25

Dateline: Saigon

The passport stamp said I arrived at Tan Son Nhut on January 29, 1968. The next day was Tet, the lunar New Year—this time around, the Year of the Monkey—a day that in a few hours would become part of history. Vietnam's most important holiday, Tet was a time to return home and celebrate the new year with family.

Despite the holiday festivity, I was anxious to get to my hotel, shed my baggy blue suit, and take a shower. There were several decent hotels in Saigon and then the rest. The two favored by journalists were the Continental Palace, built in 1880 at the height of French Indochina, and the newer, more modern Caravelle. They were located directly across from each other on Lam Son Square, the heart of Saigon.

I had booked the Caravelle, and the ride in from the airport was like floating in an angry sea filled with a cacophony of horns and squealing brakes. Wave upon wave of motor scooters, bicycles, cyclos, rickshaws, ancient trucks and Renault taxis crowded the streets in the most hazardous manner. Piled ingeniously onto scooters were household goods in transit—beds, chairs, flower pots, cooking stoves. As many as four people perched precariously on vehicles designed for a single soul.

It was every driver for himself, with no rules of the road. Pedestrians crossed these mean streets at their own risk, since as far as I could tell no one yielded for anything and there were few stoplights and even fewer traffic police. Women navigated expertly through the peril, some in the traditional native dress of the *áo dài*. Many people wore gauze masks to filter the thick and suffocating exhaust fumes.

Saigon was malodorous. Apart from the exhaust stink, there was the pungent smell of *nuoc mam*, a sauce made from decaying fish that the Vietnamese used in abundance. The smell was so repugnant that jars of the sauce were banned from flying aboard some U.S. aircraft. The sweet scent of the many flowers gracing parks and public spaces in celebration of Tet provided a bit of relief.

With the exception of the Notre Dame Cathedral Basilica, the 10-story Caravelle was the tallest building in South Vietnam. It had a splendid rooftop bar, central air-conditioning, and a single television set in the lobby that broadcast Armed Forces TV. The favorite show was *Combat*. The tap water was undrinkable, so decanters of purified water were supplied to the rooms. The lobby had bulletproof glass.

Suspended on the side of the hotel this day was a thick woven chain of firecrackers to mark the celebration of Tet. There had to have been enough fireworks braided together to last for hours, an annoyance to tired guests. My room cost $2,500 a month. Living in Saigon was as expensive as in New York.

The first thing I did was check in with the Joint United States Public Affairs Office (JUSPAO) to get my credentials. That was a lucky move. Had I waited, I would have been unable to travel for a week, as the upcoming battles put a stop to all normal business.

Next was a visit to the Associated Press bureau on the fourth floor of the Eden Building, reached by a rickety elevator that climbed in fits and starts and stopped in jerks and jolts. The bureau consisted of a dozen or so journalists and photographers, the best news-gathering operation in Vietnam, led by Robert B. Tuckman. The 55-year-old Tuckman was the consummate foreign correspondent, and had covered the Korean War for the AP.

Above all, Tuckman was one of the most helpful journalists in a culture that favored the aloof and the selfish. I would always remember to take this lesson from him. Alerted to my arrival by the AP's New York office, Tuckman offered any help I needed.

And I needed all the help I could get, because I had no idea how to cover this war in Vietnam, a country of 68,000 square miles. Not only did I have a logistical problem, I had the issue of acclimating myself to war. That was no small thing.

Tuckman offered a welcome solution. He advised me to join one of his guys and spend a week in the field learning how to make my way around the country. As it happened, an AP photographer was leaving shortly to check on fighting in Nha Trang, a seacoast town.

The photographer was Eddie Adams, one of the AP's best, who was back in Vietnam for his third tour. Tuckman lent me field gear and then Adams and I were off to Tan Son Nhut and a flight on an Air Force transport to Nha Trang. Photographers had their own quest for acedom, and Adams was here with the idea of garnering a Pulitzer Prize. In the next 48 hours he would take the winning picture.

We reached Nha Trang, the first city attacked in the Tet Offensive. Assaults on virtually every major city in the country followed throughout the early-morning hours. The full fury of the Tet Offensive shook not only South Vietnam, but America as well. It would be the turning point in the war.

As soon as Adams and I heard that the U.S. embassy in Saigon was under attack we rushed back, hitching a ride in an Air Force C-130. The embassy building had been damaged by gunfire and rocket-propelled grenades. The Viet Cong, or VC, had killed several guards but were unable to penetrate the embassy itself. Soldiers were still picking up enemy bodies from around the compound when we arrived. There was a numbness among the stunned onlookers.

Later that day, at the press briefing dubbed the Five O'Clock Follies, General William Westmoreland appeared. It was a bizarre scene. A *New York Times* correspondent showed up in a flak jacket and helmet, carrying an M16 rifle. He sat in the front row while the general, resplendent in starched fatigues and insignia, tried to explain what had happened. In the back of the room an Army sergeant attached to the U.S. Information Agency walked in with blood on his field blouse.

The sergeant had been captured by a young VC, and as he was being led away he pulled a knife from his boot and cut the boy's throat. He left him to bleed to death in the street. "He was just a punk," the sergeant said.

The mood in the room was somber, minus the usual jocular repartee between the press and the briefers, who normally tried to put the best face on a bad war. There were reports of fighting all over the country, some of it serious. Westmoreland reported that about 5,800 enemy troops had been killed in the first hours of the offensive. He expected heavy fighting to continue for several more days.

This was now a major story, perhaps the biggest of the entire war. Regardless of what my instructions were concerning filing stories by cable, I had better start writing. There was only one small problem. Since we had decided not to use the telex, no one had given me the *Plain Dealer*'s cable address.

I asked Bob Tuckman for advice. He offered to ask for the address by sending the paper a message on the AP's wire. Then he paused for a moment. Doing so might cause embarrassment for me and the *PD*, he said. More than a thousand newspapers around the world would see the message.

I didn't care. I was hardly a world-famous name, nor was the *Plain Dealer*. I was more concerned about the aces sitting at the Headliner or the Rockwell Inn chuckling over me blowing the big one.

That day Adams cinched his Pulitzer. He captured the exact moment of execution of a Viet Cong captive by Nguyen Ngoc Loan, the South Vietnamese chief of national police, who shot the man in the head. I did not witness that exact moment, for I was down the street. But when I came upon Adams he was nervously clutching his camera, fearful that Loan would take it from him.

"He killed many of my friends," Loan said of the dead VC who lay between us. Adams backed away, jumped into the AP mini-jeep, and raced to the bureau in the Eden Building. While the film was being developed, he paced back and forth with a cigarette between his lips. He was uncertain whether the shutter had captured the decisive moment.

Horst Faas, a German photographer who already had won a Pulitzer Prize for the AP, grabbed the wet film, held it up to the light, and with a heavy accent proclaimed, "Adams, you missed it."

"Damn it, gimme that," said Adams as he reached for the dangling roll of wet 35mm film. Faas broke into laughter. He had pulled a number on his fellow ace. Adams had not missed, and in his hand was the image that would forever symbolize the Tet Offensive. The darkroom assistant, Nick Ut, would later win the Pulitzer for his photo of a young girl emerging naked from a maelstrom of napalm.

But there was no time to celebrate, as the entire country was engulfed in the fury of battle. Although the assault on Saigon had been largely repelled, pockets of the enemy formed strongholds throughout the city. The 12-hour difference between Saigon and Cleveland meant breaking a curfew in order to get copy to the telex office so it would arrive before deadline. During the hours of curfew, the streets were patrolled by nervous white-uniformed Vietnamese police. We called them white mice.

Street fighting broke out everywhere as Vietnamese troops dealt with resistors. The day after his triumphant photo, Adams and I were caught in cross fire on a narrow street called Nhan Vi. We lay in the gutter listening to the distinctive, deadly sound of the VC's AK-47s. The buildings around us housed shops shuttered by heavy metal grating.

Suddenly one of the gratings parted. A thin, veiny hand beckoned, and we darted into the shop, two men seeking asylum. Inside we found a mother and father with 10 children, along with the grandmother who had waved us to safety. One of the children, a boy who called himself Peter, practiced his English. He said that the VC had killed many in the neighborhood. The grandmother brought us Cokes and apologized for not having ice. The shooting subsided after an hour, and with the silence we made our escape, thanking the elderly woman for the hospitality as the rest of the family bowed in a goodbye.

The next day did not get any better, only this time I was with Peter Arnett driving through Gia Dinh on the outskirts of Saigon. We were dressed in bright sports shirts and not looking for trouble. Nonetheless, it found us.

As we drove past a group of concrete houses we heard a firefight break out. Again, the distinctive clatter of AK-47s filled the air, followed by the retorts of different sorts of weaponry. Arnett wanted to see who was fighting. It was a group of ARVN forces, South Vietnamese, who had pinned down some fleeing VC.

As we made our way toward the South Vietnamese troops, a furious exchange of fire erupted and we took cover in one of the houses. Prone on the dirt floor and deafened by the shooting, I looked up at the roof made of flattened soft-drink cans and saw periodic glimpses of sky. The rounds were piercing the roof. I looked at Arnett's face and he was perspiring.

"This is bad," he said. Arnett had been covering the war for six years, so he knew what he was talking about. The firing continued, punctuated by grenade blasts.

Suddenly the door opened and a harried American sergeant, an adviser to the ARVN, began swearing at us. "Get the hell out of here now," he commanded. "You fools are going to get overrun by the dinks."

We needed no further encouragement. We scrambled to our feet, ducked our heads, and ran for it. I remember running through flowerbeds, looking down and passing a prone Vietnamese soldier firing a Browning Automatic Rifle, a vintage World War II weapon that was far too heavy for the diminutive trooper. The gun was ejecting shells at a furious rate.

Arnett was ahead of me, running toward a five-foot stone wall. I was breathless with excitement and exertion by the time I reached the barrier. I pulled myself over it and tumbled into a cemetery. The tall, heavy tombstones provided excellent shelter from the fusillade behind us.

Arnett took cover, and I found a place a few tombstones away. Both of us took a while to catch our rasping breaths. It had been an adrenaline-filled you-bet-your-life escape.

I hadn't fully recovered when I noticed an elderly man with a wispy white beard crawling toward me. In one hand he held a wooden tray with bottles of beer. I could hardly believe my eyes.

"Beer 50 piasters," the man managed in fractured English. "Drink beer, no die."

From behind a tombstone Arnett yelled, "For God's sake, don't overtip him."

It was just another day in the war.

That night I returned to the hotel to sit at the rooftop bar and watch the war from afar. The sky was streaked with red and green tracers, and parachute flares lit the night so brightly that roosters began to crow. The deep thud of artillery reverberated through the attenuated darkness.

The Caravelle hosted many different sorts: traveling dignitaries, politicians, journalists, professors, diplomats, technicians and the merely curious. They were all on the roof oohing and aahing over the light show as if it were the Fourth of July at home. To me, the sounds and flashes of illumination meant that people were dying.

A few days later I was watching the same scene, only this time the beer in my glass was rippled by a new noise. B-52s were making their bombing runs so close to Saigon that the very foundations of the city shook. A man next to me was also watching the spectacle. He was Walter Cronkite of CBS News.

Cronkite invited me and several other correspondents to join him for a beer, and we spent the rest of the evening talking about the Tet Offensive. I didn't say much, having been in-country for only two weeks, but the others took a very pessimistic view. The attack had stunned Washington, and Cronkite thought it wise to see the results for himself. It was clear that the CBS anchor, considered one of the country's most influential newsmen, had serious doubts about the war. Cronkite's subsequent reports would convince President Lyndon Johnson not to seek reelection.

The street fighting continued for several weeks and spilled into the spring, when the communists launched a second offensive that just added to their body count. Urban warfare, with snipers abounding on narrow streets, was the worst. Streams of refugees transporting their worldly belongings on scooters, carts and bicycles provided cover for nimble VC who moved like ghosts through the disfigured neighborhoods.

You learned to be extra cautious when moving through this sordid scenario, especially when the numbers of escaping refugees reduced to a trickle. That was a time for alarm, for behind the retreating population came the enemy. In May, four Australian correspondents failed to take heed, turning a corner in their mini-jeep to suddenly confront VC attackers. Three of the writers were summarily shot while begging for their lives while the fourth escaped, making his break just as the vehicle rounded the fatal corner.

A few days later, another correspondent, Charlie Eggleston from United Press International, was killed in a firefight inside the French military cemetery near Tan Son Nhut. He was firing at the enemy with a rifle when he was shot between the eyes. I had met Charlie a few days earlier and was surprised to find him carrying a weapon. Very few journalists were armed. The military frowned on the practice, mainly because of uncertainty regarding competency. It also violated the Geneva Conventions. Somehow I always thought, foolishly, that noncombatants had a certain immunity in battle. Only once, during a fight in the Mekong Delta, did a soldier thrust a rifle at me, saying I might have to carry my own weight.

CHAPTER 26

The Odds and Ends of War Reporting

Coinciding with my arrival in Vietnam, the fierce Tet Offensive had been an anomaly. With the fighting in Saigon generally subdued, I began to experience the day-to-day oppressiveness of the real way the war was fought.

Normal warfare involved countless hours of humping rice paddies in the hot sun or exhausting treks on jungle trails in the mountainous north where snakes hung from the trees like light cords. At night swarms of mosquitoes attacked every bare inch of your body, your lips numb from thick applications of ineffective repellent. During one ambush I was lying in a rice paddy along a canal when a fish swam into my shirt, scaring the shit out of me.

The frustration was that most of the time nothing happened, and when you are supposed to be writing about a war you need things to happen. You could write only so many stories about meaningless patrols and aimless afternoons in knee-high mud. Days of monotony would pass. Then suddenly, everything around you would erupt in a fierce, indelible fury.

Nearly every foray had its genesis in the rooftop bar of the

Rex Hotel, across the square on Nguyen Hue Street. The Rex housed JUSPAO, where daily briefings on the war's progress were held. Correspondents had derisively named the proceedings the Five O' Clock Follies, for it was a show put on by the government to give the illusion that things were going well and we were winning the war.

In the hotel was a large room where representatives from each military service branch maintained tables with various handouts and maps. It was like a travel bureau, and the public affairs officers manning each table were friendly agents happy to send you off to an adventure of your choosing. At least, that's how it appeared.

The real value of the press officers, however, became apparent when meeting them for a beer upstairs in the bar. After they got to know you, there would be a conversation that went something like this: "We've got something in two days that you may find interesting," an Army major would say. "We can pick you up at 0600 in front of the Rex and get you to the helipad out at Hotel 3. Bring everything."

That meant come dressed with a flak jacket, helmet, jungle boots and two canteens. It was always best to bring some of your own C-rations. I tied mine in a sock that hung from my belt. You didn't want to overload no matter where you went.

Helmets and flak jackets were hard to come by. While the military provided correspondents with transportation and lodging at press camps, it offered no legitimate way to purchase the necessary field equipment. Those items had to be acquired either by scrounging or by black market purchase. In my case, Al Chang, a retired Army sergeant and veteran AP photographer, took me to the 3rd Field Hospital in Saigon.

There, in a pile of discards stripped from the dead and wounded, I picked through the remnants to find a helmet and jacket that were not damaged or bloodied. I bought my jungle boots on the black market, which consisted of a stall near the main market. Black-market boots were preferable to the regular leather boots that rotted from the heat and water. Many units, especially the Marines, had not been issued the new boots, but they could be found on the vast black market filled with American goods of every type.

If you left from Hotel 3, the helipad at Tan Son Nhut, chances were that the unit you would join was nearby. This meant you could spend more time in the field. Straying farther from Saigon meant using unproductive travel time, and since the whole idea was to file stories I wanted to write as many as I could. Given the circumstances, I had a strange fear of being recalled to Cleveland.

I worked out a routine. On longer trips up north, I'd spend 10 days away from Saigon, return for a week's worth of writing, then head out again. Sometimes I had to screw up my courage to get back out to the field. I usually traveled alone to avoid conflicts over stories with other writers.

The helicopter was like taking an odd and awkward bus to work. Sitting in the open door gave you a panoramic view of the lush countryside as the sun reflected on the rice paddies. The chopper lifted into cool air, an invigorating relief from the heavy heat of the day. It was a rush to skim low over paddies and jungle.

Helicopters made Vietnam a different war, and in fact they were what the war was about. They required both sides to adjust their tactics. It was both fun and dangerous to fly above the countryside on some kind of crazy search-and-destroy mission.

A serious heliborne assault mission generally consisted of several "lifts," or flights of troops. The standard HU-1 helicopter, or Huey, could carry seven or eight troopers plus crew, so a number of flights were required to move sufficient forces for any given mission. Correspondents argued among themselves as to which lift was safest. Those who favored the first lift preferred the surprise it might offer. Those with a preference for later lifts cited the fact that the LZ, or landing zone, was already occupied and defended.

The argument did not have a lot of merit, for luck was really the determining factor. Whatever lift you were on was tension filled. As you descended from the cooler air, the temperature rose along with the anxiety in your stomach. The noise from the rotors was so loud that the only way you knew the chopper was drawing fire was if you saw holes in the fuselage or if someone got hit.

Disembarking from a hovering Huey with a load of troops had to done with care lest the chopper tilt and tip over. The helicopter hung in the air while you leaped the four or five feet to the ground. Sometimes the jump was even higher.

If the LZ was not under attack, the sound of the disappearing helicopters faded to an eerie silence as the troops positioned themselves, still tense from their vertical arrival. These were the signature moments of the war. They regularly repeated themselves, taking an occasional break for the monsoons that swept from the sky in torrents only to evaporate hours later, leaving humidity at 90 percent and clinging like gravity.

The war was bizarre in so many ways. One afternoon I was in a loaded helicopter heading for an LZ near the Michelin Rubber Plantation located 42 miles outside Saigon. It was said that the French had bribed the VC to allow the plantation to operate throughout the war.

U.S. troops were always harassing the enemy on the plantation's fringes and required permission to pursue them when contact was made. The VC sought sanctuary among the rubber trees, which were often destroyed or damaged during the fighting at a reparation cost to the United States of $600 per tree.

As our assault circled toward its LZ, marked by yellow smoke, the helicopter passed over the plantation and its blue swimming pool where four women clad in colorful bikinis were sunbathing. During its descent, the helicopter suddenly lurched to the left as the riflemen, most in their late teens, shifted for a better look. It was a surreal moment.

The whole place was surreal. I once saw a soldier with a portable television resting on a rice-paddy dike watching a John Wayne movie.

Meanwhile in Cleveland, the accountants were anxious. My stories featured more and more helicopter rides, and the paper's lawyers had asked whether I was insured for these flights. Executive editor Bill Ware instructed me to keep a log of my flights because insurance was $50 an hour. Knowing how hard it was to squeeze even $2.50 out of the paper to get a suit cleaned after covering a bad fire, I panicked. I didn't dare tell them how much helicopter time was involved, let alone the air strikes flown.

The idea of added insurance had never crossed my mind. I was 27, an age when you still flirted with immortality. There was no better place than Vietnam to test that flirtation. The first time I flew in a fighter on an air strike we managed to draw ground fire and finally took a hit before the afternoon was over. It's one thing to scramble for cover on the ground and quite another to sit strapped in a plane during a steep dive, the g-forces rendering you nearly unconscious. Enemy tracers reach up in lazy arcs, producing a loud "thonk" when one finds the wing.

We made eight passes that afternoon on a machine gun and were never sure we silenced it. To endure this, I pretended I was having an out-of-body experience, hoping my day would pick up later in some better place. It was like fast-forwarding a film. This useful ploy served me well.

Vietnam may have been the last great correspondents' war. Saigon radiated a sense of romance and adventure. It was steeped in French history, an exploitative past that reeked of opium dens, exotic women, pungent foods and lost wars. It also attracted lost souls. Getting accredited as a journalist was not difficult. Many who did so were freelancers who lived hand to mouth and spent as much time enjoying themselves as covering the war. Some had come seeking to make a name for themselves, others out of sheer boredom.

Freedom of movement enabled reporters to view the war's progress from different vantage points, resulting in a generally critical analysis of events. In Saigon, you received the government's view, but in the boondocks or on carriers in the South China Sea you talked with those who were fighting the war every day and gained quite another view. In future wars, reporters would be embedded with particular units, limiting their movement and their understanding of the larger nature of events.

Life in Saigon offered an interesting mix of events and personalities. When Martha Gellhorn, Ernest Hemingway's third wife, came to town, she was welcomed at an embassy cocktail party where guests were quietly asked not to mention her former husband. Even after his death, they were still on bad terms.

Sean Flynn, son of movie star Errol Flynn, was a freelance photographer. Sean had acted in some films himself, and when the local movie theater played one of them he left town to escape ridicule. Flynn was an engaging fellow and a regular at the Rex. Later, he and a friend were captured by the Viet Cong and thought to have been executed.

Ridgely Hunt was a magazine writer for the *Chicago Tribune*.

He was a Yale graduate from a prominent East Coast family and an Army veteran who had never seen combat. I met Hunt several months into my tour and helped him get acquainted. I worried because he was so anxious to draw fire. Hunt spent about a month delighting in one skirmish after another, describing the firefights over beers at the Rex as if they were from a Hollywood script. He was good company and there was a fever to his curiosity.

I chalked up Hunt's desire to prove himself to a midlife crisis when the 41-year-old told me he had just left his wife for a 20-year-old woman. He was anxious to show me a picture of his young girlfriend, speaking of her with passionate idolatry.

Several years later I found myself in Chicago with an idle afternoon. Hunt had sent me clips of his Vietnam work and I had always meant to look him up. When I asked for him at the *Trib*'s editorial department, an editor shot me a strange look. Did I not know, he asked.

Ridgely Hunt was no longer Ridgely Hunt. She was Nancy Hunt, and she was off that day. Hunt's long metamorphosis into a woman had been completed by a sex-change operation. I had to sit down for a minute.

Now and then visitors to Saigon didn't have to look for the war. It conveniently arranged nightly appearances when 122mm Russian rockets would cascade indiscriminately, causing panic among guests at the Caravelle. The primary target of these rockets was the National Assembly Building next door. More than one night I sought refuge in the bathtub, wearing my flak jacket and helmet, quivering at the overhead sound of rocket motors cutting out, then the silence of descent followed by a shattering explosion. One morning there was shrapnel on my balcony.

During one rocket attack a publisher from a Virginia newspaper lost her nerve and began screaming that we were all going to be killed. A British reporter up the hall shouted, "Madam, for God's sake, shut up. Your voice is far more irritating that these bloody bombs!"

The next morning, champagne was served at a going-away party. Tired from the previous night's ordeal, everyone flinched at the popping of each cork. There were always going-away parties, and there was always a bit of envy toward those returning to the real world.

Nobody liked parties more than Doug Warren, a 44-year-old freelance writer from Lorain, Ohio. Warren was a former professional golfer, an actor and a writer with 50-some paperbacks to his credit, a few of them available from the second-hand book stalls in Saigon. He had left behind both his job on the *Elyria Chronicle-Telegram* and his family to come to Vietnam.

Warren was a carefree soul who tiptoed through life without enough money to make ends meet, but still managed to enjoy himself. As a youth, he ran away to Hollywood. He became one of Mickey Rooney's protégés and hung around the town for years.

When I met Warren, he was living in press camps in the Mekong Delta and freelancing for United Press International. He had no money and the military camps were cheap and offered food. When he came to Saigon he would stay in a sleazy $5-a-night hotel.

Since I had an extra bed at the Caravelle, I let Warren stay with me and use the room when I was in the field. This was not a particularly good idea. He threw parties there, invited the chaplain from the 25th Division to take confession and cocktails, and made it the rendezvous point for various liaisons. More than once I came back after a week or so in the field— muddy, smelly, tired and irritable—to find the room occupied by people I did not know drinking my Courvoisier. It was only $2.50 a bottle at the PX, but still.

Warren developed a social set in Saigon, and the most stunning of the lot was Jurate Kazickas, a six-foot brunette with high cheekbones and a sweet personality who was accredited as a reporter for a small upstate New York radio station. Aside from her beauty, Kazickas was legendary for her disregard of danger. One day at Khe Sanh, the beleaguered combat base surrounded by thousands of North Vietnamese, and for a time shelled daily, Kazickas was wounded in the buttocks by a piece of shrapnel. She was taken to the battalion aid station, Charley Med, where for months exhausted corpsmen had been living through hell and red mud while treating the wounded. They were dumbstruck by their new patient.

Warren liked to tell the story that upon seeing Kazickas, a young Navy corpsman—in true MASH fashion—turned to the surgeon and jokingly asked if he could pull the shrapnel out with his teeth. Kazickas gave the corpsman her jungle boots.

My favorite Kazickas story was the day a lumbering four-engine C-130 cargo plane was about to take off from Vung Tau when it came to a sudden halt. The pilot had spotted her near the runway. He opened the window and asked if she wanted a ride. The last time I saw her was in Hong Kong, where she was preparing for a trip on the Trans-Siberian Railway.

CHAPTER 27

Lambacher

It was around 11 a.m., check-in time at the Caravelle, and I was in the lobby paying my bill with stacks of piasters. There were 118 piasters to a U.S. dollar, but you could get as much as 225 on the black market. I had a stack of them a half-foot tall. I was surprised when the Indian money changer who cashed my Cleveland Trust checks called the Ohio institution a fine bank and asked for no identification. Later, I would learn that no one bounced checks with the Indians. There were too many dark alleys in Saigon.

After I paid my bill, the concierge, a Vietnamese man wearing a stiff gray uniform and a black tie, asked for a word. He was troubled by one of my occasional visitors whose appearance sometimes upset guests.

He was referring to Terry L. Lambacher, a 26-year-old civilian adviser to the district chief of Cu Chi, located some 25 miles west of Saigon. Cu Chi was a dusty, well-populated district set amidst the rice paddies with unpaved roads traveled by water buffalo. At its center was a tired French fort reminiscent of an Old West stockade. What made the place especially dangerous was the secret tunnel complex that ran for miles in the nearby jungle.

When I met Lambacher, that's where he lived, if you could call it that. The ride from Saigon to Cu Chi was fraught with numerous obstacles: land mines, snipers, ambushes, errant artillery, any number of booby traps. Given the circumstances, Lambacher would drive into Saigon armed to the teeth with a Swedish K, an AK-47, several grenades and a large knife. When he would appear in the lobby of the Caravelle with all that fire-power hanging on him, he was indeed a scary sight. I told the concierge that I would advise Mr. Lambacher of his indiscretion.

Lambacher was from Independence, Ohio, and had dropped out of college to join the Army. In 1965 he became a Green Beret assigned to a Special Forces team not far from Cu Chi. After his tour, he joined USAID, learned Vietnamese, and became an adviser whose job was to help the district civil government with building schools and providing aid to the villagers.

Tet had rendered that job impossible, and Lambacher ended up many a night in the old French fort fighting for his life. Cu Chi was undermined by a labyrinth of Viet Cong tunnels that stretched for 75 miles and offered cover for nightly intruders bent on attacking the district headquarters. Forty years later I would crawl into the tunnels, now a tourist site. For a dollar a round you can shoot an AK-47 or an M16 at targets. I politely declined.

For a reporter, Lambacher was an incredible source. You could not just wander alone around Vietnam; it was too dangerous. I knew six journalists who had been captured and executed by the Viet Cong. Lambacher provided the opportunity to travel to places I would otherwise never have seen. He showed me how the VC operated in the hinterlands and the warning signs of trouble.

If no water buffalo were in the paddies, if no birds were in sight, and if no children were playing, chances were good that

the VC lurked somewhere near. In that case, it was best to get
out of the area as fast as you could. We often traveled by motorcycle, following the dirt tracks of military vehicles to avoid the
mines.

One afternoon we rode west to the Cambodian border. A
small market in a shady glade served about a thousand customers each day. For sale were American medicines and foodstuffs,
obviously black market goods. The market sold toy helicopter
gunships that shot sparks, French cookies, Philippine beer,
champagne and treasured Levi's jeans.

Mr. Binh, the Vietnamese police chief for the sector, sought
us out. The VC checkpoints, he said, had alerted the market to
our presence, and many of the black market goods normally on
sale, mostly medicines, had been concealed.

"You see that man under the tree?" Binh asked. "He is a VC
tax collector, and he watch to see how many Lambrettas use the
road and how many passengers they carry. At the end of the day
he tell drivers to pay."

Apparently, this area was a neutral meeting place where
goods were exchanged freely regardless of politics. A sort of
Switzerland in the swamps, it was an example of how those
in the countryside coexisted. Among the shoppers were young
men of draft age, which meant that unless they were Viet Cong,
they should have been in the South Vietnamese military.

Soon the Cambodian police official for the area, Chief Kinh,
approached us. Binh introduced me as a *bao chi* (journalist),
and Kinh motioned to a market stall that appeared to be a
restaurant. He treated us to a bottle of Ba Mui Ba, a Vietnamese
beer allegedly made with formaldehyde.

I could tell Lambacher was growing uneasy. He asked Kinh
whether there were any VC on the Cambodian side of the
border. The chief just shrugged. Binh confided that there were

three platoons of VC in the vicinity, but they were a hundred meters away.

"Are you sure they are not here now?" Lambacher asked.

That's when I noticed a group of young men glaring at us.

"Please finish your beer," Binh said, smiling. "It would be good to go now."

We tried to look casual as we moved toward the motorcycle. I got on behind Lambacher and held my breath. I was waiting for a shot to ring out. The bike started up and we were moving out when Lambacher turned in a circle and gave the Vietnamese the finger. I hung on for my life as we accelerated up the road back into Vietnam.

"Why the hell did you do that?" I shouted, shaken from the encounter.

"They weren't going to do anything," Lambacher said. "That market is too important to them. They get penicillin and other medicines there for their troops. It's all stolen from the Americans. If something happened the military would investigate and the market would be closed."

Corruption was rampant in Vietnam. The concrete and tin that the U.S. provided to build housing was often stolen and sold to the VC, who in turn used it to build bunkers and tunnels. In Quang Tri, 12 miles of railroad track had been stolen in broad daylight. You could only learn things like this from someone like Lambacher, who was living among the people. The people protected him, too, especially the kids.

The Vietnamese are fascinated by big people. Standing over six feet tall and weighing 220 pounds, Lambacher earned the name *trau nuoc*, "water buffalo" in Vietnamese. Kids loved him because he would do things like throw a concussion grenade into a stream to kill fish for their families' dinners. They saved his life once when they warned him of a Viet Cong ambush.

French friends of Lambacher had a certain rapport with the VC, providing him some notion of their activity in his hostile district. One day we traveled to Tay Ninh to see the Cao Dai Temple, a colorful structure that represented a Vietnamese religion blending Christianity, Buddhism, Taoism, Confucianism and 19th-century Romanticism.

The temple looked the way the religion sounded. It plays a role in Graham Greene's classic novel *The Quiet American* when Pyle, the book's protagonist, is stranded overnight on a nearby road infested with communist guerillas.

It was late afternoon when we began our return, speeding along in a four-wheel drive vehicle. This was a bad time of day to be alone on the road, for at sunset the Viet Cong silently took over the countryside. I was thinking of Greene when suddenly the engine quit. We rolled to a stop next to an empty rice paddy. There was no sign of people or water buffalo and the birds were mute.

Lambacher cursed and pulled an AK-47 from the back seat. He handed me an M16 and then looked under the hood. The engine mounts had broken, rendering the vehicle useless. Trang Bang was the nearest village and it was miles away.

"We have a hell of a problem here," he said. "The army will come through in the morning but we have to find a place to hide during the night." His plan was to conceal ourselves in a cluster of palm trees and then move to another hiding place when night fell.

"If Charlie is here, we've been seen," he said. I couldn't believe this was happening, me standing there with the rifle as Lambacher booby-trapped the vehicle with a thermite grenade. "If I don't do it, they will," he said.

Just as he was about to wire the grenade, a cloud of dust came hurtling toward us out of nowhere. It was a truck and it was going like a bat out of hell. Lambacher waved for it to stop, but it was clear the driver was not going to yield. Cursing, he lifted the AK to his shoulder and fired off five rounds over the truck cab.

The truck screeched to a halt and the driver, a middle-aged Vietnamese man, stepped out, shaken and begging forgiveness. Lambacher found a tow rope in the truck and made the man attach it to our vehicle. Then we raced nightfall to Trang Bang.

When I saw the film *The Quiet American* a couple of years ago, the scene on the road to Trang Bang brought back anxious memories. It reminded me that after a while I thought twice about spending time with Lambacher, even though he helped me to view Vietnam through a different lens. There was a certain naïveté in the conduct of the war by the Americans, and the fact that the government was misleading us was slowly becoming a reality.

Lambacher would go on to serve the State Department in Lebanon, Africa and Paris and in an anti-terrorism role. We became lifelong friends. In 2010 I gave the eulogy as his ashes were cast into his favorite trout stream near Vermilion, Ohio. He served his country well.

CHAPTER 28

Cleveland's Unhappy Warriors

Meanwhile, there was spotty communication with the newspaper. Bill Ware wrote now and again, and the accountants complained about missing receipts for bags of rice I bought for a village called Trang Bang that Terry Lambacher said would ensure safe passage. I had no idea what readers were thinking or if they were even interested in the war. The foreign/national desk did not pass along story ideas or comments on my coverage. I rarely got to see my news clips, which probably prevented disputes with editors. It was up to me to decide what to write, and I had mixed feelings about that. It was great to have freedom, but it also felt like I was writing in the dark in terms of reader interest.

One story that I knew would engage readers was the 1002d Supply and Service Company, an Army Reserve unit based out of the Schlegel Armory in Garfield Heights. Six of the men in the Ten-O-Deuce filed a lawsuit in federal court charging that it was illegal for the U.S. government to call the unit to active duty in Vietnam without Congress declaring war or the president proclaiming a national emergency. The case was considered by the U.S. Supreme Court, but the unit lost and shipped out in October to Phu Bai.

Upon arrival in-country they drove their trucks 60 miles from Da Nang only to be greeted by a heavy mortar attack. The filth, smells and ankle-deep mud were overpowering to the reservists, who had to build new bunkers and endure sanitary facilities that were disgusting even by Vietnam standards.

Phu Bai was north in I Corps and Marine country and was home to the 101st Airborne. The publicity of the lawsuit made the Ten-O-Deuce infamous upon arrival. It was billeted next to the paratroopers, which led to some unpleasant incidents. The gung-ho collective of paratroopers and Marines considered a military unit attempting to shirk its duty by going to court a patriotic sacrilege of the first order.

Phu Bai was not one of my favorite destinations. I once spent a scary night in a bunker there while the base was shelled. It was the jump-off to places like Hue, Khe Sanh and other points north to the DMZ where almost all the fighting was against North Vietnamese regulars.

It took all day to fly there, and when I arrived I was surprised to be greeted by a lieutenant from the 101st. The Saigon public affairs people had alerted him to my interest in the Ten-O-Deuce, and they essentially wanted to head off an embarrassing situation. I was going to stay in the bachelor officers quarters of the 101st because the troops from the Ten-O-Deuce were being teargassed by irate paratroopers. "Sir, we wouldn't want to subject you to that," the lieutenant said. "You can understand the difficulty here."

There were 200 soldiers in the Ten-O-Deuce, and of the six who had led the court fight only one ended up in Vietnam. For a time, the unit suffered ridicule and gas attacks along with charges of being draft dodgers and cop-out artists.

But that changed quickly when it became apparent that the Ten-O-Deuce's job was supply. In the service, supplies are like gold, and knowing someone in supply is akin to having a wealthy patron. The unit also provided services such as washing 3,000 pounds of clothes a day, making ice cream and carrying out graves registration.

"This lousy hole is the most unreal place on earth," one company member wrote home to his wife. It wasn't. There were a few other places like Khe Sanh that vied for that honor.

The Ten-O-Deuce returned to Cleveland a year later, having suffered no casualties.

The other local story that interested me concerned the whereabouts of the former motorcycle gang members I had followed to Parris Island a year earlier. I figured they were up north and I needed to go to Khe Sanh anyway. It was in the final stages of a 77-day siege and observers were trying to determine what had been achieved. The jump-off point to the combat base was Dong Ha, where the Marines were headquartered. I arrived there the day after the ammunition dump had been hit by North Vietnamese artillery; a vast amount of ordnance had cooked off.

Artillery was new and scary to me. You needed experience to judge the difference in sound between incoming and outgoing fire. The problem was compounded by the similar sound a C-130 made when it reversed its engines upon landing. That spinning incoming-like noise sent your nerves into spastic palpitations.

I checked in with the Marine press officer and began to make arrangements to get into the Khe Sanh combat base. That's when the door opened and in walked a familiar face. It was Major General Rathvon Tompkins, the former commander of Parris Island, who had recently taken over the 3rd Marine Division engaged at Khe Sanh.

It was Tompkins who had been so enthusiastic to accept the

Euclid bikers Charger Charley and Blinky in what he called his "school" at Parris Island. He recognized me immediately and didn't hesitate to help.

"We have to find those bikers," Tompkins said. "We'll find them and I'll go in with you and see how the boys are doing. We'll go tomorrow morning." I hadn't planned to get my courage up that fast, and my face must have showed it. The general shrugged it off. "This is nothing," he said. "You should have been at Iwo Jima." Tompkins then ordered an aide to see if he could locate either of the gang members.

When I got to the helicopter the next morning the aide informed me that the general had been called elsewhere and would not be making the trip. There I was, the only passenger in a large CH-46 helicopter that could carry 25. "Listen carefully," the crew chief said. "They often begin to shell on our descent. We are going to hover over the runway adjacent to a trench line. You will egress from the back, and roll right into the trench. We are not going to land, so be ready when I give the signal to go."

I wouldn't have expected less of Khe Sanh. Along with Tet it was the big story, and officials, especially those in the White House, feared it would fall like the ill-fated French garrison at Dien Bien Phu 14 years earlier. Khe Sanh had been under siege for five and a half months, taking fierce shelling and threatened by an estimated 20,000 NVA. The stench from the dead North Vietnamese was so bad that air strikes of napalm were called in to incinerate the bodies.

I looked from the helicopter at the terrain below and saw the hills that had been contested early in the battle. Scarred by artillery, they were occupied by Marines who had endured difficult conditions and continuous fighting. Somewhere out there had to be the bad boys from Euclid.

But I was not destined to find them that day. As advertised, the CH-46 hovered and I made my exit, clutching my helmet and rolling ass-over-tin-cup into the trench while a dozen nearby Marines laughed at my ungainly arrival. I had been advised to stay with the Seabees, the Navy construction battalion, because they had the best bunker on the combat base.

The base itself was a scar of red earth covered with bunkers, trenches and all forms of debris that gave it the appearance of a garbage dump. One dare not wander too far from some form of cover lest the "little people," as the Marines referred to the NVA, drop a few rounds on the campgrounds.

The Seabee bunker was secure and substantial, a tribute to its engineers. It was from the Seabees that I learned Khe Sanh would soon be abandoned. Given that it had been such a big story for months, the evacuation was stunning. JUSPAO prohibited correspondents from reporting troop movements in advance. By the time I returned to Saigon the whole press corps was aware of the situation at Khe Sanh, but only one writer, John Carroll of the *Baltimore Sun*, broke the story. His credentials were temporarily revoked.

Other than that and a few incoming rounds, my trip was uneventful. There was no word of the bikers and it was probably useless to wait.

Twenty-one years later, I was on a WERE radio talk show when a woman called and said she was Charger Charley's mother. He was living in Florida, she reported, and no doubt would love to hear from me.

She gave me his number and I called that night.

"Charger, this is Mike Roberts, the reporter."

There was a long pause. "You know, every time you show up you bring me trouble," an angry voice finally responded. "This morning my wife left me. Remember when we got busted in

Euclid? And then you did us no favors showing up at Parris Island and telling the Marines we were punks."

I got Charley calmed down enough to learn he was a mechanic at a Mercedes dealership and that he had been living in Florida ever since getting out of the service. Then came the kicker.

"You know, some gook shot me through the lung while I was waiting for a ride off the hill to go to Khe Sanh," he said. "Bullet went right through me. I was lying there waiting to be med-evaced having a cigarette and watched the smoke come out of my chest. It was weird, man."

I didn't tell him I had been at Khe Sanh looking for him. I was afraid to.

CHAPTER 29

Kim and Kimchi

I met Mr. Kim, a reporter for a South Korean newspaper, on the helicopter that was taking us to the *USS New Jersey* off the coast of North Vietnam. The World War II battleship with its 16-inch guns had been taken out of mothballs in order to shell coastal targets. The shells were the size of Volkswagens. Kim and I were to be the first reporters on the ship. The trip was considered a gift to me by the Navy, which earlier had lost me for a week on the fleet in the South China Sea.

I had been trying to reach an offshore destroyer. To do so I had to land on one of the carriers on Yankee Station and then be taken by helicopter to the ship. There was a miscommunication somewhere and I ended up flying from one carrier to another for a week until I finally gave up and flew back to Saigon. After I wrote about being lost at sea, the Navy's public affairs people offered the battleship story as an apology.

Kim was young, energetic, friendly and spoke singsong English. He was quirky in his directness. He also was proud of his heritage and the Korean military effort in Vietnam, which consisted of about 50,000 troops. Someday, he insisted, I must accompany him to Qui Nhon and spend time with the Korean Tiger Division.

Kim could be embarrassingly direct. Upon our arrival on the *New Jersey* we were met by the ship's captain, who was a bit apprehensive about his first experience with the media. He was greeted by a question from Kim.

"Captain, how many men on your ship smoke marijuana?"

I shuddered. We were going to be on this ship for a week, and after that question the captain and his officers were not going to trust our intentions. The captain made light of the situation, but Kim insisted on an answer.

"We'll ask around," the officer said. And every day after that, Kim would ask if the captain had a count on the marijuana smokers aboard. I finally told Kim it was a secret that they would not even tell me.

A few weeks later Kim visited me at the Caravelle Hotel. He was pleased to announce that the general of the Tiger Division was sending an aircraft to Saigon to take both of us to Qui Nhon, halfway up the coast in South Vietnam. "You see big battle there," Kim said, his eyes bright with anticipation. "Korea soldiers are number one."

We made the flight and were met by a jeep that whisked us off to Tiger Division headquarters. I was sitting between two Korean soldiers who, to my alarm, began rubbing the hair on my forearms. Many Asians don't have much body hair and are fascinated by it. This visit with the Koreans would be as much a cultural experience as a war story.

The general had ordered a lavish lunch for us, and we sat at a long table with the division staff. Kim chatted away in Korean, occasionally breaking off to tell me how pleased everyone was by my presence.

Before me was a bowl of kimchi, the national dish of Korea,

often served on the battlefield to boost troop morale. Made of fermented cabbage, hot peppers and numerous spices, it burned my tongue and I spit it back into the bowl. I had lost face. It was awful and I felt awful for everything being awful.

All eyes at the table were on me as the general uttered an order to an aide who arose and left. A few minutes he was back with a tub of ice cream. He set it before me while Kim honked with laughter like a lumbering goose. I apologized for my social gaffe, but no one understood me.

Lunch was over quickly and we moved on to the main event of the day—the destruction of the hamlet of Ky Son where some 300 North Vietnamese regulars had dug in with 50 two-man bunkers. This was an ugly task.

The Koreans were made for it, though. With no political pressure to hold them back, they did not operate under the same rules of engagement as the Americans. In fact, they were known for their fierce and brutal conduct on the battlefield. The North Vietnamese mightily feared them.

"We go now," Kim said, taking me by the arm and walking out to a row of helicopters. Troops in full battle dress were lined up waiting to board the lead helicopter for the first lift. As we joined them, I got a sick feeling, and it wasn't from the kimchi.

Shit, I thought. This was going to be the all-time scary ride, and we weren't going mix it up with a bunch of rice farmers with rifles. Instead, we were heading toward the battle-hardened 18th Regiment of the NVA.

Ky Son was only five minutes away in the valley below us. As we set down amid the firing, my thoughts alternated between prayer and profanity. One of the Korean soldiers had been assigned to watch over me, and as soon as we alighted from the helicopter he guided me to some cover beneath a cove of palm trees. Kim was up with the first assault group, waving me to follow. He was crazy. I shook my head. I could barely breathe, and I no longer cared about losing face.

It seemed like the fighting went on for hours, but it only took 45 minutes for the Koreans to overrun most of the bunkers, throwing grenades and satchel charges into the fortifications. The dead and dying were everywhere. Medics were attending the wounded. Several prisoners were being held in a group. They had discarded their uniforms for black peasant garb, hoping to escape.

Kim was gleeful. Two of the captives were officers, considered valuable finds. Looking scared and tired, they didn't match the fearsome reputation allotted them by American intelligence. This was a rare opportunity to talk with newly captured enemy soldiers.

The problem, of course, was that the conversation had to go through a Vietnamese interpreter, then through Kim, and then to me. One of the officers, from Hanoi, became contemptuous and said he was fighting for independence.

The other officer was frightened. He had never seen an American up close before and he bowed several times as I approached. He praised his captors as very good soldiers, but when I asked what he thought of the Americans the interpreters began to giggle. Kim said they were too embarrassed to relate his response.

I was relieved the afternoon was over. I had now been in Vietnam for eight months and was getting a little spooked. You could not keep doing this forever. Time was hardly on your side. In the aftermath of all the excitement, I lost contact with Kim. I began to walk through the detritus of the battlefield in search of him. The dead looked so pathetic.

An American major, an adviser, rushed up to me, quite agitated. "Were you just with those two prisoners?" he demanded. I nodded. "Where the hell did they go?"

"I don't know," I responded, "they were with the Koreans."

"Don't you know better than to leave prisoners alone with these people?"

"No, I mean, why?"

"Because they shoot them. That's why the NVA are so scared shitless of them."

I was stunned by my naïveté and deeply angered at myself. If what the major said was true, however, the only thing I could have done was to find one of the Americans, and by then the prisoners would have been gone. The major walked away cursing. I never knew what happened, because Mr. Kim would never tell me.

"Remember, marijuana on ship was a secret, so this, too, a secret," he said.

I hoped it was a joke.

CHAPTER 30

Back in Time

The helicopter dropped me off in a clearing in the middle of dark hills and medieval jungle. The Special Forces captain eyed me suspiciously. He had not expected my arrival here at Mang Buk, deep in the hostile wilds of the Central Highlands of South Vietnam. This remote place was occupied by a tribal culture uncivilized in almost every way except war.

"What are you, some communist spy?" charged Captain Jack Moroney when he met the helicopter. "No one said you were coming."

Earlier, at Special Forces headquarters in Kontum City, I had made arrangements to visit the camp, but apparently no one had bothered to forward the information. It was clear that Moroney was not happy. He ordered me to follow him into the heavily fortified stockade that was the center of his command.

"Don't leave my sight until I confirm your presence with my uppers," he said. He seemed agitated. "But right now we have to find the damn monkey. He's escaped again."

Moroney had a pet monkey and was anxious that the Montagnards, the tribal folk who hosted his 12-man team, had stolen the animal. These people ate everything, and monkey was a delicacy. While other team members searched for the little beast, Moroney gathered a handful of smoke grenades and began throwing them down the series of escape tunnels beneath the camp complex.

Billows of purple and yellow smoke wafted from the tunnel orifices and then, emerging from the colorful clouds, came the monkey—small, scared and screeching.

"There's the little shit," Moroney said as the trembling creature leapt to the captain's shoulder and embraced him. The Montagnards in the camp had all stopped to watch the pursuit of the errant monkey and broke into excited laughter at his appearance.

Visibly relieved, Moroney turned his attention to me. He radioed Kontum and asked if they knew they had sent a communist spy posing as a Mike Roper (the code name for a reporter) to his camp. The radio crackled in response.

"Roger, that is affirmative. We knew he was a spy and we sent him up there to test your security. You can shoot him now."

Moroney laughed. He said he couldn't shoot me, but instead had to take me to meet the village chief. That might be an even worse fate, because visitors were expected to drink the chief's potent rice wine. Strong men had been known to suffer its effects for days. The "Yards," as the Americans called them, were serious drinkers.

The chief lived in the village below the Special Forces camp. His house, on stilts, could only be reached by climbing a rope ladder. Each new arrival to the camp had to honor the chief by undergoing this ritual; otherwise, it was thought, the elder's good fortune would be lessened and his life shortened.

The wine was indeed potent. It was deceptively sweet and numbed your tongue and cheeks. But the resourceful members of the Special Forces had devised a way to get the chief drunk before his guest succumbed.

"Budweiser," Moroney said. "The chief can't handle a Bud. So we bring along a six-pack and he goes lights-out before we do. You still have to be careful going down that ladder, though."

Moroney's other advice was to avoid looking into the wine cup. You drank through a straw and put your hand over the cup so you wouldn't see the dead flies and other bugs floating in the wine. You drank slowly while the chief faded off from the beer.

To the Yards, flies, spiders, beetles and ants were edibles, sort of like potato chips or peanuts. You would see people leaning against a tree and talking while plucking insects for snacks. In the jungle, they would find bunches of wild bananas and leave a trail of peels behind, marking their presence.

Mang Buk was a trip back to another age and civilization. The only way in was through the air, and the weather and mist made even that hazardous. Women in the village went bare breasted, animals were sacrificed to deities, and water buffalo and elephants were worshiped. The Yards were known never to lie and lived by strong but simple codes. One afternoon I sat with some of them to watch the first movie ever shown in the village, *The Great Race* with Jack Lemmon and Tony Curtis. Scenes of race cars in New York made their eyes widen and their voices pitch in excitement.

Although the war was not theirs, the Yards were entrapped by it and had been fighting as mercenaries since the days of the French. The Americans employed them to patrol the dense jungles that hid supply routes from the north. They were fierce fighters and extraordinary marksmen. One 13-year-old boy could shoot your eyes out with a carbine at 100 meters. Another teenager was an expert with a mortar.

Only a few of the Yards at Mang Buk could speak a form of mottled English. Many of them had picked up strange names from both the French and the Americans, names like Beaucoup

Kilo, Donald Duck, Willie Mays and Sam Spade. Ho Chi Minh was the best drinker in the camp.

In 1967, the year before, the Yards at Mang Buk had amassed an enemy body count of 88. Forays into the gloomy jungle with them were always an adventure. They were terrified of lightning and wore colorful necklaces to ward off evil spirits. Lurking in the dense triple canopy of foliage were tigers and 37 different species of poisonous snakes. Spitting cobras were said to rear up on the narrow trails. Back in Saigon I had found an old pre-WWII travel brochure advertising the adventure of hunting man-eating tigers in the wilds of the Central Highlands. Now, men were the favored prey.

As we took our passage through this nocturnal world, the Yards moved silently with a certain dexterity and vigilance. This was their home, and they could track an intruder even through a stream bottom. I was struck by their stealth—until they found a grove of cinnamon trees, a valued commodity in Vietnam. They made the discovery with wild yelps and calls, violating the sanctity of silence, and began ripping off cinnamon bark and stuffing it into their packs and shirts and pockets. They could sell their harvest to the Vietnamese, who would find a market for it.

As the American advisers attempted to quiet the Yards, I made my way to a tiny clearing. There was a gravestone for a soldier who had *mort pour la France* in this awful place. The date of his death was 1954. If only the jungle could speak of its past.

I stayed a week at Mang Buk. In that time the Yards defeated the Special Forces in volleyball and were given Sunday off, only to indulge in a drunken spree for which they were made to stand at attention and severely reprimanded.

Beneath the team house was a concrete bunker with cots.

Hanging on the walls were packs and helmets arranged so that in the event the camp was overrun, they could be quickly grabbed for an escape through one of the tunnels. With the aid of the Yards and the Vietnamese Special Forces, the advisory team figured they could hold off a force of 1,000 attackers.

Flying high at night was the camp's guardian angel, an ancient DC-3 that had been equipped with Gatling guns so powerful they could spray every yard of a football field in one pass. Dubbed "Spooky," the gunship lingered throughout the night like a bird in search of prey. The camp's mortar fired occasional rounds at distant jungle pathways to forestall any enemy movement. Its angry jolts made sleep only intermittent.

After several days, Captain Moroney approached me with a weather report. He was concerned that we were due for some bad storms that would ground all aircraft. A resupply chopper was due to arrive the next day and he advised me to take it.

"It was great having you," Moroney said. "But the last time we had bad weather we didn't get a helicopter in here for 40 days. Believe me, you don't want to spend 40 days in Mang Buk." That was a frightening thought. How would the newspaper justify a 10-part series on the life and times of a remote Vietnamese village?

The next day I took the helicopter and went back to civilization, if that's what you could call Kontum City. In a way I was sorry to leave this story. It was so different from the rest, offering a rare glimpse into the past. As we lifted off and made a wide sweep to gain altitude, I looked down on the camp and saw puffs of yellow smoke.

It looked like Moroney's monkey had escaped again.

CHAPTER 31

Never-Ending War

There were no weekends, just an endless stream of numb and numberless days. The troops counted the days until their tour was over. I had no schedule. It was November and the monsoon winds were blowing from the northeast. By now I had become part of the place, acclimated to its swelter and dampness, comfortable but cautious of its dangers. I was always fearful, though. Vietnam would claim 11 journalists that I knew, many of them photographers.

After 10 months, I knew from my travels and experiences that we could not win the war. In fact, we should not have even been here in the first place. The French had stigmatized the people with a brutal reign. The man in the rice paddy driving his water buffalo for a meager existence couldn't care less about communism or democracy. He just wanted to be left alone.

Out in the South China Sea, the carrier pilots flew daily missions over the north, dodging missiles and MIGs to bomb bridges, roads and truck parks. I considered the pilots to be truly authentic observers of the war, for they were smart and in a position to see firsthand its vicissitudes. Despite increased bombing, they told of more and more truck traffic heading south.

The U.S. Navy, except in the rarest of circumstances, does not allow alcohol to be consumed aboard ship. Thus I was surprised one night on a carrier to be invited to a pilot's quarters where a group of fliers were drinking bourbon and scotch. The flight crews suffered fatigue, so the higher ranks apparently looked the other way. I was surprised they included me, a relative stranger, in their soiree.

One pilot joked that the war would be a lot easier for all parties involved if a battalion of Navy Seabees was stationed in Hanoi to blow up bridges. Conversely, an equal number of Vietnamese would be assigned to a carrier, and for every bridge blown they would push an aircraft over the side.

The drinking and the black humor were telltale signs. At the Rex in Saigon, we would all join in on the nightly rendition of the Animals' "We Gotta Get Out of This Place." Each night the volume would increase. All these pieces fit together to give you a clear mosaic of a war gone bad.

Wherever you went there were good Americans trying to do their best for a Washington that was lying on a daily basis. In fact, the whole war was based on a lie that over the years would unravel like a Machiavellian nightmare.

But in November of 1968 there was the feeling that the war had peaked and at best was a stalemate. Richard Nixon had been elected president and Lyndon Johnson was about to leave office, yet another victim of the Tet Offensive. Tactics in the war changed with a new commander, but there was even more Potemkin to the Five O'Clock Follies than usual.

I was hoping to be home for the holidays, so when Bill Ware's letter arrived I was sure it was an end to my assignment. I was right about that, but wrong about home. Tom Vail had been serving on a State Department advisory board and was alarmed by reports that the Middle East was on the verge of another war. Would I please proceed to that part of the world?

Another war. Just the thought of it sent me to the roof of the Caravelle for a midafternoon drink. I remembered Don Robertson's warning about animal stories, only this time it was war stories. There was nothing attractive about a tour of the Middle East, a gray and ghostly place trapped in time and harboring centuries-old tribal and religious disputes. On the other hand, I really couldn't turn down the assignment. There was an unforgiving nature to the *Plain Dealer*.

Before setting out for the Middle East, I went to Hong Kong for a much-anticipated Christmas break. I felt an incredible sense of relief as the plane lifted off from Tan Son Nhut. A year of stress evaporated, and I could feel a softness all around me. The soft music permeating the cabin, the soft seats, the soft voices of the flight attendants, and the euphoric feeling of being delivered from danger. After months in fatigues, even my clothes felt soft.

Still, I also felt a sense of abandonment. After my many months in Vietnam, a piece of its story belonged to me. It always would.

Then in its final years as a British colony, Hong Kong still adhered to some of the Crown's traditions. My hotel, the Hong Kong Hilton, overlooked one of the world's great harbors. I watched one day as British warships fired off a salute to the incoming *USS Hancock*, a carrier from the South China Sea. There was a historic nuance to the gesture. Hong Kong was lively, forgiving and incredibly inexpensive. I paid $50 for a Rolex watch. When I returned 40 years later, the same model cost $5,000. You could have a custom monogrammed shirt made for $2.50. I didn't bother to launder them. I just called the tailor in the morning and a new shirt was delivered for that day.

The Foreign Correspondents' Club of Hong Kong was the meeting place for journalists passing through that part of the world. Everyone exchanged the latest news from troubled spots and tips on how to navigate the dangers. It was pleasant to end the day at the club, looking out at the bay with a San Miguel beer. Americans were still banned from travel in China and Mao Tse-tung's Cultural Revolution was in progress, feeding a host of China watchers stationed in Hong Kong.

I spent one afternoon in Hong Kong's New Territories region with the British army's Gurkhas who patrolled the border. The Gurkhas, special troops recruited from Nepal, were considered to be among the most ferocious fighters in the world. Their hallmark was the *kukri*, a knife that once unsheathed had to draw blood. A British officer told me not to ask to see one, for then the Gurkha would have to draw his own blood before replacing the weapon in its scabbard. They had been assigned to the border because the Chinese had made a practice of kidnapping regular British troops. There were no such incidents once the Gurkhas appeared. We looked out over a vast valley into China and saw an ominous parade of thousands of Chinese demonstrators.

On New Year's Eve I boarded Pam Am's historic around-the-world Flight 1 and began my journey to Beirut via New Delhi and Tehran. It was a long, cold, lonely flight. I reflected on the revelry that was taking place at home in celebration of the arrival of 1969 and wished I was at Pat Joyce's tavern on East 9th Street. Foreign reporting had its exciting moments, but they arrived amid long stretches of depressing solitude.

CHAPTER 32

The Unholy Land

As the plane descended into Beirut that gray morning, the view of snow on Mount Lebanon provided a chilly greeting for a tired traveler. A much more alarming sight was the charred remains of 14 airliners destroyed two days earlier by Israeli commandos. The property of Arab airlines, they were blown up to retaliate the terrorist hijacking of an El Al plane.

The raid was surgically precise. No one was killed. Explosive charges had been placed in the airplanes' nose and wing wells and detonated one after another, destroying some $44 million worth of aircraft. The noses of the planes lay on the ground like cracked eggshells. An airport worker told me that several of the commandos had stopped in the airport restaurant and paid for cups of coffee with Israeli money.

That day I checked into the Hotel Saint-Georges, a legendary old-world hostelry situated on the edge of the Mediterranean Sea. It had the reputation of being a nexus of Middle Eastern intrigue, a place where journalists, spies and politicians mingled, drank and fed on rumors.

The bar was occupied by men with waxed mustaches and red fezzes who were fingering worry beads, members of the Lebanese parliament I was told. Harry Reasoner of CBS News and *60 Minutes* had just arrived and said New York was expecting another outbreak of war. The next day we began to make forays into the Lebanese countryside to see if we could detect any military preparations.

My first piece on the Middle East described how the raid on the Beirut airport symbolized the balance of power in the region. The Lebanese military was inept, I wrote; a handful of Viet Cong could have made a better show of repelling the Israelis.

The hotel had a telegraph desk. I wired the story to the *Plain Dealer* only to receive a rude awakening. The liveried concierge informed me that Lebanon's censorship office had put a stop on the wire. Any outgoing stories needed the approval of the authorities.

"However," the concierge said in a conspiratorial tone, "there is a way to bypass the censors." He was a well-groomed man versed in the needs of his clientele, having spent his working life in their service. His teenage son was training as a bellhop and would no doubt follow in the family tradition.

Across the way from the St. Georges was the Phoenicia Hotel, a modern building that towered skyward. It was here that Pan Am's flight crews spent the night before flying on to New York. "You must arise early and seek out an American stewardess and tell her of your need to get your story to your newspaper," the man said. That meant getting to the Phoenicia at 5:30 a.m. with the story in an open envelope and a few American dollars for postage. The envelope was open so that the courier could see there was nothing suspicious about the request.

The plan worked astonishingly well. My stories would arrive in Cleveland in two days, faster delivery than any mail service could provide. I tipped the concierge with a wad of Lebanese bills and won his invaluable services for the next four months.

I had not come prepared for the change in climate and was advised to go to Hamra Street. This was Beirut's most fashionable avenue, with coffeehouses, cafés, boutiques and clubs. It was here that well-to-do Arabs from throughout the Middle East came to play and break their Islamic vows by drinking fine scotch. I bought a thick turtleneck sweater and a coat and yearned for Saigon weather.

The many areas of dispute in the Middle East are deep, uncharted and beyond lasting resolution. To itemize them would require volumes. In my lifetime they have gone from bad to worse to uncontrollable. The story never ends.

In 1969 my assignment came at a time when the region was still recovering from the devastating Six-Day War in which Israel thwarted a combined attack by five Arab nations that were supported by eight other Middle Eastern countries. Israel captured the Sinai, the Golan Heights and, the biggest prize, Jerusalem. In the wake of this stunning and humbling defeat, terrorist groups were energized for revenge. Among them was Al Fatah, led by Yasser Arafat, a man who was receiving a lot of international attention.

Despite the tensions, this was a time when a correspondent could roam relatively safely while pursuing a story in the Middle East. Today, that would be impossible.

I received a letter from Tom Vail, who asked that I focus on the Arab side of the story, which he felt was not getting enough coverage. I didn't realize it at the time, but by visiting the Arab countries first, we aroused the ire of Cleveland's Jewish community. However, no Arab country would permit you to enter if they knew you had been to Israel, so it was better to visit there last.

The obvious story was the rise of Al Fatah, the most prominent anti-Israeli group. The question was how to get to the guerrillas and determine their political impact. I started with the military attaché at the U.S. embassy, who was of no help. The political officers provided a good briefing on the movement's genesis, but offered no guidance on how to make contact. They were a bit disdainful of my desire to talk to Al Fatah.

So I went to Roy Essoyan, bureau chief for the Associated Press in Beirut. A legendary figure in the wire service, he had earlier broken the story about the split between the Kremlin and China, which got him expelled from Moscow. Essoyan, like Bob Tuckman in Saigon, was thoroughly gracious and helpful. Men like this were the backbone of American journalism abroad.

Essoyan said that to make contact with Al Fatah I would have to go to Jordan. It is a short flight from Beirut to Amman, and I arrived at the hotel in the early afternoon. The fedayeen or guerrilla movement was rapidly formalizing, with about a dozen organizations operating openly in Jordan with King Hussein's reluctant blessing. Jordan's vast network of Palestinian refugee camps were breeding grounds for the fedayeen.

Finding Al Fatah was no difficult matter. Not far from the city's old Roman amphitheater the group had its own public relations office staffed to facilitate foreign correspondents. The office was in a stone building guarded by a single rifleman with a yellow grin and a harmless demeanor.

Al Fatah, at the time the largest of the liberation groups, had clerks as well as fighters, and one of the former ushered me into a drab room and produced a printed form for visiting journalists. The director of public relations, a balding man named Ahmed, asked for a picture. I carried several and handed one to him. He peered into my face, matching my image with my visage.

"When was this picture taken?" he asked.

"Last year," I responded.

"You looked better then," he said sarcastically. I probably did, I mused. Ahmed said they would consider my request to meet the fedayeen, but I would not be able to meet with Arafat. I was told to return to the hotel and stay there.

Nothing happened the rest of the day as I paced the lobby, drank too many cups of sweet coffee, and napped. I went through the same routine the next day, staring out at the seven hills on which Amman rested. By evening I began to worry that I was going to be stiffed. I was getting ready for bed around 11 p.m. when there was a soft knock on my hotel room door.

The man on the other side of the door was short and heavy-set, in his mid-30s with a thick shock of black hair and a crooked front tooth. He wore jeans and a rumpled leather coat. Tucked into his waistband was an automatic pistol. His right index finger was missing at the knuckle.

"I am Sam," he said. "You will be gone from this place for two days. You need not bring anything. Just come with me."

Sam and I walked out of the hotel to a Land Rover where two other men sat. The night was chilly and I was glad to have a coat. I was told to get in the back seat, where I was blindfolded. We drove for what seemed several hours, the car swaying on turns, adding to my disorientation. The men spoke in Arabic, smoked strong-smelling cigarettes, and did not address me. I was not at all sure that I was doing a smart thing.

We stopped briefly at what I was told were Jordanian police checkpoints. The police didn't seem to be bothered by a blind-folded man in the back of a Land Rover. We drove on until one of the men had to relieve himself. My blindfold was removed and we were on a side road, a rough-cut path in a ravine.

As we proceeded, the vehicle threatened to topple several times until we reached flat ground before a hill of majestic pine trees. A sentry appeared wearing a traditional white *keffiyeh*, and behind him a number of armed men emerged from what looked to be fighting positions. The moonlight gave the men a ghostly appearance.

When we reached our destination, I was surprised to find a makeshift camp set amid darkened Roman ruins. Broken columns and statuary lay over a clearing where I could see perhaps 20 squatting men, all of them dressed in camouflage, their faces covered by scarves. Armed with a variety of Soviet weapons, they huddled around a small fire and, in Islamic tradition, used their right hands to eat from a community dish. They were friendly, though few could speak English. They earned the equivalent of $45 a month and all the glory they could conjure.

I asked Sam where the sun would rise in the morning. He seemed puzzled by my question and then pointed to the east. At that moment my biggest concern was the Israelis. I knew they flew frequent air strikes on the Arab guerrillas, and out here in the open we were vulnerable to a morning attack coming out of the sun. That night I found a broken chunk of column that gave me cover, laid a rug next to it, and slept. It was a foolish gesture.

Though well camouflaged, the fighters dug tunnels and caves, some out of bedrock, to protect against the quick and deadly air strikes. I was allowed to see only a small section of the camp, but it appeared thoroughly fortified.

In the morning the fedayeen took some physical exercise, an uncoordinated and indifferent effort that drew laughter from a few concealed faces. Their actions seemed both childish and ominous. Though deadly in their intentions, they were too careless and carefree for soldiers. They attached a certain romance to their mission.

After a quick breakfast, the men gathered around a blackboard where an officer, a lawyer I was told, sketched plans for an operation against an Israeli fuel depot. This exercise may have been for my benefit. I couldn't understand Arabic, but I could see that the mission would require crossing the Jordan River, no small feat since the Israelis heavily patrolled the area.

The plan was to cross the river in a small boat and attack the depot with rocket-propelled grenades, then withdraw in an orderly fashion. The men energetically practiced the covering action for the withdrawal, but it was hard to imagine them having much success. What ignited their spirits was a lifelong hatred of Israel. At a Palestinian school I saw this hate being taught literally from the time children could read.

The swift and crushing defeat of the Six-Day War intensified the Arab desire for revenge, but they did not seem to take into account the necessity of proper battle training. Emotion and stirring desert music could go only so far in a war with the Israelis.

A Russian diplomat in Cairo had told me that his country's advisers to the Egyptian army were frustrated by the inability to convince their clients of the need to maintain the Soviet tanks they were driving into battle. For every hour a tank is operated, many hours of maintenance are required. "They felt maintenance was beneath them," the Russian said. "They wanted to leap into a tank and ride it to war as if it were a stallion."

The mind-set of the fedayeen seemed similar, and while I had yet to see the Israelis in action, I knew that their reputation for preparedness and execution on the battlefield could not be matched by the men here who played at war. It was as sad as the pure hated that motivated them. Together those two elements would deliver them to death.

Near the end of my first full day at the camp, Sam walked over to me. The men, he said, wanted to know if I would go with them on the raid into Israel. I didn't dare tell him that not only did I not want to go with them, I wanted to be out of this camp before they went over the river. If any damage was done on the raid, a retaliatory air strike—or worse—was certain.

My stammer and hesitation indicated that I wasn't going, and Sam mustered a weak smile. Thankfully, we left the next morning. I was again blindfolded until we reached Amman. The driver insisted I hold his AK-47 so I might feel like a fedayeen. I hung around town for a few days, sensing a deeply anti-American mood. When a friendly Jordanian guided me through a mosque, the police arrived to question my presence.

I waited to see if Sam and his Al Fatah friends would actually mount their raid. As far as I know, it never happened.

Given all this, reports out of the Middle East consisted mostly of interviews with diplomats, military attachés, students, educators and fellow correspondents. To add to the reporting problems, countries like Syria, Egypt and Iraq had broken off diplomatic relations with the United States, leaving those embassies with skeletal staffs and represented by other nations like Belgium and Spain. Political officers in the U.S. embassy in Beirut advised reporters not to travel to Syria and Iraq.

But there were stories in those places, and after the Iraqis hung nine Jews as spies in Liberation Square in the heart of Baghdad, I decided to go there.

CHAPTER 33

Baghdad

I was accompanied by an elderly British reporter, a man who had spent his entire career in the Middle East, careening from crisis to crisis, a man so cynical, salty and menacing that Iraqi passport-control officials, no slouches themselves in the bad temperament department, wilted before him.

"You open that bloody bag and I'll see to it you are flogged," he stormed at one customs agent. I cringed, and reasoned that his arrogance represented the final vestiges of the British Empire.

In early 1969, Baghdad was about as grim a place as you could find. It reeked of evil and death. Though modern and somewhat spectacular, the city was devoid of joy and laughter and humanity.

Since the beginning of the year, 22 people had been hung in the square after televised trials, a morbid theater designed to further terrify an already terrified populace. The prosecutor wore a pistol in court. Defense attorneys were allowed two minutes to defend their clients and then plead for mercy. The alleged Israeli spies, many Western diplomats believed, had not been spies, or even Jewish, but rather inmates from an Iraqi insane asylum. The sole purpose of the government's show was to instill fear in anyone with militant thoughts.

We were escorted around Baghdad by an Iraqi government spokesman, a weasely fellow who spoke reasonably good English, wore the darkest of sunglasses, and prattled on about Iraq being the cradle of civilization and the oldest culture in the world. The hangings of the nine Israelis, he said, had been necessary to protect that culture from its enemies—the Jews— and, besides, nations had every right to execute spies. Whereupon the obstreperous Englishman interrupted with his own thoughts on Iraqi civilization.

"Blokes were having lunch in the square while the unfortunates were squirming in their death throes," he said. The mood had been somewhat festive. A soft-drink bottling company trucked its employees to Baghdad so they could witness the hangings.

I had earlier talked with Marcel Dupret, the Belgian ambassador to Iraq. The televised trials, he said, were a sham. When one defendant was accused of writing reports to Israeli agents, his response to the court was that he could neither read nor write. I asked our Iraqi spokesman about this. He paused, fingered his worry beads, and smiled. "Yes, but the man could hear, could he not?" he said. "There are many means and ways of spying. The only thing we are concerned with is the question, and I take from Shakespeare, to be a spy or not to be a spy?"

I had another question for our wily guide regarding an American who was unable to obtain an exit visa. At Dupret's request, I had visited with Paul Bail, a 46-year-old from Houston who worked for Esso as a technician in Iraqi oil production. In late 1968 Bail had been arrested and charged with working for the CIA. He was tried and found guilty, but released. Unable to leave Iraq without an exit visa, he was granted sanctuary by the

Belgians. Bail was pleasant enough given his ordeal, but he was in no position to speak to me on the record. He worried that the nightmare he was living would never end.

The government spokesman responded that Bail was not allowed to leave Iraq because the ongoing investigation might possibly yield new information—perhaps unearthing another Israeli spy ring. Iraq's clemency toward Bail, he said, was another example of the country's civilized nature. Bail was freed several months later.

That night the Brit and I ate at an outdoor stand on the Tigris River. Our dinner consisted of freshly caught fish along with cold bottles of Amstel beer. It's funny how you remember things. The fish, cooked over a special type of wood, was the best I've ever had. While we were eating, a bearded man approached us with his palm out. His clothes were unkempt and the cloth on his head soiled from perspiration. I girded myself for an outburst from my companion.

Instead, the Brit reached into his pocket for some coins, then pressed them into the man's hand. He spoke to the man in Arabic, a surprise to me. Later he would tell me that he generally concealed his linguistic ability, for it enabled him to eavesdrop, a decided edge for a reporter.

Meanwhile, the Brit and the beggar had moved away from the passersby on the riverfront and were conversing in hushed tones. Then the Brit beckoned to me. "We are going to a place that you must never reveal," he said. "We are going to meet with those who resist the regime. The people there can face death if they are caught defying the fools who govern."

He didn't have to worry about me revealing anything, for I had no idea where we were going. A cabdriver was taking the three of us to an older part of the city where the streets grew narrower, the streetlights grew dimmer, and robed figures lurked in the shadows. It was film noir, with Baghdad as the ominous setting.

The cab dropped us off at an intersection with rows of two- and three-story buildings that appeared to house shops and garages. Then we walked for a block, the Arab watching to see if we were being followed. We turned into a dark alley and waited for a few minutes, then proceeded a dozen steps to a large door. The Arab knocked, the door opened a crack, and there was a hurried exchange.

We descended down a long staircase into a murky basement where the pungent odor of cigarette smoke commingled with the smell of benzene and printer's ink. Several Arab men in workers' clothes, pistols in their waistbands, huddled around an ancient platen printing press.

The Brit explained that these men were members of an underground opposition force that published an English-language newspaper critical of the government. It was a dangerous business, one that carried the death penalty if they were caught. The heavy, hurried clank of the printing press stamped out its crime as the nervous men gathered sheets proclaiming the most recent hangings of eight more alleged spies, this time all of them Muslims.

In their hurry, the printers had misspelled the word "death" in a 48-point, red banner headline: DEAHT. After returning to Beirut, I wrote that Iraq was a place you were anxious to leave. "It is medieval and mad. It is the crib of civilization and it could be its Omega."

The ensuing years would underscore my prophecy.

CHAPTER 34

On to the Pyramids

When Roy Essoyan heard that I was leaving for Cairo, he called me into his office at the AP bureau in Beirut. He needed a favor. A friend of his in Egypt desired some paint that was unavailable in Cairo. Would I mind escorting eight gallons of it? I would not have to do anything other than keep a watchful eye as the paint cans were unloaded. The friend would meet me at the airport.

I didn't think much of it until I was met by a Russian jeep driven by a tall, blond, muscular man. He was pleasant, speaking broken English with a Russian accent. The paint was loaded into the vehicle. An Egyptian official sitting next to him stamped my passport and ushered me through customs without the usual rigmarole. Then the Russian drove me downtown to my hotel, pointing to the pyramids off in the distance. All this was quite unusual.

After the Suez Crisis in 1956, the Russians had become patrons of Egyptian leader Gamal Abdel Nasser, helping to build the mighty Aswan Dam and supplying and advising Egypt's vast military. Following the Six-Day War, in which the Egyptians suffered 16,000 dead or wounded, a large contingent of Russians was now helping to rebuild that military. Much to the Russians' frustration, however, societal divisions in Arab culture impeded the training. Egyptian officers looked down on their troops, threatening military unity.

I checked into the Nile Hilton and made straight for the Associated Press bureau run by Joe Dynan. The 57-year-old Dynan would work for the wire service as a foreign correspondent for 31 years. His first AP assignment abroad was the Tokyo bureau in 1941, four months before the bombing of Pearl Harbor. He spent seven months in an internment camp with other Americans before being traded for Japanese diplomats held by the Americans. The exchange took place on a neutral passenger ship, the *Gripsholm*, in Mozambique.

Dynan later covered World War II in the European Theater and did lengthy service in the Middle East. A friendly man with a keen sense of humor, he was thoroughly knowledgeable about the region. He wore his admirable travels well, and you had the sense of being in the presence of someone who had very little left to see in the world.

Over lentil soup in his apartment, Dynan explained the situation in Cairo. Like elsewhere in the Middle East, Americans were not in vogue there. Nasser had broken off diplomatic relations following the war, and the Spanish were left looking after U.S. interests. In reality, a skeleton staff of maybe a dozen Americans was manning the embassy.

Dynan explained that my movements would be restricted to Cairo, and there was a chance at some point that I might be followed. There was a once-a-week briefing by the government spokesman, Dr. Zyat, who took only written questions and responded only with empty answers. Don't be loose and crazy about town, Dynan cautioned. Oh, and *The Fugitive* was running on Cairo TV in Arabic.

I mentioned escorting the cans of paint from Beirut and he nodded, then related the story behind the delivery. As part of the break in diplomatic relations, Egypt had cut off the AP's wire to New York, a major blow to the flow of news from the Middle East.

To rectify the situation, the resourceful Dynan made a deal with the Russian news service TASS, which agreed, in the collegial spirit of journalism, to send AP copy on its wire to New York. The paint was part of the deal.

One of the Russian officials connected with TASS, who was suspected of being a KGB agent, was having trouble with his wife. She wanted their apartment painted, but the war had caused a shortage of materials. The woman insisted on a fresh coat for the walls. If not, she was going back to Russia.

It appeared that the flow of international news may have rested on the eight gallons of paint I delivered that day. It was a great story of how an insignificant incident could affect the world community, but, of course, it couldn't be told at the time.

Despite the dreary aftereffects of the war, Cairo was a fascinating place, teeming with movement and people, its poverty troubling, its history filled with civilization's mysteries. One afternoon I visited the pyramids with one of the foreign service officers who acted as a caretaker in the shuttered U.S. embassy. We sat in the sun and looked at the Sphinx for the slightest change in expression. I asked the official what he did now that we no longer had formal relations with Egypt.

"American tourists come here by the dozens," he said. "And a lot of them are older and unfortunately some of them die. It's my job to identify them and arrange for the bodies to be sent home. That is morbid work. People don't understand that they should get their traveling done when they are young."

I was learning that the Middle East was not a story you could compartmentalize with easily understood time lines and reference points. It was a place where history never paused. Like a river it ran on and on, flowing from an incomprehensible source.

But the waterway that interested me was the Suez Canal, the great excavation that linked the Orient to the European continent and was of great strategic and economic value, generating daily revenues of $1 million for Egypt. The canal had been closed by the war; 10 sunken vessels blocked passage, trapping another 14 ships with their crews in the various lakes between the locks. I was curious about life on those vessels and made a formal request to visit them.

If nothing else, the French and the British left a bureaucratic legacy in their colonies designed to hold time at bay. Officials at the government press office said a permit for my visit would take a week to process. I would have to apply for papers establishing my identity as a foreign journalist. That would take some more time.

When I told Dynan of my plight, he suggested attaching a few Egyptian bills to my applications to see if that might grease the wheels. For about $25, I got my permits and papers in two days along with a minder named Ali, a thin, dark-skinned Egyptian in his early 20s with a bad cold. He was new on the job and suspicious.

Ali had no doubt been told to regard me as a possible spy, and under no circumstances was he to allow me out of his sight. It got so bad that he would follow me into the bathroom. The canal was east of Cairo, an 80-mile drive through the desert with its monotonous and monochromatic dunes. A black ribbon of highway wove in and out of the yawn-inducing sandbanks.

Ali conversed in Arabic with the driver, a white-haired man with a trim mustache. I had no idea what they were saying, nor was I curious. Ali sniffled and wiped his nose on his shirtsleeve.

Suddenly, up ahead, coming over a rise toward us, was a military convoy. Tanks, trucks, jeeps and, most impressive of all, huge missile carriers. A surprised Ali ordered me to cover my eyes. The convoy stretched long, and when a massive tarpaulin blew off the missile it was covering, revealing the ugly projectile in all its lethal repose, I peeked through my fingers.

Ali freaked and squawked in Arabic so rapidly it sounded like he was praying for his life. Then in nervous English he admonished me to keep my eyes closed. The scene was so funny I couldn't help but laugh. He took that as an insult, and after the convoy had passed he pouted all the way to the canal. A spy would not have to work hard in Egypt.

We took a launch out to an American ship, the *African Glen*, trapped in the Great Bitter Lake, and found life in the dormant canal lively. The crews of the 14 immobilized ships had banded together to form an organization called the Great Bitter Lakes Society. It had its own postage stamps, Olympic games, dinners, lifeboat races and T-shirts.

"Yeah, and when they dredge the silt out of the canal they are going to find more beer cans than mud," said Jack Rodriguez, the first officer of the *African Glen*. One of the ships was filled with beer and another loaded with steaks, which meant that the crews might get bored but never thirsty or hungry.

Society membership had grown to 700, the number of crew members who had served on the stranded vessels, which alternated personnel every three or four months. The cargoes on the various ships were valuable and had to be maintained until the canal reopened. Thousands of rotting apples had been dumped in the lake, along with 200 tons of rice.

I tried to get pictures of the marooned fleet, but Ali kept blocking my lens with his hand, shaking his head and mumbling no, no, no, through his sniffles. When I asked for a shot of

Rodriguez, I had to let Ali look through the viewfinder to make sure no parts of the canal were visible. The Egyptians were so paranoid about the ships in the canal that they banned cameras and stationed police officers on several vessels to make sure no Israeli spies were aboard.

At night the crews could sometimes hear artillery duels across the canal, as Egypt still considered the war to be ongoing. The *African Glen* would remain trapped in the waterway until October 10, 1973, during the Yom Kippur War, when it was sunk by missiles from an Israeli aircraft despite being plainly marked as a U.S. ship. A contemporary account of the incident said the vessel was blocking the Israeli troops' view of the canal.

No one spoke on the drive back through the desert. It was plain that Ali did not want to be here and trying to talk with him produced only grunts. The silence made me reflective. There was something strange and even pathetic about what I was witnessing in the Middle East. Such a waste of wealth and humanity, all adding up to a meaningless future for people like Ali.

A few days later I visited the Museum of Egyptian Antiquities in Cairo where in one room rows of glass cases displayed the mummies of dozens of pharaohs. It symbolized a celebration of a past that Egypt struggled to escape.

Back at the *Plain Dealer*, my reports from the Arab world were generating many irate letters from the city's Jewish community, some even accusing me of being a dupe of the Palestinians. I was unaware of the discontent until my return home. Years later there would still be some in Cleveland who thought I was anti-Semitic. One cannot appreciate the vexations of the Middle East without truly engaging in issues that produce deep, emotional reactions on both sides.

CHAPTER 35

The Israelis

Two weeks later I was on the opposite bank of the Suez Canal in the Sinai Desert, shivering in a bunker with soldiers of the Israeli Defense Force and wondering whether Ali had gotten over his cold. We had driven nine hours from Tel Aviv through a featureless landscape that was home only to a few nomadic Arabs. Their presence in the distance was marked by the pinpoints of cooking fires.

Approaching the canal we came upon the Mitla Pass, a strategic site in the desert that opened the route to the waterway. It was here that the Egyptian army had taken one of its worst defeats in history when its armored columns were caught in the pass by Israeli air strikes. The evidence of a slaughter was still evident, with the carcasses of burnt-out trucks, tanks and jeeps littering the sides of the narrow road. Clothes, gas masks, canteens, cooking utensils, small arms and other military paraphernalia were strewn about as if something terrible had ripped them from the bodies of the now-ghostly troops. All of this was preserved by the heat of the desert. The only movement was the skeletal trucks' engine fans rotating in the wind.

We pressed on through the desert to Port Tewfik at the southern end of the canal where the so-called Six-Day War was still in progress. Occasional artillery duels broke out and snipers exchanged fire, making it dangerous to wander around the sands. Huge billows of black smoke rose from a petroleum depot on the Egyptian side of the canal. The Israelis had responded with an artillery barrage after enduring random fire from the recalcitrant foe.

It was strange covering both sides of a conflict. There was such a stark difference between the opponents. The Arabs approached war in a mystical, almost romantic state while the Israelis were methodical, precise, technical and tough. Much of this had to do with their cultures—and with the fact that Israel was so outnumbered.

The Israeli troops were curious about Vietnam. Why, they asked, had the Americans not yet won a war that they had been fighting for six years? I explained that the Viet Cong were very good soldiers who were fighting for their homes, much like the Israelis were fighting for theirs. Fighting for your homeland is an unparalleled incentive.

The next day the troops insisted that I get a good look at the Egyptian sniper positions. We crawled through the sand until we were 50 yards from a group of palm trees where the snipers hid, strapped high among the fronds. They would wait patiently—an entire day, if necessary—for the one shot that would kill an Israeli. The Israelis were patient hunters themselves, and all along the canal the lethal cat-and-mouse game played out while the rest of the world thought the war was over.

Israel's environment was far different from the rest of the Middle East. There was no palpable tension like there was in Baghdad and Cairo. And there was color, greenery, a modern feeling in contrast to the tired, monotonous tones of the past. Perhaps because Israel had adapted to so much hardship since its founding in 1948, the way it existed was embraced as the norm. It was a happier place, with a bright ambiance, and people moved with a purposeful gait that spoke of the future.

But it was also a relatively small and close-knit place. One day I was at the censor's office getting ready to file a story when I came upon my old companion from Baghdad, the British reporter. He was bombastic as usual, this time berating a clerk for striking a paragraph from a story on Menachem Begin, who had just been named a minister in the Israeli government. The offending paragraph identified Begin as the terrorist leader who during the British occupation of Palestine blew up the King David Hotel in Jerusalem in 1946. The censor was unrelenting.

"That is the God's truth! The bloody man was a terrorist," the Brit blurted. "Put it back in the story."

"That might be true," the censor said. "But he is my uncle. It stays out."

Begin, of course, would go on to become Israel's prime minister and to share the Nobel Peace Prize with Egypt's Anwar Sadat for negotiating a peace following the Yom Kippur War.

But the one quality that set Israel apart from its neighbors was a tough determination. It was a hardness born of the Holocaust, a heritage so terrible that those who inherited its legacy pledged never to let the world forget.

All this made the Israelis resourceful and vigilant. I learned this one afternoon at an army base near Tel Aviv. I was being briefed by an army major on guerrilla activities along Israel's borders. The business-like major was turned out in immaculate khaki with knife-sharp creases, his sleeves precisely rolled at the biceps. On the wall behind him was a detailed color relief map of the Jordan Valley. He took a retractable pointer from his breast pocket and clicked it into place.

"Mr. Roberts, on March 15th you were here," he said, indicating a spot on the map. "The next day you moved to this point, and as you departed for Amman you traveled on this route. Tell me, what kinds of weapons did these Palestinians carry?"

I was stunned. I had no idea of where I'd been with Al Fatah, but the Israelis knew my precise movements. I also realized it was a test. If I revealed any information about my time with the Palestinian guerrillas, then perhaps I might do the same later when it came to the Israelis?

I told the major that I was not a weapons expert. He just smiled and said, "Even after a year in Vietnam?"

It was a subtle encounter, but it made plain the situational awareness that the Israelis possessed regarding hostile border activities. At the end of my meeting with the major I asked to accompany an Israel Defense Forces (IDF) patrol along the river. He said it could be arranged, but thought it foolish. "There have been deaths," he murmured.

The patrol consisted of a World War II half-track and a squad of infantry. We motored along the Jordan River, a .50-caliber machine gun manned and at the ready. Despite the familiar feeling of anxiety that percolates in harm's way, the outing was uneventful. The young Israelis were curious as to why an American would be interested in them. When I told them it was my job, one soldier replied that Americans usually came to Israel only to plant trees and then went home.

A few days later I visited the Golan Heights on the Syrian border, a strategic point that the Israelis had taken in the Six-Day War. The area was festooned with land mines, which dampened my appetite for this kind of reporting. This feeling was underscored later when Bill Tuohy of the *Los Angeles Times* and I were visiting a commercial mining operation in the desert. We were talking to the mine superintendent when an explosion rocked his office.

Tuohy and I hit the floor in unison while the bewildered superintendent stared down at the two of us. Tuohy had just won a Pulitzer Prize for his reporting out of Vietnam and, like me, was suffering from an aversion to loud noises. The explosion was the routine dynamiting of the mine, but it left us shaken. Maybe it was time to go home, I thought.

One Sunday morning I sat in my room at the Tel Aviv Hilton contemplating the rest of my day. I was tired of sightseeing but felt the kind of loneliness that inactivity only worsens. I needed to do something, and then the phone rang.

A friendly female voice said that several tourists from Cleveland were visiting her home in Herzliya, a suburb not far from Tel Aviv. A brunch would be served at noon. Would I like to come?

Would I like to come? I asked for directions.

Herzliya reminded me of an American suburb, as did the woman's living room with its big bay window. About two dozen people milled about with drinks in their hands, some speaking Hebrew and others English. The hostess, a charming woman in her late 50s, introduced me to a few of the guests, none of them Clevelanders. I was anxious to talk with someone from home.

Nearly 45 minutes later the hostess said that someone in the kitchen wanted to meet me. There, sitting at a table, was a man with a black eye patch, a figure both famous and feared in the Middle East. It was Moshe Dayan, the Israeli defense minister and military commander.

Dayan cradled a whiskey glass in his rough hands. He was a small man who could exude boundless charm, but when called upon could manage a devastating battlefield. His face was creased in an unusual pattern reminiscent of terrain. We talked for an hour. My guess was that this meeting had been arranged by someone from Cleveland in reaction to my reporting from Arab countries.

Interviewing Dayan was like dealing with a master swordsman; he parried questions with rhetorical thrusts that had an edge of ridicule. We talked about Vietnam for a while. He characterized it as a war that neither side could win—a hollow declaration. He then went on to deliver delightful one-liners that were amusing but uninformative.

By happenstance, I knew about something Dayan was working on. My father's cousin, Lieutenant General Elvy B. Roberts, commanded the First Air Cavalry in Vietnam, the first all-air mobile unit of its kind and a military curiosity. Dayan had spent several months with General Roberts, ostensibly as a correspondent for an Israeli newspaper. He was actually studying airborne operations. The helicopter was more efficient in the desert than in the heavy air of Vietnam.

Following the Six-Day War, the U.S. found itself embroiled in diplomatic controversy when Israel asked to purchase HU-1 helicopters and F-4 Phantom jet fighter-bombers. The jets would allow strikes on every Arab nation without refueling, and the helicopters would add to the tactical reach of the IDF. The purchase was a sensitive topic that the Israelis avoided talking about publicly.

Ironically, two days before while I was standing on the hotel balcony overlooking the Mediterranean, an HU-1 helicopter had swooped by, its distinctive "wop-wop" familiar to anyone who has spent time in Vietnam. I hadn't read any stories about these helicopters having reached Israel, so I decided to challenge Dayan directly. "When did the Hueys arrive?" I asked casually. He paused with his drink and squinted with his one good eye. "We have no such helicopters," he said. "Do you think you could help us get some? They are such wonderful things."

I told Dayan I had seen one over Tel Aviv and asked if he had learned much about them during his time with the First Air Cavalry in Vietnam. I took some joy in seeing that I had caught him off guard, even if only momentarily. He went on to praise the helicopters and noted how well they would function in the desert, but never acknowledged possessing them.

A few days later I again saw a Huey over the sea and wrote a piece about it, but the censor killed the story, citing military security. Not long afterward came the announcement of the sale of both the helicopters and the jets, and Middle East tensions escalated that much more. In 1973 they would erupt again in the Yom Kippur War.

After four months in the Middle East I was tired of shuffling from one sad and dreary place to another, never staying long enough to have more than a beer or two with anyone. The only news I was getting was from the BBC radio, and the high point of my day was listening to its serialization of Charlie Chaplin's autobiography. Besides, the story in the Middle East was as old as the Bible itself, and it was tough going up against that storyline. So I was happy to get a letter from Bill Ware telling me to head to Paris and the Vietnam peace talks.

It was April in Paris, but not like the song said. Spring was just arriving, and the sunlight stirred the sidewalk cafés to life. But the wind was furious, forceful enough to require a heavy coat.

The peace talks made it easy to concentrate on the city, for they were empty of news and full of recrimination, accusation and frustration. To begin with, the North Vietnamese, the National Liberation Front, the South Vietnamese and the United States could not even agree on the shape of the negotiation table. The actual proceedings were held in private, but the four sides gave a weekly briefing in the Postal Ministry building.

The North Vietnamese demanded immediate and unconditional surrender, while a bored U.S. spokesman responded by accusing the opposition of refusing to negotiate. The South Vietnamese, wearing well-cut French suits, said they had been ordered by their president to say nothing. As for the Viet Cong, this was the first time I'd ever seen one of its members who wasn't dead or captured. That contingent wore poorly tailored black suits, their spiky hairstyles resembling nipa palm. During a break in the proceedings, I referred to the Viet Cong as "Charlie," much to the horror of a Canadian reporter, who reminded me that here they were known as the National Liberation Front. It was one of those moments when you wanted to say, "You had to be there."

The best thing about the talks was that they took place only on Thursdays. That left six other days of the week to explore Paris. I didn't tell the *Plain Dealer* editors that I had bought a copy of Ernest Hemingway's *A Moveable Feast*, a memoir of his days in Paris in the 1920s. In the book he carefully listed all the addresses of his apartments, his friends' apartments, and the bars and restaurants he frequented. Using it as a guide, I spent hours and miles trudging through the city. The addresses were there, but the people, of course, were long gone. The North Vietnamese embassy was near Gertrude Stein's former house.

It would take almost five years to negotiate the peace. In the meantime, thousands of lives were lost on both sides. Reporting on the peace talks was like watching water evaporate. It was finally time to head home.

When I left Paris, the officials at El Al were suspicious. My passport was filled with stamps from Arab countries, which made them wonder why I wanted to fly an Israeli airline to New York. After suffering a spate of hijackings, El Al had gone to extraordinary lengths to safeguard its planes. I thought it might be worth a story if something happened, so that's why I chose the airline, but I didn't tell that to the man interrogating me in a room behind the ticket counter at Orly. In later years, El Al flights were attacked several times. My flight was uneventful.

CHAPTER 36

Home

Baseball fields were my first sight of home. As the plane flew into New York they were welcoming landmarks, symbolizing something familiar and stable, a part of America that remained the same in an ever-changing universe. In days to come I would both sense and see great changes in the America I knew. Much had happened in the 15 months I was gone and not a lot of it was good.

The nation had suffered the assassinations of Martin Luther King Jr. and Robert Kennedy, the war had turned America's youth against its government, drugs were rampant, and racial relations were at knife's edge. When I left, the newspaper used the word "Negroes" to describe African Americans; now we simply wrote "blacks." New social references appeared, words like "lifestyle" and "Ms." Many gays and lesbians no longer pretended to be straight.

The gap between the emerging youth culture and those over 30 had widened. It was a gap created by music, antiwar sentiment, drugs and a growing resentment of authority, especially in government and business. This had not been evident in Vietnam, but that would change as well. People were tired of the war, and it surprised me that so few colleagues asked about Vietnam. And there was something about the city that did not feel right, either. I sensed the same with the paper.

The Glenville riots had severely scarred the Stokes administration, and the downtown business community that drove so much of the city's agenda had begun to abandon the mayor. They had invested in Stokes with the hope that a black mayor could quell unrest in the black community. They had even created a fund called Cleveland NOW designed to aid that community, but recoiled when it was revealed that the militants at Glenville had been armed with weapons purchased from the fund.

The *Plain Dealer* was not left unscathed, either. There was internal bitterness over the paper's refusal to challenge official accounts of the riots. In a lengthy piece, a team of *PD* reporters raised the question of whether police had provoked the shooting. The story was never published, so instead the *New York Times* wrote about it. This and other issues had left the city room a crypt of cynicism.

All this would come into play for me later, but for now I was trying to adjust to a new reality. No longer was I living out of a suitcase and rushing from airport to airport. Life again meant finding a parking space and paying bills. I found myself angered by little things like waiting in line or in traffic. Returning veterans complained of the same annoyances. Everything seemed slow.

I gave several speeches on the war in which I concluded we were unlikely to win. I also doubted that the South Vietnamese had the capability to hold off the North for very long. A couple of City Club members alluded to my lack of patriotism. But for the most part even the most stalwart seemed tired of the war.

When I got around to reviewing my personal finances, I was surprised to find over $20,000 in my bank account. There was something odd about this figure, and when I checked with Cleveland Trust, I burst out laughing. The *Plain Dealer* accountants had been so intent on tracking my expenses that they overlooked the fact that the newspaper had overpaid me. The deal had been $11,000 to cover the war, but $22,000 had been deposited. For the slightest moment I considered larceny, but instead I reported the error.

When I presented the matter to Roy O. Kopp, the newspaper's secretary-treasurer, he was startled. Impossible, he maintained. Two days later he was on the phone demanding a reimbursement check from me. In its memo line I wrote, "Refund for one war $11,000."

In welcoming me back, Bill Ware was cordial. Throughout my travels he had been my chief correspondent, and he had indicated that upon my return we would discuss a new assignment. He laid it out immediately. I was being assigned to the paper's Washington bureau as soon as I took a few weeks off.

In the meantime, Terry Lambacher came home on leave from Vietnam with bleak and despairing reports. We drank beer in the Flats under the Main Avenue Bridge while he explained to a group of pot-smoking hippie girls how much C-4 plastic explosive it would take to drop the bridge into the Cuyahoga River. It was a bizarre conversation designed to startle them, and it produced the intended effect. It turned out that Lambacher was the only one I could talk to about the war, and I delayed leaving for Washington until he returned to Vietnam. He would remain there for several more years.

CHAPTER 37

The Nation's Capital

In the summer of 1969 Washington was still a lazy southern town with few good restaurants, abundant and inexpensive liquor stores, unrelenting humidity, a dearth of cabs, waves of tourists and 313,478 federal workers. It had a culture of its own, a complex vocabulary of bureaucratic jargon and a reverence for seniority. It also had the Nixon administration, which was stiff, uncomfortable and consumed by the war. While not yet there, Washington was on its way to becoming the international city we know today.

The paneled bar atop the National Press Club building at 14th and F Streets offered some respite from the heat and was a refuge for fading journalists engaged in relentless political rhetoric. The old-timers still debated who was responsible for Pearl Harbor. Washington was an industry of its own, providing work for countless members of the media who regarded the place as a journalistic mecca and scrambled to be part of it.

I had a different feeling about Washington. So much of it was just words, and writing about those words gave one the sense of being a stenographer and not a reporter. Unless you were a columnist or editorial writer, your job was not to interpret the words but to simply relay them to the public. Doing otherwise brought accusations of biased reporting.

Simply put, the process allowed politicians to lie. Over time the lies would accumulate to the point where levels of reporting had to change in order to challenge the lies, until finally the media came to view the political system with contempt and vice versa.

The ability to lie and mislead in Washington was aided by the complexity of government. Few reporters were experts in the arcane worlds of budgetary and bureaucratic minutiae. Only papers like the *New York Times*, the *Washington Post* and to a lesser degree the *Wall Street Journal* possessed enough staff to really cover Washington. Second-tier papers like the *Boston Globe*, *Baltimore Sun*, *Los Angeles Times* and a few others could do significant reporting, but had to focus their efforts carefully to make an impact.

The *Plain Dealer* was on the third rung of Washington bureaus in terms of importance. It was staffed by three reporters and a bureau chief, the fastidious John Peter Leacacos, a 38-year veteran of the newspaper and a man whose drooping eyelids and dreary manner brought to mind actor Peter Lorre. Jack Leacacos was somewhat withdrawn, imperious in an old-world manner, and contemptuous of everything and everyone. He was also the holder of the Order of the Crown of Italy and the Order of Saints Maurice and Lazarus, which carried no weight in the Headliner.

Leacacos served the newspaper abroad for nearly 10 years after World War II, traveling the world from one story to another and living in Rome. He had attended Harvard and during the war rose to the rank of lieutenant colonel in the Allied military government in Italy. Phil Porter once told me that in a wild moment Leacacos had driven a jeep up the Spanish Steps in Rome.

There were no wild moments for Leacacos and me. He did not welcome my arrival, making me wait for 45 minutes while he read the newspaper before acknowledging my presence. Thereupon he lectured me about the responsibilities of a journalist in Washington.

He said I was to cover the Department of Housing and Urban Development which, given all the great stories going on, had the appeal of working in a coal mine. Among my duties was attending embassy cocktail parties in order to convey Jack's greetings to the various ambassadors, all of whom seemed to be somewhat at a loss as to who he was. Being diplomats, they offered gracious responses, especially the Russian ambassador, who was effusive in extending his regards to a man whom I suspected he had never met.

Then there was the matter of our status as a bureau. One day I called the White House and told the telephone operator that I was from the Cleveland *Plain Dealer*. What airline was that?, she asked.

When the paper was sold, so the story went, publisher Tom Vail insisted on keeping the bureau separate from the Newhouse operation in Washington. In a way, the bureau was a mail drop for Vail, a channel for invitations to the White House, occasions he relished so much that he later self-published a book on the nine U.S. presidents he had met. The White House felt that Vail's visits satisfied any obligation it had to the *Plain Dealer*, which deprived the bureau of legitimate news opportunities.

To further exacerbate our awkward status, the foreign/national desk in Cleveland held the bureau in contempt and handled our copy like butchers at a charcuterie. Often they used *New York Times* wire copy instead of our stories, and many times would challenge a story's lead because it differed from that of the *Times*.

My colleagues at the bureau, Bob Havel, 44, and Sanford "Whitey" Watzman, 43, were accomplished journalists mired in a frustrating situation. It was like being on the outside looking in at others gathering good stories. Watzman was one of the newspaper's best reporters. Havel would later become the spokesman for the U.S. Department of Justice.

We indulged in a lot of black humor. Havel wrote the lyrics for a mythical musical called *The Back Page*, a spoof on the famous newspaper play *The Front Page*. We accepted our lowly station in Washington, but were puzzled by the lack of direction in the Cleveland office.

Leacacos was remote, operating the bureau with a quirky hand. The mood in the office was somber and unwelcoming, and other journalists on our floor rarely visited. One day Jack called us in and pronounced the office a citadel of squalor, ordering everything removed from our office walls. He then instructed us to go to the National Gallery and each spend $15 on art posters in the museum's gift shop. We spent a whole day looking at art and drinking beer.

A few days later two workmen arrived to paper an entire wall with a world map, a gigantic mural that dominated the office. A short man with a mustache and a beret who worked at the Italian embassy directed the application of the map, exhorting the workmen in his native tongue, which they did not understand. Leacacos was pleased by the map and for once beamed broadly. The map fascinated me, too.

Leacacos wrote a weekly column called "Clearing the Fog," which often dealt with world affairs and the activities of the U.S. State Department. One day he wanted me to accompany him to an interview with U.S. Secretary of State William P. Rogers. We were to spend 45 minutes with Rogers and focus on U.S. relations in the Middle East following the Six-Day War.

My job, Leacacos said, was to simply sit there and witness how an interview should be conducted with a high-level public official. What took place was both amusing and amazing. Our bureau chief spent the majority of the time telling Rogers about his views on the situation east of Suez. It was more lecture than interview, and I mentioned this on the way back to the office.

"You have to understand," Leacacos said. "Just because someone has a title doesn't mean that they know anything."

Meanwhile, I kept walking past the map every day, marveling at its size. From time to time I would catch Jack also admiring the results of his foray into interior design. One day after an interview in the Pentagon I wandered around the immense building and came upon a shop that sold military paraphernalia. Inspiration struck.

In the shop were packages of miniature tanks, planes and ships designed to be affixed to maps representing military exercises. I bought them all.

I started with the ships in the North Sea, the tanks sweeping down Russia's steppes, and the planes in the eastern Mediterranean. Each day I added a few more pieces to the invasion force and moved it just slightly closer toward its objective, Western Europe. Days went by without Leacacos noticing the intruders on his map.

And then one day when the four of us were in the office along with our secretary, Miss Kennedy, a man from building security appeared.

Security, Leacacos said, had been called in to investigate the meddling with the map. Jack was certain that the map's operations were being sabotaged late at night. It had never occurred to me that anyone would think this was anything more than a prank pulled by an office smart-ass. Besides, everyone else in the office knew I was the culprit.

Everything had now gone too far for me to admit to the crime. The security man said he would take it up with the building manager. The main suspect was the night cleaning crew. Jack ordered Miss Kennedy to remove the invading forces. I locked my desk drawer, which contained reinforcements.

That night I stayed late at the press club, far past the cleaning crew's hours. I was certain that the security people had checked the map after the offices had been cleaned.

Slipping down to our floor, I went into the office, arranged the remaining planes, tanks and ships around Washington on the map, and then got out of there. I came to work the next day a little late. A slew of building officials were listening patiently while Jack Leacacos ranted about office security.

I beat a hasty retreat, vowing never to touch the map again. I also got rid of my spider-shaped punch, which I had planned to use on the plastic rubber trees that graced the entrance to the office.

Several months into my Washington tour, our bureau was directed to cover the White House on a daily basis. I drew the assignment and along with 40 or so other journalists made the trek each day to the 11 a.m. press briefing. We would return at 3 p.m. for an "information opportunity." As virtual captives of the press room, reporters spent a lot of time exchanging thoughts and gossip.

The careers of a few senior White House correspondents reached back to the Franklin Delano Roosevelt administration. They lamented change, especially the arrival of television, which intruded on the late afternoon cocktail sessions that FDR frequently held with the small group that covered the White House. He mixed the drinks.

Over the years presidents had distanced themselves from the media, holding infrequent press conferences and using press secretaries and television addresses to bypass direct contact with reporters. In that first term, the Nixon White House was tightly buttoned. The president had a historic dislike for the media.

The Nixon administration launched a war on the press, largely through Vice President Spiro T. Agnew, who in a speech accused the major television networks and newspapers of providing negative, one-sided coverage. News of Agnew's speech broke late in the day, and Leacacos was directed to get responses from Ohio's senators and local congressmen.

Dick Feagler from the *Cleveland Press* was in town and had stopped by the office. We planned to go to the press club. I was introducing him to Leacacos when the call came from Cleveland to get on the story.

"You're from Cleveland, right?" Jack said to Feagler. "Well, you get on it, too." He apparently thought Feagler was with the *Plain Dealer*, and in a rare moment of collaboration the opposition contributed to our endeavor. Leacacos never knew.

One afternoon at the White House I was talking with two other reporters when press secretary Ron Ziegler came up to us. "The president wants to see you guys," he said.

The three of us thought this was some kind of joke at our expense, but Ziegler ushered us into the Oval Office. There was President Richard Nixon in his shirtsleeves, his tie loosened. He invited us to sit down and then put his feet up on his desk. His smile was genuine, not one of those for-TV grins, and he seemed at ease. Without the glare of television cameras, he seemed a different person.

Nixon talked about the peace efforts in Vietnam and his determination to end the war honorably. He bantered back and forth with us in a genuine display of communication. Nixon seemed a happy man that afternoon. It was 16 months before the Watergate burglary.

I spent about a year covering the White House and wrote a lot of copy, none of it memorable. I enjoyed traveling with the press corps and taking a Marine helicopter from the White House lawn. Banking over the city to Andrews Air Force Base was a spectacular ride, a far different experience than previous helicopter flights spent hunched in fearful anxiety.

Some presidential trips made for long days. Nixon would fly across the country and give three or four speeches, each of which required a story or update written against tight deadlines and phoned in between flights to the next city. Reporters would rush up and down the aisle of the press plane asking what the others were using for a lead paragraph. Editors on the telegraph desk liked to compare and criticize leads, much to the reporters' frustration.

On a November day when the temperature hovered at 32 degrees, some 300,000 demonstrators descended upon Washington to demand that the United States immediately withdraw from Vietnam. People passed by in waves, chanting and waving flags and placards, clearly angered by the course of the war. Veterans appeared wearing faded fatigues and I cringed at the sight of Viet Cong banners. This was a country that none of us had seen before.

Bob Havel and I roamed the mostly peaceful crowds, a strolling sea of humanity that marched to the cry of "One-two-three-four, Tricky Dick, stop the war."

The demonstrators were mostly draft-age young men, hirsute in leather, jeans and boots. I could not help but wonder what their counterparts in Vietnam must have thought. Some returning soldiers were being jeered at and spit on.

I remembered a black Army sergeant from Detroit who had only a few days left in-country when our patrol was ambushed at a river crossing. I was working my way across the river on an air mattress, pulling on a line strung between the banks, when we were fired upon. Plumes of water splashed skyward as the rounds danced across the river. As I approached the opposite bank, the sergeant grabbed me by the shirt and literally lifted me from the river to safety.

He then took over an M60 machine gun and provided cover fire so the rest of the platoon could move to safety. It all happened in a blur. Later, as night set in and the troops were eating their C-rations, one by one they came to the sergeant and gave him their ration tins of pound cake, his favorite dessert. They were rewarding a heroic action through the simplest, most meaningful gesture they could offer.

The esteem they held for that man was boundless, and that moment may have been a highlight in his life. A year later, as I watched the protestors, I thought of him returning home to a ghetto, met with scorn, a meager job and racial hostility. America's slap in the face.

In the beginning, I tried to shake the war. I tried to ignore the experience and move on in my career to something else. But the war loomed everywhere. There was a deep-seated division in a country unwilling to accept that it had made a mistake. Washington that fall was the epicenter of the nation's misery.

Across the river at the Pentagon, some of my military contacts were returning from their tours in Vietnam. As we became reacquainted, I learned of the failing morale, the increased drug usage, and, worst of all, the discouragement among the young officer corps, the future of the armed forces. Generals were caving to the political whims of the White House and ignoring the realities on the ground. Many troops would die simply because two presidents did not want to be the first American leader to lose a war.

I proposed to Leacacos that we report on military morale. He hesitated, but finally agreed. I spent more than a month visiting bases across the country and interviewing more than 70 junior officers who candidly laid out their grievances. They were given the option of remaining anonymous.

The interviews were sobering, and somewhat alarming. Most officers thought the war winnable, but the bungling of politicians unable to articulate its purpose was leading to defeat at home. The military had no hero, no revered figure who could defend it. They blamed the media, television in particular, for framing a false picture of the war. Some said that the My Lai massacre had been portrayed as a commonplace incident rather than the atrocity it was.

To many, the greatest issue was the dissolution of the service's integrity and the public's disrespect for the uniform, two factors that could affect the quality of recruits to the officer corps. Surprisingly, many were against the idea of abolishing the draft and building a professional military. They felt that a citizen military brought the country closer to identifying with its armed forces.

Rereading those articles 50 years later was a haunting exercise. By most historical accounts, the war was not winnable, and political meddling was detrimental to the cause. A professional military came to pass and generally excelled, and the media suffered from the effects of Vietnam even though it was largely correct in reporting the course of the war.

CHAPTER 38

Crazy Horse

Foment seemed to be everywhere in 1970, and not all of it concerned the war. More than a hundred years earlier the government had seized Native American lands and never compensated tribes for their loss. That was the reason *Plain Dealer* photographer Dick Conway and I found ourselves atop Mount Rushmore looking down on George Washington's head and watching a group of Native American protesters, some of them from Cleveland.

They were protesting a claim dealing with the Sioux land that had been pending in Washington since 1954. They also wanted the name of the mountain changed to Mount Crazy Horse after the great Sioux chief.

Conway and I evaded National Park Service rangers and climbed up the back of the mountain, a somewhat treacherous endeavor involving sharp rocks, deep ravines, and nasty vegetation that pricked your skin and snagged your clothes. The climb was exhausting. When we reached the top we found about a dozen Native American men and three or four Native women in a giddy mood. They were smoking marijuana. Liquor and white men were prohibited from the mountain, but as newsmen we received special dispensation.

The weed instilled a bravado that was almost humorous, except for the seriousness of their threat to dump several gallons of red paint onto George Washington and make him an honorary Indian. Wanting good light for his pictures, Conway was anxious to know when they planned the baptism. As for me, I wasn't sure I wanted to be around if they carried out their plan. This was Second Amendment country, and out there in the hills likely was a passel of guns clutched by itchy trigger fingers eager to avenge George Armstrong Custer.

After a few hours of boasting by Russell Means, head of the Cleveland American Indian Movement, it became clear that there would be no apocalypse this day. Means was as much an actor—he appeared in several movies—as he was an activist. He was a handsome man with a provocative personality and a month earlier had led 50 Native Americans in an assault on the mountain. Years later when Dick Jacobs bought the Cleveland Indians, he discovered that the team was paying Means' movement $30,000 annually to keep protests over the Chief Wahoo logo to a minimum. Jacobs canceled any future payments and welcomed the protests.

Native American protesters occasionally painted their faces and whooped war cries that echoed off the mountain and sent chills through bewildered tourists while bored park rangers looked on. The whole thing was theater, but the drama carried an effective message about a genuine grievance.

After dining on some truly bad beans and macaroni, Conway and I decided to depart before nightfall when weather conditions on the mountain became cold and windy and sometimes snowy. I took a shortcut across the Badlands in our rental car. My poor driving on the rough terrain caused Conway's head to bounce off the windshield and put a crick in his neck, locking his head in a sideways position.

We were out in the middle of nowhere but Conway insisted we find a chiropractor. We actually did locate one in a small town several miles from the mountain, but he wanted $10 to straighten Dick's neck. Conway figured the paper's accountants would never approve the expense. So we drove miles to another South Dakota town where we found a chiropractor who did the job for $5.50.

We wondered what the Cleveland Clinic would have charged.

CHAPTER 39

Of All Places, Kent State

Monday, May 4, 1970, began as a carefree vacation day in Cleveland. I was in town preparing to get married in two weeks and stopped in at the paper to meet Joe Eszterhas for lunch. We had not had many opportunities to get together over the past two years, and I looked forward to hearing his story about obtaining pictures of the My Lai massacre in Vietnam. The photographs, first published in the *Plain Dealer*, were an international scoop.

It was a glistening spring day that made you feel good to be alive. It was about 11:30 a.m. Eszterhas and I were ready to head down the hallway when John Rees, the day city editor, stopped us.

"Hold it, guys!" he shouted. "We have a shooting at Kent State. Looks like the National Guard shot some of the kids who were rioting. You better get down there now." It seemed like every time I left the building, a story broke.

The trouble at Kent had been brewing over the weekend. An antiwar demonstration had blossomed into a full-fledged disturbance that threatened the college town. A small ROTC building had been burned down on Saturday night, and Ohio

Governor James Rhodes had ordered the National Guard to the campus to restore order.

Who did we have down there, I asked. Rees said no one. Great. Walking into another blind situation and playing catch-up in the midst of chaos, I thought. The paper had covered Sunday's events with two reporters and bold headlines, but when Monday morning broke we had no staff on campus. Our student correspondent had been arrested on Sunday, so there was no one to cover the aftermath of what had been a tumultuous day. Kent State coverage was the responsibility of the state desk run by Wilson Hirschfeld.

But on weekends the city desk took over the coverage, and whoever was in charge on Sunday failed to assign reporters to the campus on Monday morning, despite the urging of one reporter who asked to stay. I thought it was a mistake that rivaled the Manry story.

Eszterhas and I took the turnpike down to Kent. At the toll booth we heard the attendant tell a motorist that the National Guard should have shot more kids. The war had divided the country, with anger bubbling over into everyday life, stoked by the Nixon administration's rhetoric about peace with honor. The day before, the president had called college demonstrators "bums."

The Kent State demonstrations had been triggered by an incursion of U.S. troops into Cambodia in an effort to destroy a North Vietnamese logistics center. Ironically, although I would not learn this for several years, the incursion was led by a relative of mine, Lieutenant General Elvy B. Roberts.

The Cambodian mission originally was to be led by a Vietnamese general, but a visit to his fortune-teller warned that he would be killed if he took part in the fight. The man listened to the soothsayer and backed out. At the last minute Nixon asked

General Roberts, whose tour in Vietnam was up in a few days, to take over the operation.

When we arrived on campus and took measure of the situation, I was sick with anger. I was angry at the naïveté of the students in confronting heavily armed men. I was angry at the Guard for its lack of discipline, and at the paper for ignoring what clearly was going to be a dark moment in American history.

There were four dead and nine wounded.

Eszterhas and I split up and began to assemble the pieces of the story. He worked on the student angle and I took the Guard, which I knew was going to be reluctant to say anything. I sought out its leader, Brigadier General Robert H. Canterbury, and persuaded him to make a statement on the shootings. I wanted him to comment sooner rather than later because it was only a matter of time before the *New York Times*, *Washington Post* and other national media would descend on the scene.

As I talked to guardsmen it became clear that in the effort to break up a student gathering, the troops involved had been hastily organized—an ad hoc group, not an organic unit—with no direct chain of command. Confused, and sensing peril, they shot into students who were hurling stones as well as insults. It was the perfect recipe for tragedy.

The students had no idea of the power and range of the deadly M1 rifles that the Guard carried. I remember thinking had I been there at the time of the shootings, I would have been too frightened to have stood and watched. I had seen too much in Vietnam. When you cover a tragic situation you learn to shield yourself from emotion, but the senselessness of what had taken place here left me drained.

Meanwhile, I was making progress toward convincing Canterbury to issue a statement when from above a small helicopter bearing the markings of Channel 5 arrived, delivering the legendary Dorothy Fuldheim. Fuldheim, a television personality in Cleveland since the inception of the medium, had a reputation for bombast. Today she was a grandstander.

"General, how many did your men murder today?" Fuldheim shouted in front of the camera at the beleaguered Canterbury, and with that came an end to a possible statement from the National Guard. It was another example of television putting itself first rather than the story. Months passed before the Guard would comment on the incident and, when it did, little was revealed. I had no respect for Fuldheim.

By not addressing the situation, the Guard left room for rumors to circulate, rumors about snipers, shadowy figures lurking in the fringes of the crowd, the usual communist conspirators and evil provocateurs of darkness. At one point, General Sylvester T. Del Corso, head of the Ohio Guard, posed the possibility of a sniper, which was quickly dismissed. Conspiracies rose like smoke from a fire, all of which had to be checked out in the hopes that a grain of fact would solve the puzzle.

Nearly 50 years later, the cause of the shootings would remain a mystery.

In the midst of the turmoil that day, Eszterhas, ever the enterprising ace, called a New York publisher and sold a book on the shootings. We didn't know it at the time, but the book would put us at odds with one of the country's most famous authors.

Another thing we didn't know was that the *Akron Beacon Journal*, aided by its sister newspaper the *Detroit Free Press*, had staffed the event so superbly that its reporting would win for them the Pulitzer Prize. I was troubled by the way the *Plain Dealer* had failed to cover the demonstration; that lapse on Monday morning was a disaster. I had not worked from the newsroom for three years and was out of touch with the personnel, motivation and awareness that it possessed. We stayed on the story for the next few days and I learned something troubling.

It was similar to the problem we faced covering the civil rights situation in the early 1960s. Editors did not have the vision, or perhaps the concern, to see where events were leading. In the days that followed they would caution us not to turn the dead students into martyrs, a notion we had never entertained. There was fear on their part of further dividing the community. They were clearly taking sides on the issue, even if they didn't realize it, just as during the days leading up to the Hough and Glenville riots.

I surmised there was no sympathy among some editors toward the antiwar movement, and that fact played a part in the *Plain Dealer*'s careless coverage that day at Kent State. To me, the newspaper's breakdown at Kent said a lot about its lack of awareness.

We simply did not have the discipline or the leadership to handle major, fast-moving stories. Tom Vail's dream of winning a Pulitzer was no closer to achievement than the day he became editor. I began to wonder if he even knew that.

My anger lessened a bit when Eszterhas and I were granted a four-month leave to write the book. It was something that Vail did not have to do.

We split the chapters between us, with Eszterhas concentrating on the students and the counterculture while I took the Guard and the related events around its activities. We each claimed two of the dead students and wrote long profiles of their lives and how they were killed. I wrote about the two girls, Sandy Scheuer and Allison Krause. Eszterhas focused on the two boys, William Schroeder and Jeff Miller.

Over the next four months we worked day and night, seven days a week. We interviewed students, professors, administrators, police, public officials, guardsmen and victims. The saddest part for me was sitting in Youngstown and Pittsburgh with the parents of the two girls and listening to their anguished recollections of their daughters. In many ways it was a dreadful summer.

We spent hours pondering the 13 seconds in which the shootings took place. Despite many investigations by the FBI and others, no clear conclusions were drawn as to who and what caused 61 rounds of .30-caliber ammunition to be fired that morning. Many rounds had been fired into the air; otherwise, there would have been wholesale slaughter on Blanket Hill.

When you listen to the recording of the shooting, a single shot is heard, then a pause followed by the fusillade. I always thought that the guardsman who fired first triggered the others, many of whom had their backs to the students at the sound of that first shot. Whether he panicked or simply fired a warning shot will probably remain known only to him.

Of the four students killed, I believe that three were hit by errant shots, while the fourth, Jeff Miller, may have been purposely hit as he waved a flag at the forefront of the crowd. A pool of dark blood marked the spot where Miller died.

One day we were in a college hangout in Kent waiting to meet some students when I looked down the crowded bar and saw an older man sitting there. He looked out of place among the youthful throng. I asked Joe if he knew him. "Nah," he said. "Probably just some guy who hangs around here."

But the man looked strangely familiar. I walked over and said hello and asked who he was.

"I'm James Michener," he said.

"The writer?" I asked.

"Yes, I'm here doing a book on the shootings." Michener

had written *Hawaii, Return to Paradise* and *Tales of the South Pacific*, among other books. He wrote best sellers the way most people changed clothes.

I didn't tell him who we were or what we were doing, but I was shaken by the news. I walked back to Eszterhas and said as casually as I could, "Oh, that guy. It's only James Michener."

Eszterhas just shrugged it off. "Screw him," he said. Michener's presence would spur us on, and months later would result in a tumultuous moment on national television.

The stark division in the country became profoundly evident during our research for the book. Many students considered anyone over 30 as untrustworthy, even an enemy. In return, many older people felt repulsion toward the youth culture. It was as if America had been on mental cruise control when it passed into the 1960s. And then assassinations, civil rights, Vietnam, drugs, and rock and roll jarred the national sensibilities, creating a break with the past. The future was long hair, jeans, loud music, psychedelics, sexual liberation, and rejection of what came before.

We had to navigate through all of that in the student interviews. Most of our time was spent convincing students that we were not some extension of the establishment. If we had trouble with that at our ages—Eszterhas was 25 and I was 30—Michener at 63 must have found the generation gap a wide abyss.

In all probability, Michener came to regret writing *Kent State: What Happened and Why*. One Kent State professor published a study of the errors in the book. The book was funded by the *Reader's Digest*, a publication known for its conservative leanings. A *New York Times* review saw this attitude reflected by Michener, and many felt that the book was a defense of the Guard. The Nixon administration placed blame for the shootings on frenzied students. Michener pointed to outside agitators, revolutionaries, as the igniting ingredient for the tragedy. That was never proved.

Our book, *13 Seconds: Confrontation at Kent State*, received respectable reviews. Many cited the fact we had written it quickly, but most considered it a worthwhile work. In revisiting the book and the events it portrayed, it is interesting that after all these years very little has been revealed about the incident that we did not collect that hectic summer. Forty-eight years later, the book remains in print.

Eszterhas was particularly annoyed with Michener, and given our competing books it was only a matter of time before our paths would cross. They inevitably did on NBC's *Today* show. Barbara Walters hosted a segment on Kent State, and it was not long before Eszterhas was accusing Michener of dishonest and inaccurate journalism, alluding that the author was more comfortable with fiction than with fact.

Walters tried to referee the dispute, but the show was forced to cut to a commercial during which viewers could still hear the rancorous row. After the show, Eszterhas, Michener and I found a bar at 9 a.m. and had a drink to calm the situation and make some peace. I felt sorry for Michener. It was clear that he was out of his element with the book.

We made a few dollars, but used them for living expenses during those four months. From time to time over the years I returned to Kent State on the anniversary of the shootings to participate in panel discussions, but the farther the tragedy receded in time, the more toxic the dialogues became. I finally stopped attending, mentally fatigued by the anguished rhetoric.

Back in Washington I covered the report by the President's Commission on Campus Unrest, which placed equal blame for the deaths on the students and the National Guard. Some have since come forward with new information concerning the shootings, but on final analysis nothing of substance has been brought to light.

It is ironic that of all the places in America disrupted by protests of the Vietnam War, Kent State bears the historical legacy that symbolizes those tormented times. The shootings also symbolize the end of the 1960s, an era fraught with pain, fear and death. Watergate was around the corner, and that would cast another kind of shadow across the country.

CHAPTER 40

Going to the Dark Side

A writer of note once said that any story followed to its end will have a sad conclusion. While I did not yet realize it, the phone call from executive editor Bill Ware was the beginning of the end of my story at the *Plain Dealer*. Ware was coming to Washington and wanted to have lunch with me, which meant something was up.

I had been at the paper now for eight years, with almost half of that time spent as a correspondent abroad and in Washington. The assignments had come so quickly that I did not think much about my career. I was living it. Never did I consider becoming an editor. The mere suggestion was repellent.

That was my immediate reaction when Ware announced that he and Tom Vail wanted me to return to Cleveland and serve as the newspaper's city editor. It was a flattering offer, but it held no intrigue. When I told Bill that I appreciated the consideration, but didn't think the job was for me, he shook his head.

"We need you there," Ware said. "We've got problems and we think you can really help."

I promised to give it some thought, but that was just a nice way of ending the lunch amicably. I really needed time to weasel my way out of this situation, which I feared was more of an order than an offer.

There were a number of things to consider. First, I had no experience as an editor, a desk-bound job that required different skills and temperament than reporting. It involved long hours and late nights. Ted Princiotto lived like a monk when he had the job, never fraternizing with the staff. Even worse, you had to deal with about four dozen different personalities, a more troublesome problem than covering the day's news.

And then there was the meddling from the front office.

Rationally, there was little to attract me to the job. Emotionally, however, there was one draw. Perhaps I could change the culture of the paper? This was a dangerous and foolish thought, and I toyed with it gingerly.

One day at the press club in Washington I had a drink with the former city editor of the *Chicago Daily News* and asked for advice. "Whatever you do, don't take it," he said. "The job is the pissing-post of American newspapers, which are naturally fucked up beyond any salvation."

A few days later Vail called and asked when I was going to take over the desk. I danced around the question and said I was still thinking about it. I could sense some annoyance on the other end of the line. That day I talked to Princiotto, and he did not encourage me.

"We have a situation here where the paper is putting itself out," he said. This is what he said whenever he felt the paper was full of prosaic news due to lethargic reporting. I didn't like hearing that.

I talked with Eszterhas, and he offered a different view of the situation. Take the job and fix the place was his advice. Ware talked to me again. I was being given a once-in-a-lifetime opportunity, he emphasized, and I should seize it if I wanted to ensure my future with the paper. There was another factor. I had just married Patricia Weitzel, a food writer on the paper, which meant that my days of living dangerously were probably over. It was time to settle down.

With some regret, on June 1, 1971, I became the *Plain Dealer*'s city editor, responsible for 50 reporters and a city in anguish. I wasn't in the building more than half an hour when my first problem came screeching into the city room. It was a woman whose sex-change operation we had reported on, but an inaccurate use of pronouns had reversed the procedure in print. She was so angry she had to be escorted from the building.

The other odd thing about that first day was that Terry Sheridan, one of the last of the paper's aces, quit. He cut the ribbon on his typewriter and left a half-empty bottle of scotch on his desk that remained there for several days, a memorial to his obstinacy. We had never got along well, but I felt his loss. The paper had wanted to transfer him to the Painesville bureau. Instead, he became a private detective.

A few days later, Eszterhas gave me a proof of a magazine article he had written for the *Evergreen Review*. It was a self-deprecating piece on Joe's acquisition and sale of photos from the My Lai massacre in Vietnam.

The photos had been taken by a former Army photographer named Ron Haeberle who had also attended Ohio University and knew of Eszterhas. When the My Lai story broke, the media's first reaction was disbelief. The story had been uncovered by Seymour Hersh, a freelance journalist for the Dispatch News Service, a relatively obscure outlet.

Haeberle's pictures erased any doubts that the massacre had taken place. The ambitious Eszterhas immediately worked out an arrangement where the *Plain Dealer* would be the first to publish the pictures and *Life* magazine would pay $20,000 for the national rights. The paper gave Joe a $500 bonus and received worldwide notices for its scoop. It was heady stuff.

The magazine proof that Eszterhas handed to me was for a story entitled "The Selling of the My Lai Massacre." Along with a description of the hectic events surrounding the pictures, the story contained humorous anecdotes and ironic asides. Included were references to Tom Vail's desire to be a vice presidential candidate, details of the dreaded Robert Manry fiasco, and less than complimentary remarks about other personalities on the paper.

I read the proof and voiced concern that Eszterhas was pushing the envelope. I suggested several cuts and Joe made them, but my mistake—and it was a huge one—was not advising him to kill the entire piece. At this point I didn't realize how much tension existed at the paper. Publication of the *Evergreen Review* article in October 1971 resulted in Joe's firing and a public arbitration that bared the paper's soul and embarrassed everyone involved. It also widened the breach between management and staff.

It did not take long to see that something was seriously wrong in the city room. There was a sullen resentment that had not existed when I last worked in Cleveland.

The era of the aces was a thing of the past. What had replaced it was a congregation of reporters who bad-mouthed the newspaper and went about their work in a perfunctory manner. Conversely, the editors, who remained remote in their offices down the long hall, viewed some on the staff with suspicion and contempt, regarding them almost as seasonal help.

It was up to me to resolve this division, which took a while to understand. The lack of morale was clearly hurting the paper. Even the younger newcomers were listless. The city room had the atmosphere of a public utility, and the paper read like it, too.

As best I could figure, over the past few years the paper's ineptness in certain areas had accumulated to the point where reporters lost faith in the seriousness of the journalistic mission. Once this feeling took hold—the feeling of not being important to the enterprise—came the loss of care for the organization.

While reporters often had an unusual sense of humor, I'll never forget Andy Juniewicz returning from his court beat one day. When I asked what he had for the paper, he said, "No news is good news." It was a funny line, but ironically it symbolized the sardonic miasma that had crept into the place.

One morning I came to work to find an angry salesman from the advertising department. He held a short clipping that announced the winners in an automobile sales contest. Each of the dozen or so names in the list was misspelled. The article had originated in the promotion department. That department was run by Alex Machaskee, who would later become the paper's publisher.

Machaskee was not well liked and drew hostility from some on the editorial staff. I had mentioned to him that if he had copy for the news side he should just give it to me personally and not come up to the city room. I didn't tell him that he was not welcome.

When we looked at the carbon copy of the article, all the names were spelled correctly. The piece had been handled through the rewrite desk, whose occupants claimed to know nothing, but they did add that the printers sometimes drank heavily. Clearly, what had happened was that the article had been written once with the misspelled names and then written again for the file with the proper spellings.

For someone to sabotage the paper like this was a sacrilege. The issue of trust was now in doubt in the city room.

On any given day on a newspaper like the *Plain Dealer*, there are articles that anger someone, someplace. The downtown business community was particularly sensitive to criticism and had learned that by going above reporters' heads, they could gain a sympathetic ear from certain editors. For example, the Illuminating Company complained bitterly about every reporter who covered its decades-old war with the city's Municipal Light Plant.

Complaints would be redirected to the city desk with instructions to talk to the reporter in question. Often there was nothing wrong with the way a story had been written and reporters chafed at the criticism, viewing it as a challenge to their credibility. This frequent back-dooring of the staff wore down morale to a nub. At the *Cleveland Press*, reporters would tell wonderful stories of how editor Louie Seltzer had handled complaints. He would call the offending reporter into his office to face the complainant, scold them, then give them the rest of the day off for participating in the charade.

I was in the job only a few days when Ted Princiotto spoke to me in private. He was now the night managing editor, whose main job was selecting the stories for page one and laying them out. It was a waste of his abilities, but it was one of the rungs of promotion.

Princiotto told me that in a week certain changes in management would likely generate controversy. It would be best, he said, for me not to be close to him when the changes took place. I was not sure what he meant, and he did not elaborate, but I had a sense of foreboding.

It was the afternoon of Friday, June 18, when Bill Ware called me into his office. He told me that Ted no longer worked for the newspaper. It was stunning news. Ware offered no details other than to say that he was retiring later in the year. The new executive editor would be Thomas R. Guthrie.

I stayed in touch with Princiotto over the years, and he would never tell me what transpired that day. His loss was a blow to the paper. He, more than any other single person, cared about the quality of the news coverage and worked constantly to improve it.

While I never learned what took place, my guess is that Princiotto objected to Vail's promotion of Guthrie, who had a reputation of being a straphanger, a man along for the ride. Guthrie, a Scotsman, had met Phil Porter during World War II when he was a public information officer in the Royal Air Force. After the war Porter got him a job at the *Plain Dealer*, where he served mostly as a copy editor, briefly as Washington bureau chief, and later as Vail's assistant.

Guthrie was a cheery, hail-fellow-well-met sort with scotch on his breath and office politics in his soul. He was also palsied with hip-shooting impatience. He was the opposite of Princiotto in almost every way and was someone with whom Vail obviously felt comfortable.

As Roldo Bartimole once put it, Princiotto wasn't of the right pedigree for the job. He may have been the best editor on the paper, but he had an Italian surname.

When I became city editor, I appointed Bob McGruder as my first assistant. An African American, he was coming off a rough few years covering Carl Stokes at city hall.

McGruder's leadership and reporting skills were respected by the staff. Years later he would become the executive editor of the *Detroit Free Press*. When he died in 2002, newspapers across the country carried his obit, citing him as a prominent figure in the diversification of American journalism.

I was happy when McGruder took the job on the desk, so I was caught off guard when Guthrie caught up to me in the hallway to offer his thoughts about the appointment.

"Why did you put the darky in that job?" Guthrie asked.

"What do you mean?" I said, flabbergasted.

"The darky, McGruder."

"Tom, because he knows his shit," I said. I laughed with uneasiness and dismay, feeling my sensibilities flatten as I realized that the leadership of the paper didn't get it. According to Jim Cox, Guthrie once told an editor that the *Plain Dealer* could not send McGruder to the Columbus bureau because a black man would embarrass the paper. Stokes had struck a vein of truth in his accusation of racism in the paper's front office.

CHAPTER 41

The Sad Conclusion

The fall of 1971 brought Ralph Perk's election as mayor, and we were ready for the new administration. City hall had always been a focal point of competition between the *Plain Dealer* and the *Press*, even though its importance was diminishing with time. But it remained a daily battleground for the two papers.

I was not about to let the *Press* scoop us. We put three reporters on city hall: Edward P. Whelan, George Rasanen and Tom Brazaitis. I told them not to leave anything for the afternoon newspaper.

And they didn't. Ned Whelan was an amazing reporter. We would work together for almost 20 years, and in that time he was among the city's most accomplished journalists. Rasanen and Brazaitis were skilled as well.

A new administration traditionally alternated the announcement of its cabinet posts between the two newspapers. I wanted to break with tradition and go for them all, and that's what we did. With only one more cabinet member to be named, we just needed the law director to sweep the field.

But our aggressiveness was bringing heat on the mayor from the *Press*. Perk sent his secretary, J. William Petro, to meet with executive editor Tom Guthrie and complain that our reporters were being less than ethical. Petro told Guthrie that Whelan had rifled his desk drawer.

I wasn't sure whether Guthrie's face was red from lunchtime glasses of scotch or from anger at Whelan. He demanded to know whether Petro's accusation was true. I told him no.

"Well, how can you be so sure?" he asked.

"For one, I trust Ned," I said. "For the other, he told me the drawer was locked."

Every day at 5 p.m. the editors would meet in managing editor David Rimmel's office to argue our cases for space on page one. The editors made their best pitch, and this day I was particularly animated. Whelan had just called in with the final cabinet member, which meant we had beaten the *Press* on Perk's entire executive staff.

Some of the editors applauded, and as the meeting broke up Rimmel asked me to stay behind. Looking down at his desk, he proceeded to tell me that we could not run the story on the appointment of Richard Hollington as Cleveland law director.

"Tom promised the mayor that the *Press* could have the story," Rimmel said. I was dumbstruck. After trying to create some synergy in the newsroom, to be blindsided by the publisher was cataclysmic. How could I tell Whelan and the others that the story was killed to help the mayor when I had urged them to be aggressive as hell.

"This is bullshit, Dave," I said. I left his office and walked down the hallway to Tom Vail's office, blew by his secretaries, and arrived unannounced in his presence.

"Tom, I think you have to tell Ned Whelan why we are not running his story on Dick Hollington," I said to Vail, who was bewildered by my sudden appearance. "I'm sure not going to tell him."

"I promised the mayor the *Press* could have that story," he said.

"Just think how this is going to impact morale in the city room," I responded.

Vail thought for a moment, then reached for the phone and dialed the TV newsroom of WKYC, Channel 3.

"Here is a tip for the evening news," he said without identifying himself. "Richard Hollington is the new law director. Check it out." And then without pausing he made another phone call.

"Hello, Mayor," he said. "We just found out that Channel 3 is going with a story about Hollington's appointment. We have to go with the story, too."

I didn't say anything to the reporters about this for a couple of weeks, but I had lost a lot of confidence in our mission and in Vail. Tom wanted to play the same game with city hall that Louie Seltzer had played for so long, but he didn't know how. Stokes had shunned him, and Vail viewed Perk as someone who would be more compliant toward his interests in city hall. Vail liked dabbling in politics.

More important to me was the realization that I was not long for this place. Guthrie's overt racism and Vail's disregard for the staff made any long-term improvement in the city room unlikely. Regardless of effort, the paper was destined to merely put itself out, undistinguished, uninformed and unresponsive to the community. This is what Ted Princiotto had seen coming.

Vail misjudged Ralph Perk, whose administration would be infamously bad. Many veteran political observers in Cleveland call it the worst in our lifetime. It was not long before reporters were gleefully trampolining on the administration. City hall was out of control. And in the midst of the chaos arrived Richard G. Eberling, a suspect in the Sheppard murder case, a jewel thief, and in time a convicted killer.

The obsequious Eberling and his equally unctuous partner,

Obie Henderson, gained entry to the inner circle of city hall thanks to the *Plain Dealer*'s Wilson Hirschfeld, who had quietly done Perk's bidding on the paper for years. He considered Perk to be totally honest with a moral conviction far above others in public office. Hirschfeld was naive.

Perk had ties to people close to the mob and made city hall a haven for political hacks, wandering misfits, opportunists and outright fakes. Jim Dickerson, his 450-pound chief of staff, was a man whose entire resumé was a falsehood.

Henderson, who was the chief clerk in the paper's city room, ingratiated himself with Hirschfeld, who in turn persuaded Perk to name Henderson and Eberling as city hall's official interior decorators. The twosome lived together in a dark, unfriendly house on Bradley Road in Westlake. It was filled with purloined furnishings. Many of us, including Guthrie and Hirschfeld, had been entertained there.

Eberling and Henderson robbed city hall of valuable artwork, murdered an elderly woman whom they had befriended, and killed a racehorse for the insurance money by hitting it with a car. They both died after long prison sentences.

Reporters were increasingly aware of what was taking place, and the paper's relationship with city hall was becoming tricky. We did not talk openly about what we were hearing in front of Guthrie or Hirschfeld. We knew the *Press* had begun to mount an after-hours surveillance of Perk's activities. Our paper was in conflict. Vail wanted to influence city hall, Hirschfeld wanted to maintain his agenda with Perk, and the city desk wanted to expose the corruption surrounding the mayor. It made for a toxic environment.

Meanwhile, the daily grind on the city desk was getting to me. We had reporters of various skills and experience, but many were indifferent and careless about their work. One veteran reporter misspelled a single individual's name six different ways in the same article. Another reported that U.S. chess master Bobby Fischer was playing a match on East 6th Street when he was actually in Denver. Still another was routinely late to work because "there was a big dog" near his car. Few story ideas were generated by the staff, some of whom didn't read their own proofs let alone the rest of the newspaper or the *Press*.

"No one seemed to know." That's a phrase used when a reporter is too lazy to make an extra phone call, and it was increasingly slipping into the paper. Roy Adams brought a pillow to work to sleep in the library. Adams was also known to wear a gas mask during services at St. Sava Serbian Church. A dispute among the parishioners had become so contentious that someone had thrown a tear-gas canister into the midst of Mass, and Adams wanted to be prepared for another attack. A priest called the paper to complain.

It got so that some days I wished I was back in Vietnam. There was a lack of trust among the editors, most of whom were too frightened to make decisions. For instance, on the night of December 21, 1971, the lead story was a fatal stabbing during an altercation in the Santa Claus line at Higbee's downtown department store. An ugly holiday story, but it had all the elements of a page-one article. There was only one drawback: Higbee's was a major advertiser.

Managing editor Dave Rimmel, after some consideration, ordered that the name of the store not appear on page one, but be mentioned later in the story. I argued the issue, noting that television and radio had already broken the news and named the store. We were going to look bad in the morning when readers had to turn the page to find out where the murder occurred.

The rewrite desk was already ridiculing the decision. In the morning we did look bad, and the uproar was such that Rimmel lost his job. The advertising department had asked for the favor and he had complied. The paper's journalistic seriousness was again in question.

Rimmel was a longtime *Plain Dealer* editor who had spent most of his career on the feature side of the paper. He was decent and thoughtful, but not up to the slap and dash of the city room. My complaints about the Higbee story may well have contributed to his downfall, and for that I felt bad. I felt worse when I learned his replacement would be Wilson Hirschfeld.

Hirschfeld was a bald, soft-spoken man with riveting eyes and a tendency to move his head from side to side as if suffering from a minor tremor. A devout Christian Scientist with a pious disposition, he was 55 when he became the paper's managing editor. He had begun working at the *Plain Dealer* as a delivery boy in 1936 and rose to the city room prior to service in the Army Air Corps during World War II. He had a reputation as a tenacious and meticulous reporter with an inordinate distrust of public officials, who feared his scrutiny. But he had a blind spot when it came to certain politicians.

Despite Hirschfeld's appearance and reserved manner, he was a man of improbable celebrity. Though he never boasted of it, he was considered to be the model for the comic-book hero Superman. In the 1930s, Hirschfeld had worked on the Glenville High School newspaper with Jerry Siegel and Joe Shuster, the creators of the Man of Steel, and many accounts have it that he was the soul of Superman.

Superman's disposition toward fighting crime and evil was evident in Hirschfeld, as was a certain aloofness that set him apart from whatever collegiality existed in the city room. He was among the last of the World War II editors who lived by detail and authority. In short, in 1971 he was remote from an increasingly younger and independent-minded reporting staff.

Hirschfeld was a true believer and it reflected in his naïveté, which ultimately cost him his job. His dedication to and promotion of Ralph Perk violated journalistic tenets, a fact well known in the city room but apparently not in the executive hallway. There came a point when reporters refused to do stories based on Wilson's tips regarding Perk.

The concern over the city hall coverage was such that Guthrie began to review every story, his hand trembling as he read the copy. I do believe that things had come to the point where the less written about Perk's city hall, the happier the front office. But reporters were hell bent on exposing the mess that was the Perk administration, and they distrusted Hirschfeld because of his relationship with the mayor. Communication among the editors broke off. As for me, I had never forgotten that Hirschfeld named my off-the-record source in the Beverly Jarosz murder case.

These were unsettling days in the city room, and I was frustrated by not having the wherewithal to handle it. To make matters worse, John Rees, after 45 years working for Forest City Publishing, first with the *Cleveland News* and then with the *Plain Dealer*, unexpectedly announced he was taking early retirement. Revered by the staff, Rees was exceedingly kind to young, confused reporters and a great role model, remaining steady and solid amid the chaos of a breaking story. He once talked a man out of jumping from the High Level Bridge and kept another from slashing his throat.

Rees represented the institutional memory of the city room, his knowledge reaching back to the 1920s when he had covered the deadly Cleveland Clinic fire. I was always saddened to see veteran newsmen leave. They labored to record the history of a city and got so little back. When I asked Rees if there was something I could do to make him stay, he told me he was tired of amateurs running the place. It was a dig at Guthrie.

John's retirement seemed like a good opportunity for Tom Vail to make an appearance in the city room, signaling that somebody still cared about the staff. I called one of Vail's secretaries and made the suggestion, but he didn't show. In his stead came a hastily typed note, complete with a typo, that made the day even more awkward.

Hirschfeld took to the managing editor's job with zeal and piety, critiquing, complaining about, and commenting on the quality of the news gathering. He was going through the same learning curve that I had endured, and the lesson was just as dismal. The staff was spiritless and suspicious. What Hirschfeld did not understand was that he needed to act as a buffer between a clueless front office and an embittered staff. He was obedient to every whim and whisper that emanated from his increasingly paranoid superiors.

And much of it was petty. When reporter Tom Andrzejewski wrote a piece about a federal court trial involving a man who had lost his legs in a railroad accident, he failed to note that the defense attorneys said they would appeal the case. It was a careless oversight but hardly an indictable offense.

The lawyer involved, however, was an old acquaintance of Vail's, and his inquiry prompted Hirschfeld to turn the matter into its own federal case. Had Andrzejewski intentionally omitted the fact to make the lawyer look bad? I took exception to the harshness of Hirschfeld's reprimand and in private the conversation became heated.

And then late one night assistant city editor Jim Flanagan foolishly sneaked a can of unopened beer into the city room. He was caught and fired. Nearing retirement, Flanagan knew every street in the city and was a great mentor. The firing reduced him to tears. I argued to a florid-faced Guthrie that the punishment didn't fit the so-called crime. After much negotiation, Flanagan got his job back. And I took another step toward losing mine.

The end came on a Tuesday in February, one of those days when the sky was dark and ugly and anyone with money was in Florida. It was a fitting backdrop for bad news. I got a call at home that Guthrie wanted to see me at 2 p.m.

The meeting was brief. Guthrie said it was time to part company. I had become too much of an irritant. I couldn't argue that. If I really cared I would have asked for a bill of particulars, but I just wanted out. As I trod down the long hallway for the final time, my emotions were mixed. The promise and excitement that the paper held a decade ago was gone. All the aces were gone. The *Plain Dealer* seemed an empty place now, its pages no longer crusading, having fallen prey to the turmoil of the times.

On the other hand, the paper had been good to me. I would miss the routine and the rush of deadline, the joy of breaking stories and the camaraderie, but there was no way I could continue. We had some good people, but the leadership was taking us nowhere and there was no hope of turning the *Plain Dealer* into a relevant regional paper. Later, I reflected on how much talent we had lost, how much time and money had been invested. Good reporters are not made overnight.

My departure did little to alleviate the mounting tension that was escalating into corporate panic. If Guthrie thought I was an irritant, his remaining tenure was filled with irritation much of his own making, resulting in two newspaper strikes that cost hundreds of thousands of dollars and an unprecedented level of acrimony.

When the 1972 strike began, Guthrie was doing what he did best. He was lunching at the Cleveland Athletic Club when he got word that the Newspaper Guild had begun picketing the

Plain Dealer building. Reportedly, he called Hirschfeld and told him to ask Mayor Perk to send in police. Perk responded by dispatching six mounted policemen who charged into the strikers with their horses. It was an act that would live in infamy in *Plain Dealer* history. Another strike occurred in 1975.

After that, the executive hallway that I had traveled so often was sealed off from the city room, restricting reporters from access to the editors. A peephole and a buzzer were added security precautions. In a classic blunder, Guthrie announced his successor publicly, only to have to renege when Vail denied the promotion. The vanquished editor who never reigned was then exiled to the Columbus bureau, broken and bewildered by his bad fortune. It only got worse. One editor was replaced because he fell asleep during meetings, another because of an attempt to influence a legal proceeding.

Hirschfeld did not last as managing editor. Despite carrying out Guthrie's orders, he was fired after the horse incident. One night not long afterward, a former reporter invited me to dinner at the English Oak Room in the Terminal Tower. I was wondering why I was there when out of the shadows Hirschfeld emerged. He stood before me, head bowed, shoulders slumped, an empty man who begged that I accept his apology for not supporting me. In the end, I felt sorry, because after 38 years the paper meant so much to him. He died a few weeks later.

As time marched on, editors revolved like reels in a slot machine with no winners. Then the Newhouse organization began to hire journalists of its own choosing from outside the paper. It made a difference, but it was too late. Technology slowly began to deal all newspapers a crippling blow. Like other papers, the *Plain Dealer* became a mere shadow of itself.

For reporters who covered the 1960s, it's hard to believe that the great era of newspaper journalism passed so swiftly into oblivion. I was lucky to get out when I did.

CHAPTER 42

A Whole New Gig

Three days after leaving the *Plain Dealer* I had a job. Lute Harmon, the erstwhile divinity student who had petitioned Louie Seltzer for a job on the *Cleveland Press* 10 years earlier, raised enough money to start a city magazine, a trend that was sweeping metropolitan areas across the country. City magazines were an offshoot of the New Journalism movement, giving journalists new venues for writing in more depth and detail.

It was exactly the medium that Cleveland needed, an independent voice that could address the status quo of a city mired in its past.

I had interviewed with the *New York Times* and was fairly certain that I would land something, so when Harmon invited me to dinner I was ambivalent. But I was fascinated by the magazine's potential and the opportunity to portray Cleveland as it was and not as a myth. The city prided itself on its appreciation of art and music, but it deserved better in the written word. The opportunity to write lengthy pieces was enticing, and I had done everything I wanted to do on a newspaper.

Dinner turned out to be long on talk and heavy on wine. Harmon was a salesman of the first order. He painted a picture of a slick magazine with fine graphics and incisive writing. The more the wine flowed, the better the magazine sounded.

The next day Harmon called to congratulate me on joining *Cleveland Magazine*. I protested, but he countered that he had my signature on a napkin and thus I couldn't go back on my word. When I saw the magazine's offices, I was crestfallen. Located above the Emerson Press at East 18th and Payne Avenue, they consisted of three shabby rooms with the barest essentials and no privacy.

Harmon's plan had been to work on the magazine on weekends and keep his job at the Illuminating Company. He also wanted to rely on freelance writers, which was a stretch since Cleveland is not necessarily a writer's town. I told him we needed staff writers and fast. If the magazine was going to make it on modest resources, it could not dawdle.

At the outset, my plan was to spend a year on the magazine learning to write long, and then look for a job elsewhere. Ned Whelan left the *Plain Dealer* and joined us as a staff writer. It did not take much to convince him that a future at the paper was dubious at best. With Whelan's contacts and his knowledge of the town, we gained legitimacy among the political set overnight.

Whelan wrote more cover stories than anyone else in the history of the magazine, many deftly chronicling the last days of the mob, others profiling Cleveland's most powerful players, and still others portraying the political folly playing at city hall.

And then in another stroke of good fortune, Gary Diedrichs, who had worked briefly at the paper, gave up freelancing in New York and came to town to write some memorable pieces. Diana Tittle arrived from the *Elyria Chronicle-Telegram*, bringing a rich talent to the magazine's pages. Dennis Dooley wrote of arts and culture with a special aplomb.

As time passed, Rory O'Connor captured national awards, and Greg Stricharchuk delivered fine investigative pieces. Patricia Weitzel, a former *Plain Dealer* food writer, became the magazine's restaurant critic and elevated the town's taste. Frank Kuznik wrote extensively of the stormy reign of Mayor Dennis Kucinich. Kathleen Mills, a precise and reliable copy editor, made us all look good. Edward J. Walsh played so many positions that we couldn't find a proper title for him. Aces, all in their own right.

Once the staff was in place, the magazine prospered, reaching a circulation of 60,000. Harvard University ranked *Cleveland Magazine* among the country's best city magazines. The magazine saw the city through a different lens and gave writers a voice that did not exist before.

For the 17 years that I edited the magazine, we attracted the best journalists in town. Almost everyone of note either passed through the staff or became a contributor, including Dick Feagler, Don Robertson, Bob August, Rich Osborne, Brent Larkin, Peter Phipps, Terry Sheridan, Stan Davis, Doug Clarke, Dan Cook, Jim Parker, Jim Neff, Jim Wood, Lilli Lief, John Tidyman, Evelyn Theiss, Cindy Oster, Peter Jedick, Mary Mihaly and others whose work made the magazine the must-read of its time.

Epilogue

I hadn't spoken to Tom Vail since my departure from the *Plain Dealer* in 1973. Then in the spring of 1991 I received a letter from the Sigma Delta Chi (SDX) journalism fraternity announcing that I was among four persons to be honored with a lifetime achievement award. One of the other recipients was Vail.

At the ceremony we each were given a few minutes to comment on our careers. Vail spoke first, noting how he had worked his way up in the newspaper business to ultimately become the *Plain Dealer*'s editor and publisher. Good fortune had me speaking next, and I could not resist.

"Tom was modest in speaking of his achievements," I told the assembled. "He left out his biggest achievement. The one about his family owning the newspaper."

The remark drew some laughter and Vail smiled. As we were leaving, he came over and shook my hand. I hoped that I hadn't embarrassed him.

The years passed and we both retired from the scene. Then one day in 2011 I was surprised by an email. Vail had lost the certificate from his SDX award. Did I know how he could get a replacement? I told him I could find out, but only if we had lunch together.

For the most part, the paper's staff had found Vail a curious figure, largely because his appearances in the city room were rare and fleeting. He was a devoted Anglophile and cut a Gatsbyesque figure in his fine English suits. The real buttonholes on his jacket sleeves captivated some of the editors, who fixated on them during meetings.

From time to time, in an attempt to better know the staff, Vail would host a lunch at the Union Club. For some in attendance, this would be the first and last time they would dine in that citadel of commerce. On my initial visit with several other reporters, Vail ordered a gin rickey, a cocktail unfamiliar to us beer drinkers.

Now Vail maintained an office above the Bravo restaurant on Chagrin Boulevard, and we met there for lunch. I was in the restaurant's lobby when he appeared, still trim in a splendidly tailored suit, carrying a thin book. I wasn't sure what to expect, but we shook hands and he was as cordial as ever.

"Mike, can you believe I'm 85?" he exclaimed, feigning bewilderment over his age as we made our way to a booth. He looked good.

I was a bit surprised when he asked if I wanted a drink, but I ordered a chardonnay. Vail chose a mojito, which made me recall the long-ago lunches at the Union Club when he drank gin rickeys and spoke of the exciting prospects for the paper's future.

That time was gone, and so were the paper's prospects. Vail talked about the city and shared his opinion on various personalities. For the most part we avoided discussing the *Plain Dealer*. He did wish that *Cleveland Magazine* had more meat to it, but that was no longer my purview.

I think he was uneasy that I might bring up a past grievance. But I had only one thought on my agenda. And that was to thank him for all the opportunities he had afforded me. It was a priceless education, full of adventure and challenge. It was a dream, actually. I thanked him, and he nodded and passed me the book he had been carrying. It was a memoir.

I opened the cover to find an inscription: *To one reporter from another.*

I smiled and felt the old ace in me return. Well, I thought, at least he got it half right.

*   *   *

During the 1960s, no one could have forecast the fate of newspapers. Looking back, it was the golden hour of print journalism. Technology was on a constant march, and at first it seemed that the advent of computers and improved communications would do nothing but enhance news coverage. It did, but not for newspapers. At a time when the 200th anniversary of the publication of Cleveland's first newspaper is being celebrated, there is the distinct possibility that the city will ultimately be without a printed edition of a daily paper.

In retrospect, newspapers should have been wary of technology the moment television arrived, for it foretold the future. The six o'clock news cut deeply into the afternoon papers. The *Cleveland News*, an afternoon daily published since 1905, was purchased by the *Cleveland Press* in 1960 and closed. Even the once mighty *Press* could not make it to the end of the century, selling its circulation list to the *Plain Dealer* in 1982 and then vanishing.

An example of just how unsuspecting the newspaper industry was of new technology took place in Cleveland. In the late 1990s, the *Plain Dealer* invested heavily in a new downtown headquarters and a suburban printing plant. The paper reportedly was making a 30 percent profit and viewed the future with optimism. The investment turned into a multimillion-dollar mistake.

In less than 10 years the Internet throttled the advertising base of newspapers and ate into readership. Even when papers began transitioning to an electronic format, advertising dollars did not follow. By 2006 the *Plain Dealer*, now in economic distress, had offered buyout packages to 60 journalists; 50 more were bought out or laid off two years later and an additional 47 followed in 2013. A veteran staff was gutted and replaced in part by recent college graduates hired at low salaries. Experience no longer mattered, and the paper shrank in size, content and quality. The *Plain Dealer*'s institutional memory began to disappear, along with the fine points of reporting—fact-checking, editing and follow-up. And then the paper cut back home delivery to its subscribers.

Fifty years ago, the *Plain Dealer* and its cadre of curious reporters checked daily to see how the city and region were functioning. This was an invaluable service that contributed to the safety and security of the community. The paper scrutinized politicians, supporting the search for leadership that would make the city better. It promoted culture and trends, enriching life for its readers. It helped businesses flourish.

Newspapers were once a unifying force in communities, a friendly visitor that arrived on your doorstep every day. Now people are largely indifferent to them. Many—including individuals in the highest levels of government—hold newspapers in contempt, insulting those who work at them and casting accusations of bias, idiocy and sensationalism. It is only natural for people to disdain the bearer of bad news. But in many ways newspapers have always given more to readers than they got back. Papers told you where to shop, where to eat, what to wear, how to live. They recorded your death.

In the new age of electronic devices, readers have become their own editors, seeking what they want or need to know from a vast landscape of information. The news cycle is never-ending. Social media is singular, sketchy, distant and vulnerable to manipulation and lies. Being truly informed in such an atmosphere requires critical and disciplined thinking. I am not sure that's the direction we're headed.

The credibility that newspapers once sought to project now seems a quaint notion. The romance is gone, the crackle of printed pages replaced by newsfeeds on tiny gadgets. But for those of us who were lucky enough to work in journalism throughout the tumult of the 1960s, the memory of the way it was—the excitement, the adrenaline pump, the sense of mission, the catharsis of deadline—remains, even though the ace has gone the way of the iceman.

Acknowledgments

It was the persistent urging of my friend and colleague Edward Walsh that spurred me to write this book. Walsh thought the saga of newspaper reporting in the 1960s—a key era in Cleveland's history—was worth sharing, and he finally convinced me to make the effort. The 1960s were a time of great turmoil both in this city and across the nation, which gave the task an edge. Along the way I was aided by former colleagues who also were there for the ride. Roldo Bartimole gave freely of his time, recounting his three decades of covering the city. Bob Daniels, a great rewrite man, told of the hellish week of the Hough riots. Jim Cox, a stellar newsman in both print and television, spoke of the journalistic challenges in covering the era's civil rights troubles. Tom Andrzejewski and Andy Juniewicz offered valuable recollections of days and nights at the *Plain Dealer*.

And, finally, a special nod to the estimable Kathleen Mills, who managed the editing of the book with such precision.

Thanks to all.